THE NEW DAY TRADER ADVANTAGE

SANE, SMART, AND STABLE— FINDING THE DAILY TRADES THAT WILL MAKE YOU RICH

JON D. MARKMAN

New York   Chicago   San Francisco   Lisbon   London   Madrid   Mexico City
Milan   New Delhi   San Juan   Seoul   Singapore   Sydney   Toronto

1 2 3 4 5 6 7 8 9 0   DOC/DOC   0 9 8 7

ISBN   978-0-07-150852-0
MHID   0-07-150852-X

Printed and bound by RR Donnelley.

McGraw-Hill books are available at special quantity discounts to use as premiums and sales promotions, or for use in corporate training programs. To contact a representative please visit the Contact Us pages at www.mhprofessional.com.

This book is printed on acid-free paper.

ACKNOWLEDGMENTS

B ooks are collaborative enterprises. Editors, researchers, mentors, ghosts, demons, friends and family all make their contributions. I owe several people a huge debt of gratitude for helping me with this one.

First are my wife and children. I missed a lot of 14-year-old baseball tournament games this summer, and a whole bunch of 12-year-old soccer tournaments, while working weekends to crank this out. Thanks to my awesome kids, Joe and Jane, and my wife, Ellen, for giving me the time without complaint—not to mention inspiration, love and friendship.

My researchers Anthony Mirhaydari and Adam Hirsch made major contributions. Anthony, a business lifecycle consultant, helped in particular with Chapter 6 due to his deep understanding of the way great companies prosper by cooperating with suppliers and customers. Adam, a born trader, helped a ton with Chapter 4. He's the man when it comes to spin-outs, reverse-splits, IPOs, and every other little oddity of the market where information inefficiencies flourish.

My mentors in the business also deserve a grateful nod. These are guys who have taught me the business week after week in person, on the phone, and via IM and e-mail. I would still be an absolute babe in the woods without the kindness and patient tutoring of master traders and researchers Terry Bedford in Toronto, Ed Dunne in New Jersey, and Richard Rhodes in Philadelphia. Thanks to Vic Niederhoffer for reminding me both to count and to trust my instincts. And thanks to David Anderson in Palo Alto for explaining the energy business and Lakshman Achuthan for teaching me the economics racket.

My editors and publishers have also helped me grow as a writer and analyst and connect directly with readers. So much appreciation goes out to Danielle Hart, Mike Bell, Shannon Miller and Chris Marett at ACP Phillips; Chris Oster and Richard Jenkins at MSN Money; George Moriarty and Dave Morrow at TheStreet.com; and Jeanne Glasser at McGraw-Hill.

CONTENTS

INTRODUCTION

It's a new day in the world equity markets, as volatility in stock prices rises from a four-year slumber amid widening disparities in global economic growth. With more wealth being excavated from the earth and oceans and being transformed into energy, electronics, vehicles, and homes for the swelling ranks of middle-class consumers worldwide, investors have steadily taken more risks with less confidence.

This new era of uneven but substantial growth has led investors to trade stocks with more jitters than at any time in the past four years. This sort of volatility calls for a whole new set of rules and game plans.

In this new climate, traders who formerly made money minute by minute by sprinting from buys to sells and back again, using seat-of-the-pants hunches about trends and reversals, have found that commissions and emotionalism were quickly gobbling up all their profit and mental energy. They had to change, and they have. Both cagey veterans and dedicated newcomers have slowed their pace and are becoming the market equivalent of middle-distance runners: entering positions with techniques honed in the sprint blocks, but then holding them for days, weeks, and in some cases even months to avoid suffering losses amid frenetic whipsaws.

You could say that the rise in volatility has essentially redefined what it means to be a day trader. Rather than entering 20 jumpy positions and exiting them all before 4 p.m. eastern time, active investors today are entering just a handful of positions each day and holding them until they are nicely profitable, however long it takes.

Indeed, it's appropriate to declare that the new day trader is more of a "daily trader"—and a lot healthier and happier for the switch. Instead of battling head to head with pros around the world for pennies and nickels, the new day trader is piling up the quarters and dollars with a lot less stress.

This freshened breed of active trader has come to realize that it's virtually impossible to get rich *quick* in the market—but that you can get rich at a somewhat slower tempo by lengthening holding periods and relying more on cunning, patience, and planning than on fast reflexes. The patron saint, muse, and cheerleader for many is CNBC personality and former hedge fund manager Jim Cramer. But successful traders who develop confidence in themselves realize that they don't need a guru. With so much information available now at low cost, it is easier than ever for you to become your own guru.

Self-reliance, to be sure, is a beautiful thing. It is long-lasting, energizing, and fulfilling. Just about anyone with the time to do half an hour of research a day and the desire to make extra money can join the ranks of successful active traders. If you've gotten this far, that means you.

Have you mostly been a mutual fund or index fund trader until now? Then this book is for you, too, because it will show you a way to emerge from the mob of folks who think that real outperformance in the markets is unattainable. For years, I have urged readers of my best-selling investment newsletter and columns to set their feet firmly in the active-investment camp and buy the strongest companies in the best sectors of the economy whenever their shares have slipped for one reason or another and short the weakest companies and the worst performing sectors when their shares advance sharply. I have urged readers not to give in to the notion—popular among so many pessimistic economists, policy makers, financial talk-show hosts, and self-help buzzards—that individuals should just passively buy index funds and earn the same bland returns as everyone else. I have urged readers to take control of their financial future and reach for the brass ring by actively seeking out returns that can whisk them past the passive masses and into the express lane of life—the lane that puts you in a position to pay for your kids' college education easily; create an awesome retirement; take great, not average, vacations; buy front-row tickets to professional sporting events; travel first class; or perhaps even stake out an entirely new career. It's the lane that helps you take advantage of our capitalist system and put you and your family ahead in the world.

In this book, I will provide more than a dozen fresh, clear ideas to help you achieve your goals. All are proven techniques that do not require a degree in advanced financial engineering to exploit. And, most importantly, all have been proven to work in many different investment climates.

I have arranged the book by day of the week to help you focus systematically on the dozens of opportunities that regularly arise. Without a programmatic approach, it's easy for your trade research to deteriorate into a hodgepodge of methods picked up here and there, without rhyme or reason. I encourage you to focus on one methodology per day, forcing yourself into the sort of routine witnessed among successful professionals and advanced amateurs of all disciplines.

To symbolize the sort of discipline, routine, and single-minded focus required for success, it may be helpful to think of the new day trader as a bird of prey. A hawk harnesses its unusually strong vision and brainpower to well-honed intuition and total desire. A hawk needs to eat 10 to 20 percent of its weight every day in order to thrive, just as a day trader may wish to risk 10 to 20 percent of his or her capital every day.

Most importantly, a hawk plans, calculates, swoops, and executes on its mission with a grace unsurpassed in the animal kingdom. There is no wishing, or praying, or hoping, or waiting for luck, or dependence on outside experts, or complaints about the weather among hawks. Their world appears to be do or die, but it's actually more subtle than that. Hawks don't have a 100 percent success rate, and they don't aspire to one. They know that if they mess up an attack, they will get another chance. They don't pout, or storm about, or curse their fate and give up after a miss. They just regain altitude and try again. Hawks' resilience and determination provide a perfect paradigm for the active trader who wishes to make money consistently over many months and years in the market.

So how shall we plan and execute like a hawk? Week by week, day by day, hour by hour. I'll offer an approach to successful daily trading that works for me, but by all means modify it to suit your own skills, time, emotions, and belief set. I propose that you start your week on Sunday afternoon and continue on to Friday afternoon. Take a break on Saturdays to count your blessings and enjoy the profits of your efforts.

Sundays

- **Timing.** Possibly the most important determination you will ever make as an active investor is the direction of the intermediate-term market trend. If you get the three- to six-month direction of the market right, you know whether you should primarily take long positions or short positions. Some traders will tell you that they can take both successfully, but it's usually not worth the trouble. That's because when the market is generally rising, selling short is mostly a loser's game. You will learn from me and two other experts how to decide on the direction and likely longevity of the intermediate trend and how to recognize "oversold" and "overbought" conditions that will allow you to lighten up or double down on positions to exploit short-term wiggles within that trend.

- **Cycles.** I will explain the most important cycles at work in the equity marketplace, including the 20-week and 40-week cycles. I will present quantitative and anecdotal evidence of these cycles and show how they can be exploited by active investors.

- **Multimonth momentum.** I will explain why observations of stocks' relationship with their 10-month simple moving average may be the simplest yet most effective weapon in our toolbox. Stocks that are emerging from long downtrends and preparing to rebound back toward their highs must eventually switch from being under their 10-month moving averages to above them. This transition typically occurs slowly at first and then picks up speed. I will show how to find these stocks and exploit them in both short- and intermediate-term holding periods.

Mondays

- **Sector relative strength.** You will learn a new way of exploiting the well-known insight that at least 60 percent of a stock's movements come from the popularity of its sector. I will show how to create sector relative strength charts at the Web site Stockcharts.com that will provide insights into which sectors are in favor during any given week. Special emphasis will be given to showing that the best time to buy into sectors is when they are emerging from a long period of disfavor, such as occurred quite unexpectedly with energy providers in 2004, broadcasters in the fall of 2006, and auto parts makers in late 2006. Investors who were quick to jump on those surprising trends made a lot of money before the trends became evident to all, and then promptly waned.

- **Swing trading.** Throughout this book, I will use a wide variety of "swing trade" methodologies to explain how to take short-term advantage of long-term change. In this chapter, though, I will describe the five simplest and best chart patterns to look for and how to execute buys and sells based on them. These will include double bottoms, bull and bear flags and invalidated head and shoulders.

Tuesdays

- **Earnings, event, and seasonal edges.** You should trade stocks only when the probabilities are clearly in your favor: not because you think you can read a chart better than 10,000 professionals who have been at the game many years longer than you, but because the stock faces a price event, earnings date, or calendar day that has proved to be a successful directional predictor in the past. I will show you how to use the remarkable resources available at a subscription Web site called Markethistory.com to trade stocks only when the odds are clearly in their favor. For instance, you will learn that when a particular company reports earnings in January at a time when its stock is above its 200-day moving average, the shares tend to rise over the next 18 days by an average of 6.3 percent.

Wednesdays

- **Spin-offs.** Corporate orphans provide great opportunities for active traders, as they are typically overly hated and misunderstood, providing traders with highly exploitable price information asymmetries for many weeks and months. You'll learn what to look for and how to trade them.
- **Initial public offerings.** This is another very misunderstood corner of the market. I will show you how to get information about new offerings, track them and trade them in their first week, month, and year.
- **Postbankruptcy stocks.** Companies that declare bankruptcy very quickly become pariahs on Wall Street. They are seen as failures and are shunned by the crowd. Yet very often bankruptcy courts shear off debt and other obligations from struggling companies, leaving them in great shape. When formerly bankrupt companies refloat shares in new IPOs, they are usually ignored by the retail investors whom they previously burned—but bought avidly by savvy institutional investors. I will explore this phenomenon and show how you can make a fortune in this much hated corner of the market.

Thursdays

- **StockScouter.** In 2001, I invented and helped to develop a stock rating system at MSN Money called StockScouter that has been incredibly successful—trouncing the broad market by a wide margin since its inception. In my previous book, *Swing Trading*, I showed readers how to take advantage of the system for long-term investing. In this book, I will show you how to exploit StockScouter for trading over one-month and and six-month holding periods.

Fridays

- **N power.** One of the most powerful and least understood forces at work on stocks is what I call "N power," which is the power of the "new." New management, new products, new distribution, and new highs are all observable changes at work in the marketplace that active investors can monitor and exploit. I will provide examples and show how to buy the shares of companies that are undergoing life-changing shifts of power and purpose. Most investors are typically skeptical about the prospects for changes that will affect companies positively, so I will show how to battle that tendency by looking for key fundamental and technical success factors. Fridays are a good time to reflect on what you have learned during the week and what has really changed, which makes it an ideal time to consider what's really new in the news and lay plans to act upon your insights.
- **Ecosystems.** Another hidden force is at work on companies when they are participating in an industry that is undergoing

secular change in the way its value is weighed by the marketplace. Very often this happens not just in a sector, but in a product cycle. A great example of an ecosystem that is boosting the shares of a small but far-flung subset of companies today is commercial jet aircraft production. As Boeing prepared to build its most radically new plane in two decades in 2006, called the 787 Dreamliner, it boosted the shares of titanium producers, aluminum smelters, cockpit makers, forged aluminum parts makers, landing gear makers, and the like. This chapter will help you understand not just how to recognize these ecosystems—whether local, national, or global—but also how to determine where the greatest short-term value is being created.

I hope you will have fun with these ideas and really execute on them. I want you to advance to a whole new level of understanding of the short-term forces at work in the market and to achieve your financial goals with fewer impediments. So now let's get started.

SUNDAY

Everything comes too late for those who only wait.
—Elmore Hubbard

There is no investment industry occupation or advisory niche that is more reviled in academic circles than that of the market timer. Professors, mutual fund executives, and professional financial advisors swear that they have studied market timing to death and can prove, without a scintilla of doubt, that no one can consistently forecast the market's major ups and down.

The orthodoxy holds that the only market timing strategy known to work reliably is the long-term hold. This belief condenses to a marketing slogan: "It's not market timing. It's time in the market."

Of course, this is utter nonsense aimed at encouraging mutual fund investors and financial advisory customers to keep their money in one place and never move it—no matter how badly it performs. The industry has built its great Manhattan and Boston skyscrapers and its executives have built their seaside mansions on the strength of this simple but misleading concept.

How do we know it's wrong? We will get to that at length in a moment. But for now, just keep in mind that virtually all of the great traders and investors of the past century have been market timers of one type or another, from Jesse Livermore at the turn of the twentieth century to Warren Buffett today.

Livermore, the subject of the wonderful 1920s-era fictional work *Reminiscences of a Stock Operator,* made one of his early fortunes by timing a clever series of short sales and purchases upon learning of the great San Francisco earthquake of 1906. (Of course, he lost it all later—but that's another story). Buffett is famous for world-weary comments to reporters that he sees nothing to buy while at the same moment easing his funds, with exquisite timing, into a set of purchases of railroads or gas pipelines or mortgage lenders.

Indeed, the mere notion of buying low and selling high is a form of timing. One of the industry's top timers points out that if you simply buy when you have money to put at risk and sell when you need the profits for something else, you are engaging in a form of timing. My late father, a master salesman and storyteller, used to have a funny line on this point. He would ask a new customer at a lunch to identify the secret of comedy. And then, before his companion could answer, Dad would blurt out, "Timing!" That was good for a laugh, proof that it was true. And let's not forget one of the great predators of the animal world, the hawk. Do you think hawks randomly pick the time to swoop down on their prey? Not a chance. They patiently wait for the right set of circumstances and opportunities to line up and then dive for the kill. If they didn't exquisitely time the moment that their dinner bell rings, they'd be a very extinct set of birds.

For the purposes of timing the market in an effort to be a successful daily trader, most people lack the superb go/no-go instincts of the hawk, unfortunately. So we have to rely on more artificial methods. To be consistently successful, you need to focus on timing methodologies that have stood the test of time, not just ones that you feel intuitively might work or that are sent to you as a tip by the guy in the next cubicle.

After studying numerous methods over the years, I have come to realize that it's best to take a big-picture view when it comes to timing. So here's the big thought: You want to be long in a bull market and neutral or short in a bear market. And in each case, to augment your returns significantly, you want to make big bets against short-term countertrend moves. I know that this sounds almost ridiculously naive, but if you are a relative beginner, you might be amazed to learn how well this approach works out.

Short selling in a profound, prolonged, persistent bull market is pretty much a loser's game. Every time you find an index or sector or stock that is faltering and should topple over, it tends to find support and buyers. Wall Street's graveyard is filled with people who called tops too early, trying to lean against the tide.

One of my favorite stories along these lines came out of an interview that I once did with the legendary hedge fund manager Michael Steinhardt. He told me that his research had suggested that network equipment maker Cisco Systems (CSCO) should be sold short during the epic bull market of 1991, and he kept that position on for two years. By the time he covered, he had lost $250 million. Yes, the great Steinhardt lost a quarter of a billion dollars on a single trade by going short during one of the biggest technology bull markets in history.

By the same token, it is possible to be long certain sectors or market capitalization groups during a broad bear market, but it's hard work. The tide is against you. The bear market of 2000 to 2002 was something of an exception, as it presented some great opportunities to be long energy, small-cap stocks, regional banks, and real estate investment trusts. But even in those cases, the gains were relatively muted and subject to a lot of whipsawing.

Does this mean that you just sit back once a trend is established? Not at all, because some of the really big money to be made in the market occurs at times when you can identify and effectively trade extreme countertrend rallies. That is, during bull markets, there will occasionally be strong, short-lived jolts to the downside, and you need to get long with as much of your cash and borrowing power as you can stomach. And likewise, during bear markets, there will occasionally be strong, short-lived jolts to the upside, and you'll need to learn ways to go heavily short into them.

Indeed, perhaps the most important elements for success in timing as an active trader are to understand when major trends are starting and ending, how long each is likely to last, and how to distinguish short-lived countertrend zigs and zags from true reversals. Markets spend most of their time in bull market mode, but the media and experts are always trying to scare the public into thinking that a bear market is right around the corner. So you need a variety of means to reassure yourself that the bull is in full gear even when it appears to be faltering, as well as ways to determine if it is, in fact, time to batten down the hatches and put your bear on.

To make gobs and gobs of money in equities, your best bet is to go heavily long near the initiation of a major uptrend, or bull market, and to take money off the table or go short near the start of an important downtrend, or bear market. You don't have to be exactly on time in either case, and it's a lot better to be a little late than way too early.

That might sound easy enough, but how do you carry it off?

Fortunately, a lot of data have accumulated over the years to help us pinpoint the initiation of major uptrends and big downtrends, and that's what we're going to study. I want you to use your Sundays to determine whether the market is currently in a major uptrend or downtrend, and make sure that you set your mind to set up your hunt for new positions for the week appropriately. And at the same time, I want you to take time on Sundays to determine the possibility or likelihood of a countertrend rally in the coming weeks and to contemplate what you would do about it.

Why do I specify major uptrends and downtrends here, if we're talking about day trading? It all has to do with focus.

At Microsoft Corp., where I worked for half a decade, the program managers are great at helping product development teams shut out discussion of extraneous topics so that they can concentrate on what's really important. They call this process the identification of "nongoals." In the case of market timing for our new style of day trading, our nongoal is the short-term investment horizon, or anything less than two weeks. We are going to focus like laser beams on the one- to six-month horizon.

So here's the deal: We're going to start with the mysterious art of determining the expected start and end of intermediate-term cycles. Then we'll move on to determining the launch of major new trends out of those cycle inflection points. And then we'll go on to a study of tradable countertrend rallies.

Cycle Seekers

Analysts who study intermediate-term market timing can be divided into two groups: (1) those who focus on trying to understand and *anticipate* the market's hidden cycles of ups and downs, and (2) those who strictly seek statistical *evidence* that an up or down cycle has already begun or is beginning at the moment of study. As a practical matter, I recommend that you try to straddle both camps. Look out on the horizon and have an assumption as to when cycles are likely to commence, but don't actually act until there is real evidence that the cycle has actually commenced.

Our guides for this study will be two masters of each sort of inter-mediate-horizon market timing, Tom McClellan and Paul Desmond. Each is a pro's pro and has a unique approach to this difficult but important task. We'll start with McClellan.

Natural Rhythms

Analysts like McClellan who study cycles in the market think that their work is no more unusual than using a calendar to "predict" which months will be warm and which will be cold. If we were in a primitive society that didn't understand the seasonality of weather, a forecaster in midwinter who predicted warm weather in six months might be considered a prodigy. To cycle guys, the world of stocks and commodities is underpinned by mathematical, natural, and even biological patterns that are invisible to the naked eye.

Even if you do not believe in cycles, it's important that you rec-ognize that many others do. If the views are strong enough—and are acted upon with strong buying or selling—they can become self-fulfilling prophecies. It's the George Soros theory of "reflexiv-ity" at work, in which things happen because people expect them to happen. If the smart-money institutional consensus belief is that a timing method or strategy works, it will continue to do so even if it makes no sense to academic researchers or common sense.

Many major hedge funds use cycle work to help them plan their year. It tells them what might happen, based on a variety of tested theories. Yet they don't use cycles derived from Elliott waves, Gann patterns, seasonality, presidential cycles, lunar phases, 20-year cycles, and 40-month cycles in isolation. Instead, they overlay numerous successful cycles from a variety of sources to see how they all line up. Some call these points of intersection *balance points*, and they lead to further investigation. Once balance points are pinpointed, research managers study a calendar and scrutinize the major and minor U.S. and foreign media and trade journals to try to figure out what news events might spark the downswings, upswings, and, most importantly, major reversals that the cycles foretell. They trust their cycle work without knowing exactly what will lead to inflection points, but they always seem to feel safer, intellectually, if they can find a good story to support the math.

Cycle work, in other words, tells traders when major investment events might happen, but it rarely says why. Some people need to know why, and that may include you. But you should know that other very successful cycle traders are comfortable following the cyclical patterns without pinning down reasons for them.

McClellan, the Lakewood, Washington–based editor of the *McClellan Market Report,* is one cycle guy with a strong long-term record who straddles the line between those who simply forecast and follow cycles and those who must know why they occur. He publishes his views on a variety of cycles, and then speculates in his advisory service on why they might work.

A former engineer and Army helicopter pilot, Tom has an unusually good pedigree for this work. His mother and father invented the McClellan Oscillator, a tool that is widely used to study market breadth, in the 1960s. Since then, the senior McClellans and their son have invented another 100 methods to measure market cyclicality.

In a series of interviews, Tom told me that only two fundamentals matter in the market: how much money is out there, and how interested people are in investing it. Cycles thus depict millions of individuals' on-again/off-again desire to commit their hard-earned dollars to paper assets, a rhythm that may have a hidden biological or psychological dimension.

Tom observes that timing is important because it is one of the few things over which traders actually have control. The market determines the buy and sell price of an instrument, but the trader determines when it is purchased. So if you can control only one thing, you might as well try to get good at it.

He approaches market timing in this way: A study of cycles helps us understand what is *supposed* to happen. But he thinks you should not start a trade until that *expected* event actually does happen.

Now let's focus on one big cycle idea that should work well over a full one-year span during 25 percent of your entire future career as an investor.

Third Year of Presidential Cycle

The presidential cycle is probably the best known of the major cycles in the market. I won't belabor the details, because it is so well covered in other books. But the key point is that each of the years of a president's term has certain tendencies that have persisted, with important exceptions, throughout many of the past 100 years.

As you might expect, however, most of these cycles have deteriorated over time to the point that very few of them occur reliably enough to provide us with important timing clues.

For decades, you could count on market weakness during the first year of a presidential term. The reason: presidents try to jump-start their administrations with attempts to manage the economy in ways that scare investors, whether by changing the tax code, launching new entitlement programs, or altering long-established norms in communications, drug policy, and the like. These changes, which are usually sold to the public as "reforms," disturb investors because their ultimate impact on corporate profits is unknown.

First-year weakness was an insistent cycle during the first part of the twentieth century, and it worked recently in the first years of the two terms of the George W. Bush administration. Yet it doesn't work reliably enough to count on. The initial years of the two Bill Clinton terms, for instance, were amply positive at +7.1 percent (1993) and +30 percent (1997). The first and second years of a two-term president's second administration, in fact, are usually not as rough as the first and second years of his first term because he usually does not spend much time telling us how screwed up his predecessor was—and therefore does not try to implement as many investor-aggravating reforms. Likewise, the second and fourth years of presidential terms also have mixed records.

However, the third year of the presidential cycle has a virtually unblemished record of being positive for stocks. In the twentieth century, with two exceptions, the market finished higher in third years. The two exceptions: 1931, with the onset of the Dust Bowl, the Depression, the passage of the anti-free-trade Smoot-Hawley Act, the collapse of the Weimar Republic in Germany, and the rise of the Nazi Party; and 1939, when Hitler marched through Poland to launch the Second World War. The Dow Jones Industrial Average plunged 55 percent in 1931 and dropped 6 percent in 1939. (In 1987, the third year of Ronald Reagan's second presidential term, the S&P 500 was up by 38 percent in August before crashing in October. It finished the year up 1.5 percent.)

In other words, unless there are very serious and unusual conditions, you can expect to trade from the long side of the market throughout the third year of a presidential term. Three recent examples—1995, 1999, and 2003—were all barn burners, with the Nasdaq 100 advancing 46 percent, 102 percent, and 43 percent, respectively.

The message is very clear: when you are in the third year of a presidential term, which is a full quarter of your entire career as an investor, you are in a fortunate and special time frame. Every Sunday in those years, when you sit down to study the major trend, you must have a heavy bias toward looking for confirmation that a bull market is well under way, even if sometimes it appears that a bear is threatening to emerge.

Forty-Week and Twenty-Week Cycles

But what if you're not in the third year of a presidential term? Well, that's a little more challenging, but we have our ways.

Just to keep things simple, if you pay attention to 40-week and 20-week cycles in the U.S. stock market, you will know how to scout the horizon for danger and opportunity and be way ahead of the majority of independent traders.

The 40-week cycle was identified and studied by an analyst named J. M. Hurst in the 1960s, but McClellan is its current leading proponent. No one has ever come up with a satisfactory answer as to exactly why this cycle exists or how it works, so all you can do is observe that it does tend to work and leave it at that. It's one of those market mysteries. If you're cynical, you could say that this cycle recurs because the institutional consensus believes that it will recur. If that's not a good enough answer, we might as well observe that it's actually more like a 38- to 39-week cycle (terms that just don't roll off the tongue as easily as a "40-week cycle")—the length of the human gestation period. So perhaps there are some natural harmonics at work.

At any rate, here's how you use this cycle. It's pretty simple. At any given time, you just look back at the most recent major low point in the market and count forward by 270 to 280 days. The next major low should be right around that future date. And if you want to cut the data a little more finely, then you should note that halfway through that period—in other words, after 130 to 140 days—there should be a less significant low point, or at least a significant pause in the action. Plus, a top typically comes around 28 days before any expected bottom.

As you can see, this is not like the presidential cycle, which you can circle on your calendar 100 years in advance. This is a cycle that slides and slips around a little, but it should give you a general feel for what to expect every four to nine months.

Let's look at a few recent examples from 2004 through mid-2007, as shown in Figure 1-1. The first significant low shown on this chart was S&P 1,063 on August 6, 2004. Of course, you wouldn't realize that this is a significant low at the time it was occurring. But when

Figure 1-1

you look back on it in October, you can see that it was a significant low. That's when you start counting forward.

An easy way to do this is to type "8/6/2004" into a cell in Excel, then in another cell type "="(the *equals* sign), click on the cell that holds the date, and then type "+270." Excel will calculate the date 270 calendar days forward, which is May 3, 2005. Now you can circle that date on your calendar and expect a cyclical low right around then. It most likely will not happen exactly then, but you can expect it within a couple of weeks.

In this case, the *actual* next low came on April 15, 2005, at S&P 1,141. That was about two weeks early, but good enough—you were expecting something around that period, so you were prepared. On the expected date, May 3, the S&P closed at 1,161, and the final low for the period after May 3 came on May 13 at 1,146. Those three levels are within 1.75 percent of each other, so you can see that you don't need to be precise. All around that time, traders who were not looking at the 40-week scorecard were probably just scrambling around, but those who were expecting a low were able to scale calmly into new purchases. You would also have noticed that the S&P 500 had traded down to its 70-week moving average at that time, which had provided support to the bull market since 2003.

Now let's fast-forward a bit to late 2005, just to look at another period. By then you could look back and see that the significant closing low came on October 13, at S&P 1,176. When you put that date into Excel and count forward 270 and 280 days, you come up with July 10 to July 20, 2006. The market actually started to deteriorate in early May 2006 and really fell apart in June, but you were looking for a final low in mid-July. The lows on July 10 and July 20 were 1,267 and 1,249, respectively. The actual July low came at 1,236 on July 18, while the low for the entire summer was 1,223 on June 13. All were within 2.9 percent of each other, so expecting the low to be on July 20 was certainly worthwhile. And that turned out to be a very durable low for the entire year.

By the time you had moved forward from that low into September and October, it was clear that the June 13 closing low was the significant low for the summer, so it was time to determine the time frame for the next 40-week low. According to Excel, the dates 270 and 280 days forward were March 10 and March 20, 2007. In that time frame, the market began to deteriorate at the end of February after cresting at S&P 1,460; it hit S&P 1,398 on March 10 and S&P 1,410 on March 20. The closing low in that time frame was March 5, at 1,374, and the midday low was 1,363 on March 14. Again, all were within 1.75 percent of each other, so you were right in the ballpark with the 40-week cycle forecast. The next 20-week low was due around August 3 (March 14 + 280 days), and it came close. On that day, the S&P 500 closed at 1,433; the ultimate summer low came two weeks later on August 15 at 1,406, a 1.9 percent difference. (The expected top was July 6, and that was close as well, early by just a week and 25 S&P 500 Index points, or 1.7 percent.) Meanwhile, the 40-week low in late 2007 was due between November 30 to December 10, with a top due around November 2.

In every case, you can see that the actual 20- and 40-week cycle highs and lows were close to their forecasted dates, but not precisely on time, so it's important to observe in real time whether a low appears to be forming before you do anything about it in a dramatic way. It's sort of like a weather forecaster telling you that it's supposed to snow tomorrow. It's a good idea to actually look out the window to see if it is even cloudy before you make plans to go skiing.

Also, McClellan warns that, just to make life difficult, the 40-week cycle seems to jump to a new schedule every six to eight years, like a person's heart skipping a beat. In the process, it can sometimes disappear for half a year or more—perhaps just to throw researchers off the scent. McClellan argues that just such a "phase shift" occurred in 2005–2006, and the 40-week cycle has been operating on a new schedule since then. The next phase shift should thus be due in 2012 to 2014, so mark your calendar.

Start of a New Uptrend

Now that you know when you are supposed to expect a new uptrend to begin, you next need a way to determine whether it is really happening. You can get lost in the day-to-day zigs and zags of the market unless you have a clear concept of what to look for from a robust new leg up in the market.

If you look retrospectively at the starts of more than 100 major uptrends over the past 75 years and sort all their characteristics into piles, you will see that they have a few clearly observable patterns—a signature, if you will, or a statistical fingerprint—that distinguish them from mere upward wiggles within a prior downtrend.

So what's supposed to happen at the start of a big move higher? Explosions, fireworks, sirens, excitement!

The full path of a trend, mind you, is much like that of a bouncing ball: a parabolic arc. At the start, though, we are concerned only with the beginning of that arc. At the point that it launches higher, the ball is traveling at its fastest rate.

A great example of the power of the initial move of a strong market occurred in the 3½ months following mid-March 2003, as shown in Figure 1-2. The Nasdaq 100 jumped to 1,300 from 950 at lightning speed. That was a 36 percent move in just 15 weeks, a real blitzkrieg. A short correction back to 1,200 occurred after that, which many market participants at the time believed marked a return to the bear market that had plagued investors from 2000 to 2002. Just as the fear reached its zenith, along came another, more modest surge that took the tech-heavy index up to 1,450.

The strength of the first surge of a major new up cycle is most easily understood in contrast to the second. It's so powerful that investors just can't believe it. The index travels quickly to the top of its 20-day moving average "envelope," as shown in Figure 1-2, and remains at the top of the envelope with only one- or two-day excursions to the bottom. It never travels below.

$NDX (Nasdaq 100 Index) INDX   © StockCharts.com
31-Dec-2003   **O** 1471.60 **H** 1474.20 **L** 1459.10 **C** 1467.90 **V** 436.3M **Chg** -2.10 (-0.14%) ▾

Escape velocity: 36% move for the Nasdaq 100 in 3.5 months starting mid-March 2003.

Gentler arc higher after initial surge: 15% move in next 3 months.

Figure 1-2

McClellan Oscillator: The Acceleration Gauge

The most important thing about the start of an uptrend, then, is that it has incredible upward energy. Physicists use the term *escape velocity* for this phenomenon. It refers to the minimum speed an object requires if it is to peel away from its gravitational field and exit its prior orbit. One of the best tools for gauging the sort of hyperenergy that can signify the start of an important uptrend is the McClellan Oscillator.

The McClellan Oscillator acts like an acceleration gauge, telling us how quickly the object—which in this case is the New York Stock Exchange Advance-Decline Line—is shucking off gravity and exiting its prior state. It does this by measuring the acceleration of advance/decline statistics.

Why? Well, it's pretty simple—elegant even. The big idea is that for a new trend to really get going, it needs to have enough power to bring all kinds of stocks—large, small, and every sector—along with it. So we want to see the advance/decline line kick into fifth gear. When there is so much money available and being put to work that even the least-deserving stocks go up, we have a very healthy condition for the start of a major uptrend.

Technically, McClellan Oscillator data are figured by subtracting a smoothed 39-day exponential average of advances minus declines on the NYSE from a smoothed 19-day exponential average of advances minus declines. When the shorter moving average rises much faster than the longer moving average, the McClellan Oscillator rises rapidly and steadily to an "overextended" condition, peaking at +150 to +200. This signals that a market has achieved escape velocity. After that point, the market has not only launched but escaped its prior orbit—and can then travel higher on its own. Even if the McClellan Oscillator turns down at that point, which it will, the market is off and running.

When does this occur? Ah, now we're getting somewhere. As active traders, we can do a lot of great work in all kinds of conditions, but we really live for this setup.

These sorts of conditions typically occur quite soon after very oversold conditions. They are two sides of the same card. One follows the other like day follows night. Very typical versions of this setup occurred in the early summer of 2006 and in the spring of 2007. In both cases, the market had been ambling along just fine in the months before, minding its own business and making money for people in a slow and nonvolatile way. Out of the blue, however, the market stopped going up. In fact, there is usually some news event—it doesn't matter what—that causes investors to lose confidence. It doesn't even have to be a period in which sellers become the dominant force the market. It can just be a situation in which buyers go on strike.

After an initially quick period of decline, investors appear to regain their bearing—but then another panic attack hits and the market plunges. Suddenly, you're in a situation in which investors are fed up with the losses they've experienced in the preceding weeks and dump stocks indiscriminately—every sector, every size—in a paroxysm of panic.

You will know that this is happening because the broad indexes are sinking, but as a patient day trader, you need to wait for a bell to ring before fading the decline by buying into it. Now you know that you are waiting for a 40-week low to occur, but there are a couple of ways to hear that bell.

One of them is a McClellan Oscillator reading of –200 or lower. When that happens, brother, you need to dip into your cash hoard to buy stocks, or go into margin, or buy options, or purchase one of the exchange-traded funds that provides double the gains of a selected index, such as the ProShares Ultra QQQQ (QLD), which delivers double the return of the Nasdaq 100.

You can see this very clearly in Figure 1-3. In May 2006, the broad market began to weaken. It slowed down, and then collapsed in a heap in mid-June. All this time, as a patient daily trader, you were waiting for a bell to ring to give you a signal, and it sounded with the decline of the McClellan Oscillator to –200. At that point, the market can definitely fall further, but you know that you are really close to a panic bottom, if you are not already there. Virtually everyone who was thinking about selling has sold, and there is a vacuum. And dispassionate students of panic—like you, I hope—are the ones who fill that vacuum by buying.

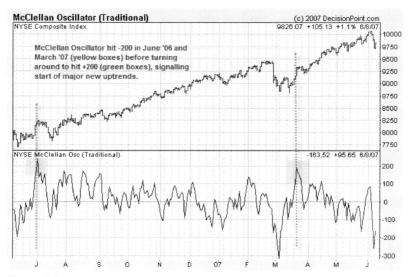

Figure 1-3

The same thing happened in the spring of 2007, as you can see on the same chart. The decline in U.S. markets started with a jolt from the blue in late February as a result of a plunge in the Chinese stock market and then continued into early March toward the 40-week low. The time to buy heavily into the plunge, as you can see, was when the McClellan Oscillator fell to –200. The oscillator ultimately fell to –300, but that's OK. After it fell below –250 during the time frame in which you were expecting a major 40-week cycle low, you should just have added to your new, leveraged holdings with confidence.

Not too much later, in both cases, the market reversed, and you were on your way to a big gain. But there was much more to both cases than a quick profit because the vacuum created by selling led to a tornado of bargain hunting and fevered buying. So many stocks of all sizes and sectors were picked up so rapidly by voracious institutional buyers that the advance/decline line shot up and the McClellan Oscillator zoomed up above +150, and then up to +200. Again, that level rings the bell. The market had achieved escape velocity and was well on its way to much higher levels.

The McClellan Oscillator is available in most professional trading software programs, such as TradeStation. If you don't have one of those, the easiest place to observe it in chart form is online at Decisionpoint.com. You need to pay a monthly subscription to access the site, but it's worth it. The Oscillator is listed in the "Indicators" section, and you can view a six-month or three-year version. You can also see the current reading for free at the McClellan Financial Publications Web site at this address: http://www.mcoscillator.com/Data.html. And finally, it is published twice a month in the excellent *McClellan Market Report*, which costs $195 per year, and in the organization's Daily Edition, which costs $600 per year.

Now occasionally a bottom doesn't look like either of these two examples on the price charts. And that is because there are two types of bottoms: ones that prices go down into, like the ones we just looked at, and ones that prices move up out of. That is to say, sometimes new bullish phases begin from a standing start after the market has been trading sideways for a while. In either case, the instructions are the same: look for a −150 to −200 reading on the McClellan Oscillator to start your buying, and then add with increased confidence—perhaps in thirds or fifths of your available funds—until the McClellan Oscillator reverses up to the +150 to +200 level.

So is the bullish phase over at that point? Not in the slightest. Remember that the move to the +175 to +200 level on the McClellan Oscillator is just the first impulse wave. There's usually some sort of rest period after that, like the two minutes following the end of the first quarter of a professional basketball game. When the oscillator goes that high, it promises that there's a lot more to come, as it suggests that money is flooding into the market at a tremendous rate. In the succeeding days, weeks, and months, the oscillator will probably never get back to that +150 to +200 level; in fact, it will make a series of lower highs. That's fine. It's not a divergence that signals trouble. It just says that the market has escaped its previous low orbit and is now cruising at a higher level, and you should be looking only for plays on the long side of the market.

On the other hand, if four weeks go by after a −150 to −300 reading without a surge back to the +150 to +200 level, then you might not be done with the bottoming process. The rocket did not achieve escape velocity, and it may have to return to Earth. If that happens, either you will have to look for other reasons to believe that a bottom has been achieved but it's perhaps not as firm as you would ideally like, or you may need to acknowledge that it is time to play defense, plan for a retest of the earlier lows, and await another attempt at an escape toward new highs.

Advance/Decline Line Immunization

What else can you look at for comfort that an uptrend will continue in place? Again, turn your gaze to the advance/decline line—that longstanding measure of liquidity. Our guides, McClellan and Desmond, both agree that if the NYSE advance/decline (A/D) line is at a high, the market is "immunized" from suffering anything worse than a 10 percent correction over the following three months. In other words, if you're in the middle of the third year of the presidential cycle and the A/D line is near its peak, if the market begins to stall and slip back by 3 to 9.5 percent and there are calls all around for the start of a new bear market, you can keep your cool and feel virtually assured that a mere correction is taking place. You are not likely to get a 1987-style crash or a 1990- or 2000-style bear market if the A/D line is at highs at the time that the correction begins.

In contrast, when liquidity is weak, only one class of stocks—such as large caps or energy stocks—may be soaking up most of the money that investors are applying to stocks. As fewer and fewer stocks participate in an uptrend, the New York Stock Exchange A/D line declines.

It can sink for a long time before an actual decline in the broad averages begins, however. As an example, the A/D line made a top in early 1998 when investors were focusing exclusively on large-cap technology stocks. No one wanted small caps or mid caps or energy producers or basic materials makers: it was all big-cap tech, all the time. The A/D line was in a long-term downtrend by the time the Dow Jones Industrial Average topped out in late 1999 and the Nasdaq topped out in early 2000. So the falling A/D line was essentially a yellow flag that warned of a problem with liquidity. A declining A/D line paired with a rising stock market is like a guy who has a diminishing income but lives high on the hog with credit cards. He can accumulate a lot of cards to keep his scheme going, but eventually the bill must be paid. And for the market, the bill was paid in 2000–2002 with a severe bear market.

Sentiment Lows

So what do you look for in sentiment at the start of an uptrend? That is a lot trickier, but one element to look for is pervasive pessimism. I know that sounds counterintuitive, but bear with me. You are likely to be tempted to look for signs of pessimism in every newspaper headline or conversation with coworkers, but there are more persuasive, quantitative ways to go about the task.

You are probably already familiar with observing the spread between bulls and bears in surveys of investors performed by the American Association of Individual Investors. Generally, when the ratio of bulls to bears extends to bullish extremes, as it did most emphatically in late 1999 and more recently in mid-February 2007, the market is due for a correction. And conversely, as you can see in the months marked by arrows in Figure 1-4, when the number

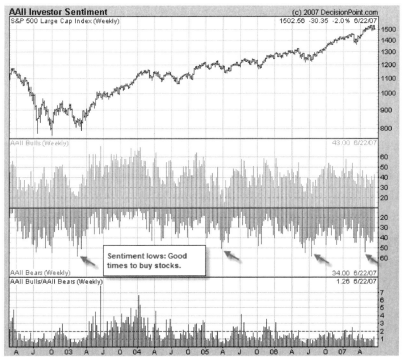

Figure 1-4

of people expressing bearish sentiment runs to extremes of 50 percent or more, it's a good time to be a buyer of stocks. (This chart can be found at Decisionpoint.com in the "Market Indicators/Sentiment" section.)

Another less well known—and thus potentially more useful—quantitative sentiment indicator, though, looks at the mood of the overall populace, not just investors. A deliriously happy public is bad for stocks, while a morose populace is great for stocks. When people think the economy is great, then it cannot get any better. Periods when people think the economy is in bad shape are when stock market bottoms occur, because things cannot get any worse. People also usually have money on the sidelines at those times, which can then fuel the advance as they make the switch from bearish to bullish.

To see the contrast, check out the monthly Gallup poll that seeks the general mood of Americans. In this survey, the poll taker asks people, "In general, are you satisfied or dissatisfied with the way things are going in the United States at this time?" The answers are published at the Gallup Poll Web site (http://www.gallup.com/poll/1669/General-Mood-Country.aspx) and take the form of the percentage that describe themselves as satisfied or dissatisfied.

When you plot the American mood against a chart of the S&P 500, you will see that with remarkable regularity the best times to invest or trade from the long side of the market come when Americans are at their most pessimistic. And vice versa. The best time to stay out of the market, or be short, is when consumers are at their most optimistic. Figure 1-5 shows the yearly averages of the absolute percentages for each answer since 1978, while Figure 1-6 zooms in on the 2005–2007 period.

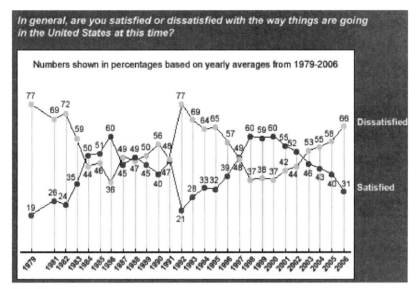

Figure 1-5

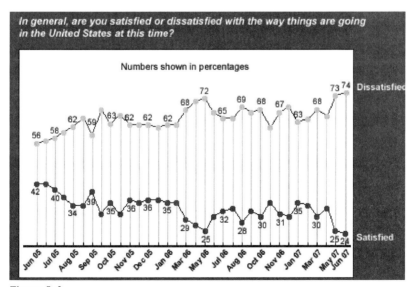

Figure 1-6

What you are looking for is the spread between those who are satisfied and those who are dissatisfied. The optimistic sugar high for the past decade came in the week of January 7, 2000, shortly before the market was about to topple into a two-year bear market. In that survey, Gallup found that 69 percent of the public believed that economic conditions were getting better, while 28 percent thought that they were getting worse. The Dow Jones Industrial Average topped out on January 14 that month, and it took almost seven years to crawl back.

Strangely enough, the general mood of Americans remained positive for most of 2000 as the bear market was just getting under way, and remained so during 2001, except for a hiccup to the downside in May and just after the September 11 attacks, and on through the middle of 2002. During virtually that entire span, the market was mired in a downtrend. Happy Americans, it seems, make for a lousy market.

Now contrast that with March 2003, just before the start of the U.S. invasion of Iraq. In polling during March 3–5, the spread hit an eight-year low at –25. And sure enough, that was just about the best time to put money into stocks in this decade. The mood has remained sour virtually every month since, punctuated with spikes of extreme crankiness around market lows in October–November 2005; May–June and December 2006; and May–June 2007. All of these times were great times to be applying new money to the market. To study the spread yourself, visit the General Mood of America page at the Gallup poll site, as indicated earlier, and copy the table given there to an Excel spreadsheet. It lists only the percent each week that were satisfied and dissatisfied. Create a column for the spread by subtracting Dissatisfied from Satisfied, and you are good to go, as shown in Figure 1-7.

Grumpy Citizens Make for Buoyant Market				
Gallup Poll: General Mood in America				
Date	Satisfied	Dissatisfied	Spread	Market Milestones
Jun-07	24	74	-50	
May-07	25	73	-48	Dow 13,628
Apr-07	33	65	-32	
Mar-07	30	68	-38	
Feb-07	34	64	-30	
Jan-07	35	63	-28	
Dec-06	30	69	-39	
Nov-06	31	67	-36	
Oct-06	35	61	-26	New Dow High, 12,081
Sep-06	30	68	-38	
Aug-06	32	67	-35	
Jul-06	28	69	-41	
Jun-06	33	65	-32	Dow 11,150
May-06	32	65	-33	
Apr-06	30	67	-37	
Mar-06	25	72	-47	
Feb-06	27	71	-44	
Jan-06	29	68	-39	Dow 10,865

Figure 1-7

Poor Timing Method: Earnings Growth Forecasts

This may be a good time to note a timing methodology that makes a lot of sense on the surface but doesn't work at all, and that is trying to time the market based on earnings growth projections. This is because there is a real disconnect between earnings growth and the stock market.

What gives? I know this goes against the conventional wisdom, but hear me out. Ned Davis Research says that the disconnect between earnings and stock results has occurred because earnings don't actually drive broad-market results—and never have.

Ned Davis, who runs an investment and economics research operation in southern Florida, is the leading proponent of this contrarian thesis. In a controversial report published in 2005, he showed that in the years since 1958 in which S&P 500 earnings growth has been greater than 6 percent, stocks have averaged only a 3.9 percent gain per year. When earnings growth has been below that level—which amounts to the long-term trend—stock returns have averaged 8.1 percent per year.

Traditionalists might say, no biggie: focus on earnings growth expectations, not trailing growth rates. But when you do the research, it turns out that the higher the expectations for stocks, the worse the results.

So add this to the conventional-wisdom bonfire: those analysts who crow about how great a stock is going to do because the company is expected to grow earnings by more than 25 percent next year may be all wet. The Davis study shows that the real sweet spot for stock market returns actually occurs when a company is expected to earn 12.5 percent or less in the next year, and the overall market's growth expectations are limited. In 2006, this was true in spades: in aggregate, NYSE stocks in the lowest quintile for expected earnings growth were the market's top performers.

Why would this be? We can surmise that the market does not discount fundamentals 12 months ahead, as is commonly believed. Instead, good news and optimism tend to lead to a fully invested market in which there are few bystanders left to make purchases. At the point of maximum optimism, the market falls over for lack of new buyers. In contrast, when news is bad and investors are feeling nervous about the future, the market has a lot of bystanders to convert into buyers and thus is in position for an extended rally.

There do seem to be some better economic clues as to future market direction, by the way. Consumer-price inflation may be at the top of the list. Ned Davis research shows that in the 49 percent of the years since 1958 when inflation has been clocked at greater than 3.5 percent, stock market returns have been subpar, at 3.9 percent per year. When inflation has been less than 3.5 percent, returns have bulled forward at a 9.8 percent annual pace.

The bottom line is that low inflation, low earnings expectations, and broad economic pessimism are the keys to strong stock market returns. When expectations for economic and earnings growth peak, cash flows into the market also peak and the only remaining direction is lower; in contrast, when expectations for growth are low, cash flows into the market bottom and the only remaining direction is up. We certainly saw this in the first half of 2007. Just as the general mood was turning increasingly sour, gross domestic product growth fell well below its 3 percent trend line to less than 1 percent, and expectations for S&P 500 companies' earnings growth fell from double digits to the mid-single digits, and then into negative territory by the third quarter. All that time, with skeptics and bears kicking and screaming, the market roared forward to new highs for the Dow Jones Industrials and the S&P 500 Index by mid-October, and the advance/decline line hit repeated new highs before ultimately stumbling. Go figure.

Pinpointing Bottoms

Now that we have some great new tools to examine on Sundays to help us understand sentiment, escape velocity, and liquidity, I'd like to bring to your attention the expertise of Paul Desmond, who is keeper of the flame and head honcho at Lowry's Reports, the oldest professional technical analysis firm in the country and one that sports an enviable 75-year record at helping institutional investors ride the major market trends.

Desmond and his team have done tremendous work on identifying the statistical fingerprints of bear market bottoms and bull market tops. They have also done a great job of helping investors identify the major intermediate trend of the market, which is where you make the most money. And finally, their analysis also helps us understand the difference between a sharp countertrend rally or decline within those trends and a real trend change. Desmond sees stock market history as a chain of long bull phases and short bear phases, each of which has a life span whose length is demarcated by historical averages.

The start of a bull market, he notes, is like the first couple of months of a human life—a time when a baby gains weight at an incredible speed. Remember what McClellan said about achieving escape velocity? It's the same thing. A baby's weight doubles within a few months, and its strength increases exponentially. Everything gets better for a child all the time as it becomes a teen and a young adult. Then, at age 28, a person's inner workings begin to slow dramatically. You don't grow any taller, you don't get any stronger, and athletes find that their vertical leap tops out. This is the age at which most professional athletes, as well as regular humans, peak physically. They may not get worse, but they are unlikely to get much better as they slide toward middle age. At around 40, some fundamental changes take place in the human body. Your skull expands, your hips widen, your hair starts to gray, your memory and hearing falter, and your strength begins to decline for the rest of your life. If you chart every human being on

Earth, you will see roughly the same pattern, with occasional exceptions that prove the rule.

Stock markets are much the same. At the start, they go through a burst of enthusiasm in which people are buying heavily into what they believe are incredible bargains. Their enthusiasm rises, and the market becomes extremely overbought and stays that way for weeks or months. Volume increases because people are pouring money in. But then you get to a point where the most enthusiastic participants have invested all they've got, and the process starts to slow. The number of stocks participating begins to diminish. The advance/decline line begins to decline as the market becomes more selective. And then you see real signs of fatigue.

As a bull market ages and the advance/decline line begins to wane, whole groups of stock begin to fall out of favor. At that point, it makes sense to begin to reduce your risk exposure by reducing your portfolio's diversification. The one element that characterizes every market top is an increase in selectivity as fewer stocks participate in advances and the market's structure becomes more fragile. At the very top, only a few favorite stocks are still pushing the major indexes higher, while most stocks are already declining.

So now that you have a view of the entire span of a market's life from Desmond's point of view, let's go back and look at exactly what characterizes the death of a bear market and the birth of a bull market.

Selling Climax

The key insight that Desmond's team has brought to the table is a simple statistical formula to identify the sort of bona fide "selling climax" that sets the final floor for stocks at the end of a bear market.

Desmond defines a *selling climax* as a final capitulation of investors in which stocks are dumped with abandon. Investors throw not only the baby out with the bathwater, but also the soap, the towels, and the plumbing. Selling is no longer based on perceived values, he notes, but rather simply on the desire to get rid of stocks. And then, once everyone who wanted to sell stocks has sold, of course, a vacuum emerges, as there is no one left to drive prices lower. That is the magical moment in which stocks are so heavily discounted that a sudden recognition of bargains spurs the start of the next bull market.

For many decades, the concept of a selling climax was limited to anecdotal observations, primarily related to total volume of trading, the number of declining stocks, and the number of new lows. But Desmond's work shows that a selling climax is actually more of a psychological phenomenon than a physical phenomenon. It's more about *intensity* than about activity.

The Upside of Downside Days

To define the level of intensity that has characterized final market bottoms in the past, Desmond's team studied data going back to 1933 and found that virtually all contained at least one day, and usually at least two or three days, of panic selling in which downside volume equaled 90 percent or more of the total of upside volume plus downside volume and in which points lost equaled 90 percent or more of the total number of points gained plus points lost that day. All of these statistics are carried in the *Wall Street Journal* every day if you want to do the math yourself. Or for $700 a year, which is a bargain, in my view, you can subscribe to the light version of Lowry's NYSE research service and have it do the math for you. (You also get a daily report on Lowry's view of the intermediate market trend and an excellent weekly report on Fridays that sums up the big technical picture in a way that, for my money, is superior to other services.)

Desmond calls these extraordinary panic sessions "90 percent downside days," and it's important to note that they do not occur only at the final bottom of a major market decline. These 90 percent downside days tend to be spread out through major downtrends, with the last in the group occurring right at the final bottom.

In fact, Lowry's work shows that 90 percent downside days tend to persist until they are followed by a panic buying day on which upside volume equals 90 percent or more of the sum of upside plus downside volume and points gained equals 90 percent or more of the sum of points gained and points lost. This one-two punch of a 90 percent downside day followed by a 90 percent upside day is the absolute signature of the end of a selling climax and the start of a new bull market.

In an award-winning paper that was circulated to institutional clients but never published widely, Desmond's team made the following observations about these 90 percent downside and upside days. I want you to know about them because they will occur at least occasionally even in full-on bull markets, and the extreme fear or euphoria that they produce can lead to more errors of judgment than just about any other condition.

- A single, isolated 90 percent downside day does not, by itself, have any long-term trend implications, since it sometimes occurs at the end of short-term corrections. But because it shows that investors can panic, even an isolated

90 percent downside day should be viewed as an important warning that more could follow.

- A 90 percent downside day that occurs shortly after a market high is most commonly associated with a short-term market correction, although there are some notable exceptions in the record.

- Broad market declines containing two or more 90 percent downside days often spawn a whole series of 90 percent downside days that are spread apart by as much as 30 trading days. Therefore, it should not be assumed that an investor can "ride out" such a decline. Impressive, big-volume "snapback" rallies lasting three or four days commonly follow quickly after 90 percent downside days. But longer-term investors should not be in a hurry to buy back into a market containing multiple 90 percent downside days if the market is broadly declining and is below its 10-month moving average.

- The 90 percent upside day that signals the completion of the selling climax usually occurs within 12 days or less of the last 90 percent downside day.

- On occasion, back-to-back 80 percent upside days have occurred instead of a single 90 percent upside day to signal the completion of the selling climax. Back-to-back 80 percent upside days are relatively rare except during these selling climax reversals.

- Back-to-back 90 percent upside days—a rare development— have usually been registered near the beginning of many important intermediate and longer-term trend rallies.

- Isolated 90 percent upside days—not preceded by a 90 percent downside day—do not have any long-term

implications. About half the time, they are followed by a
further rally. In the other half of the cases, they represent an
"upside blow-off" followed by lower prices.
- Isolated 90 percent upside days are unreliable when
triggered by a news announcement.

That's a long list, but it should help you determine situations when
a bear market might be over and when a big downward jiggle in a
bull market is a buying opportunity and not the start of a new bear.

To put it in a nutshell, the big idea is that when 90 percent downside days occur during a broad downtrend, they portend worse
action to come, not a selling climax. However, when a cluster of
two or more 90 percent downside days are followed by a 90 percent
upside day, it's time to break out the champagne and start buying
because this tends to portend the start of a big move higher. And
when a scary-seeming 90 percent downside day arrives while the
market is clearly in bull market mode, it's also time to buy because
this tends to mark the end of a correction, even though, at the time,
you will be hearing calls from pundits and the media for the start
of a new bear phase.

Countertrend Rallies

Inflections between bear markets and bull markets are rare because
full-on bear markets only happen about every four to six years, so
let's spend another few minutes thinking about the opportunities
to trade countertrend rallies.

The reason we get these countertrend declines during bull
markets is explained by research performed by behavioral finance

scholars. One of the most astute papers on the subject was written in 1993 by Shlomo Benartzi and Richard Thaler titled, "Myopic Loss Aversion and the Equity Premium Puzzle." It observed that investors are psychologically more sensitive to loss than to gain by a factor of 2.5 to 1. That is, they feel the pain of losses two and a half times more than they feel the pleasure of a profit. This leads private investors, and many pros as well, to join the crowd of sellers when the psychological anguish of loss becomes acute. Veteran independent analyst Robert Drach, who has an enviable record of accurately pinpointing bottoms and keeping investors on track during countertrend moves, has a wry sense of humor when it comes to this subject. "We too can be academic," he said, referring to the Benartzi-Thaler paper, "entitling the same subject, 'Wiggles Scare Folks.'"

Ten Percent Solution

Fortunately, there is one more statistical signature in Lowry's bag of analytical tricks to help us trade and make money from countertrend declines amid a bull market. What you need to observe is the percentage of NYSE stocks trading above their 10-day moving average, as this is helpful in measuring short-term extremes of panic behavior. According to Lowry's, when the percentage of stocks trading above their 10-day moving averages drops below 10 percent amid a broadly uptrending market, this is a panic situation that cries out for you to get your buying groove on. It often coincides with an isolated 90 percent downside day, so there are lot of sparks flying that might distract your attention.

A recent example emerged not long after the stock market began to drop on February 27, 2007. The 10-day percentage indicator dropped from a peak of 84.6 percent in February to a low of 3.7 percent on March 5, as you can see in Figure 1-8, reflecting a deeply oversold condition. Along with the fact that you should have been looking for a 40-week low around that time, the withering of the number of stocks above their 10-day moving average would have put you on the alert to buy stocks. The same extreme oversold levels occurred near the bottoms of August and November 2007, too.

Since 1990, according to Lowry's, there have been 20 cases in which the percentage of stocks above their 10-day moving averages has dropped below 10 percent. In 78 percent of those cases, the market was higher by an average of 2.98 percent in the next two weeks. In 94 percent of the cases, the market was higher by an average of 8.9 percent in the next three months. And, in 94 percent of the cases, the market was up an average of 20.1 percent in the next 12 months.

In the case of March 5, 2007, the Dow Jones Industrials went on to rally 13 percent over the next three months—showing once again that fading a countertrend rally during a bull market can yield spectacular results. And by the way, the S&P 500 sector that had performed best going into the decline—the Materials SPDR (XLB)—also outperformed going out of it. The XLB was up 4 percent for the year by March 5, versus –3 percent for the broad market. The XLB went on to gain 15 percent over the next three

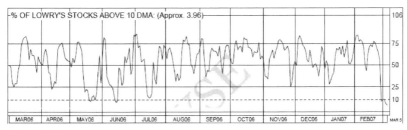

Figure 1-8

months. Meanwhile, the sector that had performed worst going into the decline—the Homebuilders SPDR (XHB)—performed worst subsequently, with just a 1 percent gain over the next three months. Likewise, the S&P 500 rose 11 percent in the two months following the extreme oversold reading of August 15. These are patterns that you will see again and again, so be sure to pay attention at times of extreme distress in the market, and use your head—don't lose it.

The Major Trend

Now finally we can get to the marquee moment, for your most important job on Sundays is to determine whether the major trend of the market is up or down—and at the same time you must think about what could change your mind. With any luck, you will come to the same conclusion for 250 weeks in a row or more, but as a day trader it is still something you must consider and decide upon.

What makes the big trend? As equity investors, we are participating in an auction market, and that simply means that buyers are pitted against sellers. For the value of the market to go up, buyers need to find a way to force sellers to hand over their inventory, which is shares of stock. They do this by offering them an increasing amount of money, until finally the holder hands over the shares. This is why the starts of bull markets are characterized by such intensity. Sellers need to be begged to hand over their shares, and buyers must bid ever higher and more intensively to make them do it.

This battle over a limited number of shares is at the heart of the market. In a bull trend, we start with the premise that buyers must be more anxious to buy than the sellers are to sell. After we have determined that this is true, then the question becomes: How much substance do the buyers have? What are their resources, and how many others are there right behind them in line with the same point of view?

This emotional and financial state is something that we can view in volume trends. If prices are going higher on a smaller amount of volume, it's suspicious. But if they're going up on increasing volume, then it's a sign that enthusiasm is strengthening and broadening.

After the whole question of price and volume change, everything else is secondary. Elements like the number of advancers to decliners, sector relative strength, and the differential between value and growth are all minor matters compared to the intensity shown in price and volume statistics.

Lowry's encapsulates these two vectors of the market in what it calls "buying pressure" and "selling pressure" measurements. Its Buying Power Index is formulated through a recipe that combines the total number of points gained by all New York Stock Exchange stocks and the volume of all stocks that gained. Conversely, its Selling Pressure Index is formulated from the total number of points declined and the volume behind those stocks that lost points.

The first chapter in all college economics texts explains to students the laws of supply and demand. But if a second chapter were written that focused just on supply and demand as reflected in the stock market, it would zero in on the need to measure the volume of supply versus the volume of demand. If that seems obvious, it's really not. Most analysts look at only the total volume of the market as a part of their approach to understanding the market's trend. But the key to really understanding the trend in a fundamental way is to understand the fuel behind each side of the buyer/seller transaction.

In case this isn't clear, let me explain it another way. Let's say that you laid the *Wall Street Journal* in front of you one morning and wanted to determine the differential between buying pressure and selling pressure. What you would do is add up the number of points by which each advancing stock gained and then add up all the trading volume of each of those advancing stocks. That's the total market buying pressure. And then you would do the same for the losers: add up all the points lost in aggregate, and then add up all the trading volume behind each of those losers, and that's your total market selling pressure.

These data are provided by the stock exchanges to the Associated Press, which distributes them to the *Wall Street Journal*, among others, for publication. But Lowry's is the only service that puts them together into a set of smoothed moving averages and charts them over time, as shown in Figure 1-9. What you find is that when buying pressure is rising and selling pressure is falling, you are in a full-blown bull market even if the broad indexes appear to be stagnant or jumpy. And when the Buying Power Index becomes dominant over the Selling Pressure Index, you simply have to conclude that buyers are in control and that every sharp dip to the downside is an opportunity to press your bets on the long side of the market—not to get scared out of the market.

Now what's kind of interesting is that when a bull market slips into middle age, and trading gets a bit sloppy, a lot of smarty-pants reporters and pundits start to call for an end to the run. But nine times out of ten, they are just speaking from their own emotions, anecdotes, and fears and not from a deep, statistical understanding of market forces. People might peak physically at 28, but still have a ton of life left in them—in fact, people can be extremely vibrant well past 55 and on

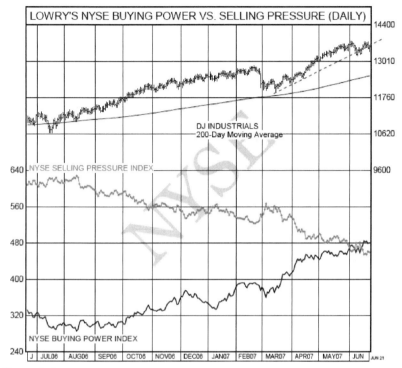

Figure 1-9

into their eighties. And likewise an "old" bull market may have moments when it wheezes or looks like it is going to sputter, but if buying pressure is rising, selling pressure is falling, and the advance/ decline line is rising, it is simply not going to keel over and die.

In Lowry's work, the most important sign to look for when you believe a top might be near is not short-term ephemera like a hedge fund blowup, or rising energy prices, but rather rising selectivity among investors that shows up in the slippage of the advance/ decline line, rising selling pressure, and falling buying pressure. Be careful, though, about acting too fast. A discernible peak in the A/D line doesn't mean that stocks will go down. It means that a top might be four to six months in the future as long as there are other confirming signals, such as a persistent, profound decline in the number of stocks above their 30-day moving averages, the number of stocks making 52-week highs, and a contraction of volume.

Even this view can go wrong, at least temporarily, because in mid-2006 it looked as if all of these factors were turning against the bull market: selectivity was rising, the A/D line was falling, buying pressure was withering, and selling pressure was rising. By July, when the S&P 500 slipped beneath its 200-day moving average for a short spell, it looked in many ways as if it was time to say sayonara to the bull market that had begun in 2003.

In your Sunday studies, you might have become quite concerned. But as you know by now, you would have been expecting a 40-week low around that time, so your antenna had to be up to sense a fake-out. And then sure enough, investors began to sniff out the fact that the Federal Reserve Board would stop its 18-month campaign to lift interest rates in August. And when this was combined with a turn-around in the previously fast-climbing price of crude oil, investors suddenly changed their mind and regained their ardor for stocks. Quite briskly, their appetite broadened, the McClellan Oscillator shot up, and the next phase of the bull market was on. As you saw back in Figure 1-3, in late July the NYSE achieved escape velocity and the market barely even hesitated in its advance until late February of the following year, seven months later.

Line in the Sand

To perform a reality check on all of these data, my final line in the sand is the 10-month simple moving average of a stock or index. A single month's close below that line is cause for concern, but once you get two or three monthly closes in a row below the 10-month moving average, it's usually lights out.

As you can see in Figure 1-10, the 10-month moving average contained the entire bull market from 1990 to 1994 and again from 1995 to 2000, with one hitch in 1998 around the time of the Long Term Capital Management hedge fund blowup and the Clinton impeachment crisis. And even though you were forced out for three months during that stretch using this line in the sand, you were back in at S&P 1,100 and remained in until S&P 1,400 in the middle of 2000. From mid-2000 through 2003, using the 10-month moving average, you were out or short the market until March 2003, which coincided with a 90 percent downside day selling climax, two 90 percent upside day buying panics, and the advance of the McClellan Oscillator over 200.

Figure 1-10

You can see the same closer up in Figure 1-11 using the exchange-traded fund that incorporates all of the stocks in the Dow Jones large-cap, mid-cap, and small-cap indexes, called the iShares Dow Jones Total Market Index (IYY). Checking on this chart every Sunday during the bear market of 2000–2002, you would have remained out of most stocks, or short the market, for 29 of 30 months. Then from March 2003 through at least June 2007, you would have been long stocks for 49 of 50 months. That's a pretty compelling guide, and that is my bottom-line recommendation for your Sunday studies.

Figure 1-11

MONDAY

Relative Strength and Swing Trading

In the popular imagination, decades are characterized by a profoundly resonant cultural pulse. In the twentieth century, for example, we know about the Roaring Twenties, the Swingin' Sixties, and the Me Decade of the Seventies.

Decades are memorialized by investors in much the same way based on the industrial sectors or market capitalization groups that were in favor for a stretch of 10 years. The 1960s were famous for the Nifty 50—large growth companies that were considered to be "one-decision," buy-and-hold-forever positions, such as American Express, Bristol Myers, Avon, Coca-Cola, and IBM. The 1970s were famous for the success of oil and gas stocks as the price of energy soared amid Mideast conflicts. The 1990s was the era of the large-cap technology stocks, as Dell, Microsoft, Intel, EMC, Oracle, and Sun Microsystems captured investors' attention amid the explosive growth of the personal computer and, later, the Internet.

In each of these eras—and for many multiyear periods within those decades—the "It" stocks worked for investors week after week and month after month. Every dip was an opportunity to buy more. The stocks rose in part because fundamental changes taking place in the national or global business environment generated outsized earnings growth, to be sure, but also in part because investors believed that they would always continue to rise. As I mentioned in the last chapter, there is virtually always a fundamentally rock-solid reason for stocks and sectors and markets to work, and then there is a layer of sentiment on top of those fundamentals that provides an extra ripple of excitement, lust, and greed. The pleasure of being right on top of secular change creates a sort of endorphin rush for investors, and they continue to bid up companies within certain groups because their behavior is continually reinforced by higher prices.

Academic studies have shown that at least 60 percent of an individual stock's advance comes from the success and popularity of its sector. And studies further show that individual stocks are beholden to both the success of the market capitalization group and its placement on the valuation spectrum between growth and value.

On Mondays, I want you to spend an hour researching sector, size, and valuation groups. Not as an academic, of course, but as a tactician. I will show you ways to determine which industrial sectors, sizes, and valuation cohorts are working at any given time, and then show you how to find the individual stocks within those groupings that will make you the most money in the coming multiday, multiweek period.

The Great Divide
Before we go any further, let me explain exactly what these categories are and why they exist.

First, you need to recognize that—like planets rotating at their equators, and at the same time rotating around the sun, which is itself rotating around the galaxy—stocks spin on five axes. Like practical astronomers, our job is to determine the varying amounts of gravitational pull, if you will, on each of them. These five axes are:

- **Sector.** Most investors see all companies in the great global economy as being divided into 11 sectors: basic industries, capital goods, consumer durables, consumer nondurables, consumer services, energy, finance, health care, public utilities, technology, and transportation. These sectors cycle in and out of favor at various points in the economic cycle, and often overlap.
- **Industry.** Each sector is subdivided into industries that will cycle into and out of favor during their group's time in the sunshine. The industries in each sector include, but are not limited to, the following:
  - **Basic industries:** Aluminum, chemicals, gold, steel
  - **Capital goods:** Farm equipment, aircraft, industrial machinery
  - **Consumer durables:** Autos, auto parts, houses, home furnishings
  - **Consumer nondurables:** Cleaning products, cigarettes, beverages, food
  - **Consumer services:** Retailers, ad agencies, newspapers, hotels, restaurants
  - **Energy:** Oil, gas, and coal explorers, refiners, and marketers

- **Finance:** Banks, insurers, brokerages, real estate trusts, credit services
- **Health care:** Drug and medical device makers, biotech, health-care plans, hospitals
- **Public utilities:** Wired and wireless phone carriers, electricity and gas merchants
- **Technology:** Semiconductor, software, PC, printer, and network equipment makers
- **Transportation:** Railroads, airlines, truckers, air delivery services

- **Size.** Companies are grouped by investors according to their total market capitalization, which is their current price times the number of shares outstanding. Arranged from largest to smallest, the bins are megacaps (over $100 billion), large caps ($10 billion to $100 billion), midcaps ($2 billion to $10 billion), small caps ($250 million to $2 billion), and microcaps (under $250 million).

- **Valuation/style.** Companies are grouped by investors into two big categories for purposes of understanding whether they are generally cheap or expensive. The two big bins are "growth" and "value." Although the distinctions are loose, the division is usually sliced by a blend of a company's price/earnings, price/sales, and price/book ratios. The half with the higher blended ratios is dubbed "growth" stocks, and the half with the lower ratios, "value" stocks.

- **Geographic region.** Companies are grouped by their nation of origin, even if they are fully multinational. The big sets are United States, Europe, Japan, Asia ex-Japan, and Latin America. But you'll also see added to this mix the individual countries within Europe, Asia, and Latin America and the broad term *emerging markets* to refer to all countries outside the West.

Many investors believe that each of these categories should do especially well at various points in the global economic cycle. The best-known model for the changing favor and disfavor of various sectors was created by veteran Standard & Poor's analyst Sam Stovall. His theory held that investors should try to anticipate the changes in the strength of different sectors.

- During a full recession and a market bottom, the Stovall economic cycle model holds, investors should anticipate the revival of consumer expectations, the bottoming out of industrial production, and falling interest rates by buying cyclical stocks (such as consumer durables), industrials, and technology.
- During an early recovery period, the model holds that investors should anticipate rising consumer expectations, rising industrial production, and bottoming interest rates by buying industrials, basic materials, transportation, and energy stocks.
- During a full recovery, the model holds that investors should anticipate the coming decline of consumer expectations, flattening industrial production, and rising interest rates by purchasing consumer nondurables (also known as "staples"), consumer services, and health care.
- And during the decline toward a recession, the model holds that investors should anticipate sharply falling consumer

expectations, falling industrial production, and the peaking of interest rates by buying utilities.

While this theory may serve as a fine architecture for institutional money managers who accumulate very large positions over a long period of time and need to have vision that stretches way out past the horizon, as a practical matter, the categories are a bit too broad and long range for daily traders. We mostly just need to understand what is happening right now and how the ground may be changing just a few thousand feet out toward the horizon.

Half a dozen years ago, it was not at all easy to see and understand which sectors, market-cap groups, and regions were outperforming the market, but the advent of exchange-traded funds, or ETFs, has made it easy to not only see all the variations in performance among our five axes, but also trade them. There's never been a better time to be a daily trader, as you'll see in a moment when I show you how quickly you can spot and profit from these wonderful new financial instruments.

Now, as I said a moment ago, certain sectors, industries, capitalization groups, valuation groups, and regions—as well as combinations of each—are always outperforming the broad market at any given time. And so it stands to reason that if you want to beat the market, you need to understand exactly which groups either are outperforming now or are on the path to outperforming after a long period of underperforming.

To determine this, we need to study the relationship of each of these groups to a market benchmark, which for the sake of this discussion we'll call the S&P 500 Index. (It's an imperfect benchmark, but it's the one almost everyone uses.) Rather than just eyeballing the chart of each group and comparing it in your mind's eye to how well you think the S&P 500 is doing, you need to create *relative strength* charts, either with a packaged trading software program or on the Web.

I'll show you how to do this on the Web, as it's effective and inexpensive.

Sector Indexes

As you might expect, just to make things difficult, there is a lack of unanimity among investors as to exactly which stocks belong in each sector, market-cap group, and so on. There's no real science to the categorization; it's not as easy as declaring that a plum is a fruit and celery is a vegetable. And as a result, investment information companies have divided the world's thousands of stocks into their own branded indexes. For instance, you may have seen sector indexes created by Standard & Poor's, Rydex, Vanguard, or Russell Investment Group, among others. For our discussion, however, we will focus on the granddaddy of them all, which is Dow Jones.

The editors and economists who have created and manage the Dow Jones indexes start mostly with the sectors that I mentioned earlier, with two exceptions. First, they lump consumer durables and consumer nondurables into one big group called Consumer Goods. Also, instead of an energy sector, they have a sector called Oil & Gas, and they put other energy sources, like coal, into Basic Materials. It doesn't really matter. Any such division works for our purposes.

Figure 2-1 depicts the Dow Jones U.S. Oil & Gas Index ($DJUSEN) from the period July 2001 to July 2007. If I were to lay a graph of the S&P Energy Select Sector SPDR (XLE) on the same chart, you would discover that there is virtually no difference. The

$DJUSEN (DJ US Oil & Gas Index) INDX   ©StockCharts.com
29-Jun-2007   **Open** 604.98 **High** 607.70 **Low** 581.13 **Close** 599.72 **Chg** -5.26 (-0.87%) ▾
— $DJUSEN (Weekly) 599.72
— MA(70) 499.66

$DJUSEN is the symbol for the Dow Jones
U.S. Oil & Gas Index. It is essentially the
same as what Standard & Poor's calls its
Energy Select Sector SPDR (XLE).

Figure 2-1

chart represents a combination of all oil and gas industries, including producers, explorers, services providers, distributors, and
pipeline operators.

Now in your mind's eye you can recall energy-related news over
that five-year period and mull the relative strength of the Oil &
Gas sector compared to the broad market. But to be effective as a
daily trader, it's much more worthwhile to plot it in order to know
for sure.

To do that, you need to create a chart that compares the
$DJUSEN to the S&P 500. You can create this kind of chart on
many high-cost trading platforms, such as Tradestation. But the
Seattle-based Web site Stockcharts.com charges just $20 per month
for the sort of advanced charting tools and data that will permit this
kind of analysis. That makes the site a bargain for all levels of
investors.

The task is pretty simple. Instead of just typing the sector symbol in the symbol box on the site's home page, type in $DJUSEN:$SPX and press Enter. That creates a chart that shows the *ratio* of the Dow Jones U.S. Oil & Gas Index to the S&P 500 Index. When the line of a chart like this is rising, it means that the index represented by the first symbol is rising faster than the index represented by the second symbol. And when a chart of this nature is falling, obviously, it means that the index represented by the second symbol is stronger than the index represented by the first symbol. The line will rise even if both indexes are falling if the downward slope of the second index is steeper than that of the first. As you can see in Figure 2-2, the $DJUSEN:$SPX relative strength (RS) chart shows that energy has powerfully outperformed the S&P 500, with brief interruptions, from 2002 through mid-2007. In 2002, both indexes were down, but because energy was down less than the S&P 500, its relative strength line rose. In 2003, the relative strength line fell because the S&P 500 performed much better than energy stocks. But the disparity between the two groups really took off in the period 2004–2007, when energy stocks exploded higher, advancing 200 percent during a period in which the S&P 500 rose by 75 percent. As a daily trader, you can certainly figure out which group of stocks you would have wanted to be trading during those very long stretches of time. In other words, although you would have made plenty of money in the stocks included in the S&P 500 in that three-year stretch, the really big bucks were to be had in the energy stocks represented by the $DJUSEN.

A chart like this doesn't have any buy and sell signals in it, however. So developing them is our next step. We can devise any number of complicated signals, but just to keep things simple, I'll show you signals using two different moving-average crossovers. The first

$DJUSEN:$SPX (DJ US Oil/Gas/S&P 500) INDX/INDX   © StockCharts.com
29-Jun-2007   **Open** 0.40 **High** 0.40 **Low** 0.39 **Close** 0.40 **Chg** -0.00 (-0.92%) ▼

In '02, the S&P was down sharply while energy was down mildly. The result is a rising "relative strength" line for energy.

Energy was much stronger than a strong S&P 500 from '04 to '07, so its RS line rose sharply.

Down a lot

S&P 500 up 50%

Down a little

Energy up 100%

Figure 2-2

will be a 13- and 34-week crossover. It's easy to create at Stockcharts.com by manipulating chart settings as shown in Figure 2-3. Visit any chart page, and under Chart Attributes, set Periods to Weekly and Years to 5. Under Overlays, set one Simple Moving Average to 13 and another to 34. Make the color of one purple and the other red, or whatever colors you prefer. Then under Indicators, type in 13,34,1 as the Parameters for the MACD.

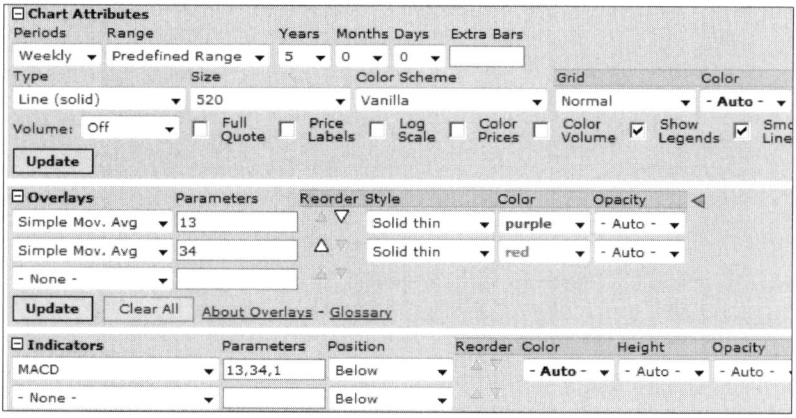

Figure 2-3

Now when you click the Update button, you will see a relative strength chart of the energy sector versus the S&P 500 with a 13-week moving average and a 34-week moving average. These two lines tend to do a very nice job of helping us determine the intermediate-term direction of an index, stock, or relative strength ratio.

When the 13-week average crosses over the 34-week average into the dominant position and slopes higher, it tells us that the stock, index, or relative strength ratio upon which it is based is strengthening and moving higher in a persistent, profound, pronounced way—and that moment of crossover is a buy signal. The crossover calls out, "Hey, look here! Medium-term momentum has changed!" That signal can certainly be contradicted, but at the moment of impact, you can consider the signal to be as good as gold. The MACD indicator is on the chart to give us a little more information. When the MACD line designed in this way touches the horizontal zero line, it gives us confirmation of a crossover. And it is a little more sensitive to the changes in the two moving averages, as it tends to hook skyward and rise a short time before a move higher in the two moving averages, giving us a sort of "head's up" that a change is coming.

You can see how all this plays out in Figure 2-4. It's the same as Figure 2-2 portraying the relative strength of the energy sector versus the S&P 500 index, but it now has our two moving averages and the MACD on it as well. In late 2003, as you can see in the bottom panel, the MACD started to turn higher. It hit the zero line in January 2004, and you can see the actual crossover of the 13-week and 34-week moving averages in the center of the highlighted box.

Figure 2-4

At the exact moment when this was occurring, of course, you didn't know that the relative strength of the energy sector was going to move into a sustained uptrend for two years. It might have seemed ambiguous or even confusing. But I have come to think very highly of these crossovers, particularly in sectors like energy that have trended very well in the past, and I urge you to do the same.

As you can see, the relative strength of energy versus the S&P 500 rose without interruption until October 2006, when the 13-week moving average crossed under the 34-week moving average, and the MACD line thus went below 0. Between those two signals, the energy sector rose by around 80 percent. Now mind you, it was only the relative strength of energy compared to the broad market that was weakening in the autumn of 2006. Energy was still pretty strong, as you can clearly see back in Figure 2-1, and it merely touched its rising 70-week moving average in October 2006 without violating the long-term uptrend. So while the relative strength crossover is something to which you should always pay attention—as it can potentially push you to trade out of one sector that's sinking relative to the broad market and into another that is rising relative to the market—it is not the only useful piece of information at your disposal.

Broadening Your Sector View

Now that you know how to create a relative strength indicator for a single sector, it's time to move on and create a view of all sectors and industries. I wish there were an easy way to do this, but there is not. Thus, you need to create this incredibly useful list in Stockcharts.com yourself. To do that, you need a list of all the Dow Jones sectors, which I have provided in Appendix A.

The next step is time-consuming, but take heart from the fact that you have to do it only once—and you will benefit from it for a lifetime of investing. You need to turn the sectors' relative strength charts into a "Favorite Charts" list at Stockcharts.com in the following way. Visit the site's home page, then click the Sharpcharts link in the left sidebar. Next click Your Favorite Charts in the left sidebar on the subsequent page, and then click Create New List in the middle of the page that comes up. The site will pop up a dialog box asking for a list name. Type in something like DJ Sector RS and submit it.

You will then see a page that looks exactly like Figure 2-5 except that the white space following Many: will be blank. In that space, you need to type in each of the Dow index symbols as shown in Appendix A followed by a colon and the symbol $SPX, and then a comma and a space. I've typed in the first two in this example. You may wish to add them in three separate lists and name them DJ Sector RS 1, DJ Sector RS 2, and DJ Sector RS 3.

Once you are done typing in the symbols, click the Add Many button and you will be halfway home. Next you need to create the 13-34 Weekly Crossover chart style. To do that, create the chart shown in Figure 2-4, as instructed. Then click the Add New button next to the ChartStyles dialog box and give it a name, such as

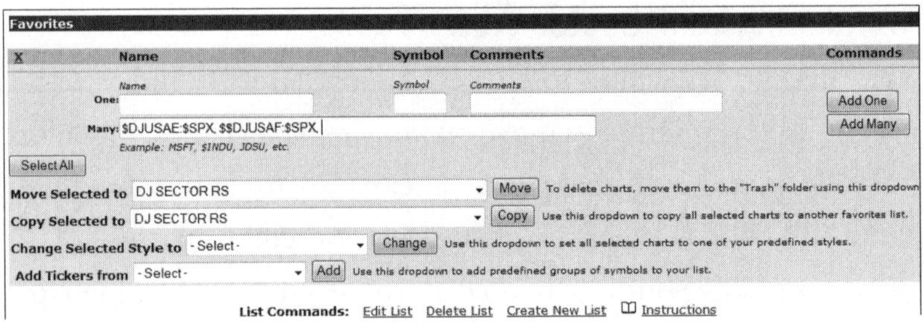

Figure 2-5

"5-Yr 1334 Weekly Crossover," choose a button number, then click Add, as shown in Figure 2-6. Now you can apply that style to any chart you are observing by clicking the appropriate gray button on the left side of your Stockcharts.com screen or by choosing that style from the ChartStyles drop-down menu.

Instead of applying this chart style to just one chart, though, you will next want to apply it to all of the relative strength charts that you wish to view. To do that, first summon up your Dow Jones Sector RS chart list by choosing the name that you have just given it from the Chartlist drop-down menu at the top of any StockCharts.com chart page. You will at first see just the first chart in the list. To see the rest, click the View All link. Now you are looking at a page that contains 10 relative strength charts. But there's a problem: they are not in the 1334 Weekly style.

To view them all in the correct style, click Edit List on the List Commands line, as shown in Figure 2-7. Then on the page that comes up, go to the very bottom and click Select All.

After all the checkboxes are instantly filled, go to the line titled Change Selected Style to on that page and choose the one you just created, which was 5-Yr 1334 Weekly Crossover, as shown in Figure 2-8. Click the Change button to apply that chart style to all of the relative strength charts on your list. And after the page refreshes,

Figure 2-6

Figure 2-7

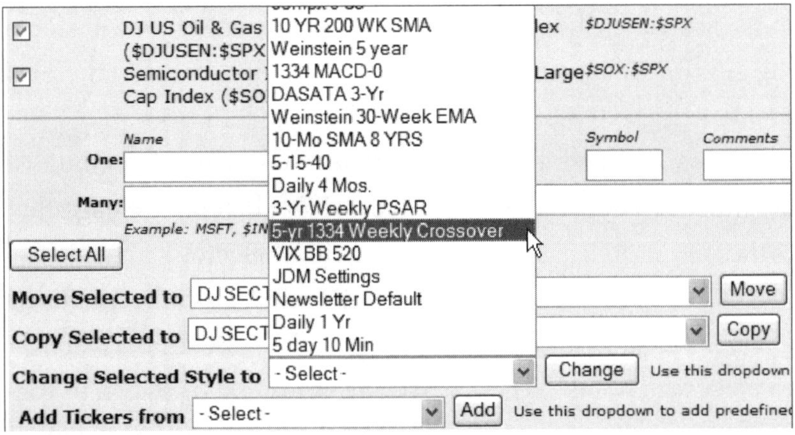

Figure 2-8

go back to the very top and change the list view chosen from Edit to 10 per page.

I know that this is a lot of work, but as I said, you have to do it only once—and you are gaining a powerful weapon in your battle against mediocrity. Now you are looking at the first of a series of pages that contain all the relative strength charts that you created earlier. And your job now is to scroll down through the pages and scrutinize each chart to find the ones that exhibit the sort of change in relative strength that tends to be meaningful and long-lasting. About 40 percent of the charts you see will show a downtrend, meaning that the sector is underperforming the S&P 500, while another 40 percent will show an uptrend, and the rest will be flat or inconclusive. If your timing work from Chapter 1 suggests that you should be looking for longs, obviously you should concentrate on the uptrending relative strength charts. If you want to put on shorts, then look at the charts that show poor relative strength.

You've already seen one strong relative strength chart from the 2004–2007 period, which was energy versus the S&P 500. Now let me show you a few other relative strength charts that worked out well so that you can look for similar ones in the future.

Relative Strength Example 1: Auto Parts, Winter 2006–2007

In the winter of 2006–2007, a great many stock groups were going well. The move out of the summer low that year was so powerful that it seemingly left very few sectors behind. A couple of sectors that had been doing badly for years, though, continued to lag — and chief among them was auto parts. And why not? Everyone knew that the U.S. auto industry was suffering from its worst slump in history, so it just stood to reason that U.S. companies that sold into the auto industry would also fare poorly.

Yet in my weekly studies of sector relative strength that winter, I could not help but notice that the auto parts sector was clearly reversing a long-term downtrend in relative strength compared to the broad market and showed signs of emerging in a real leadership position. I asked all of my market contacts for reasons why this might be happening, and no one had a clue. Yet it was clearly occurring, with the breakout coming in January 2007, as you can see in Figure 2-9.

This is one of my favorite types of sector relative strength conditions: it seems to defy logic, so most investors are skeptical. The level of short selling in most of the leading stocks in a sector like this is usually high, as that strategy has worked well for a long time. As the sector's strength reverses, the smart short sellers will get out. But many of the "dumb" shorts will stay in, adding lots of fuel to the fire, as they must repeatedly cover their swiftly losing positions by buying shares.

Figure 2-9

The auto parts industry does not have its own exchange-traded fund, so to take advantage of an idea like this, you need to find out the names of the largest companies in the sector, particularly the ones that are leading the charge. You can't rely on analyst reports because at this stage of a turnaround most professional brokerage analysts will still be bearish on the entire group and could dissuade you from your pursuit.

I recommend three simple means of finding the right stocks to trade. The first is the most direct: go to the free Web site Bigcharts.com (a unit of Marketwatch, which is itself a unit of the *Wall Street Journal*) and click on the Industries tab on the home page. On the left side of the page, you will see a sidebar with the headline Dow Jones U.S. Sectors. Click on the sector that is most likely to contain your specified industry. In this case, it is Consumer Goods. You will then see a fly-out menu, as shown in Figure 2-10. As far as I can tell, this is the only place on the Web that you can see all the charts of all stocks contained in each of the Dow Jones sector and industry indexes.

When you click on Auto Parts, the site first sends you to a page listing the best-performing stocks of that group. Ignore these results and click on a tab called Industry Analyzer in the middle of the page. On the page that comes up, change the settings of the drop-down menus: Change Sort by to % Price Increase, and change Time Frame to 3 months or 6 months. Leave the rest of the settings alone, then click the Draw button, as shown in Figure 2-11. (Alternatively, you can set Sort by to Market Capitalization to see all of the industry's charts in order from large caps to small caps.)

Now what you are looking at are the actual stocks that have caused the Auto Parts sector to make such a surprising move higher relative to the broad market. Your next move is a lot more subjec-

Figure 2-10

Figure 2-11

tive, as you must then check out the charts and fundamentals behind each of the top 20 or so stocks listed in this screen. You will without doubt find at least half a dozen stocks to pursue further.

When the sector and industry relative strength is a tailwind pushing these stocks forward against much skepticism from the crowd, you can find some real gems before the vast majority of your peers realize that auto parts is the Next Big Thing.

In this particular case, we caught on very early to the early 2007 surge in the shares of auto parts makers Johnson Controls (JCI), Cummins (CMI), TRW Automotive (TRW), American Axle (AXL), and Borg Warner (BWA). All of these stocks appeared as auto parts sector performance leaders in winter 2006–2007, and all of their charts showed beautiful 13-34 daily breakouts. Just to show you one, check out Borg Warner, a maker of auto drive-train and engine-management systems, in Figure 2-12. You can see that its shares were stuck in a long consolidation during the summer and autumn of 2006. Note that this consolidation coincided with a period of poor relative strength for the entire auto parts industry, as shown in Figure 2-8. Once the auto parts sector's relative strength changed for the better and then broke out of its multiyear downtrend, observe what happened to industry powerhouse BWA. It gapped up in the first week of January 2007, and its daily MACD 13,34,1 thrust up above the 0 line. Since this was not happening in isolation but rather in tandem with its entire group, it was a significant buy signal. You would have wanted to buy BWA on that breakout at $65 even though the stock looked "expensive," trading as it was at its all-time high. The stock went on to gain 55 percent through November 2007 versus a 4 percent return for the S&P 500 Index.

Although it is sometimes difficult to narrow your focus to a single stock in a sector when many look equally strong, it is important to simply pick one or two to ride and not become paralyzed by indecision. If the sector move is truly under way, it doesn't really

Figure 2-12

matter which you choose—they should all perform well. In this case, Johnson Controls performed about the same over that January 11 to July 6 period, while TRW Automotive was up 43 percent, and American Axle was up 58 percent. That is the value of playing sector relative strength. Oh yeah, and when do you sell? Using the 13-34 crossover system as a simple trade timing tool, you hold until the MACD line sinks back below 0. Or sell on a trendline break, as I'll explain below.

Relative Strength Example 2: Chemicals, Winter 2006–2007

As you have seen, the beauty of using sector relative strength as your guide in finding great stocks to trade on a daily basis is that it very often puts you in groups that are not initially popular with the public. When these moves start, they are usually launched by institutional investors—pension and hedge fund managers—that are focused on finding low-priced, low-risk plays outside the mainstream. Although major sector moves virtually always end up as high-growth and momentum runs, in other words, they start off in the value camp. And as a result, at the beginning of the move, you may feel that you are all alone. There will be very few analysts upgrading the stocks in these sectors, and you won't find a lot of portfolio managers talking these stocks up in television appearances.

This was certainly true with auto parts, and it was equally true with commodity and specialty chemicals in 2006 and 2007 when they began one of the most spectacular advances in recent history. Because they are a very unglamorous group of stocks, chemicals seldom appear on most investors' radar. As you can see in Figure 2-13 (which depicts the relative strength of the Dow Jones U.S. Specialty Chemicals index, $DJUSCX, vs. the S&P 500), they outperformed powerfully during the millennial bear market from 2000 to mid-2002, then fell out of favor once fancier stocks like technology and retail got their groove on at the start of the 2003 bull market. They had a nice little move in 2004, but the signal that I want you to focus on in this case occurred in April 2006.

What makes this one special is that it shows that you can read sector relative strength charts in the same way that you read the charts of stocks and ETFs. In 2006, what you had was a MACD 0-line cross in January that looked pretty good, but that may have left many investors wondering if it was for real. After all, this is not a group of stocks that anyone is dying to throw money into. You need

Figure 2-13

a lot of persuasion. And that final bit of persuasion came in April 2006 when the DJUSCX versus S&P 500 Index relative strength line moved up above its old highs of March 2005 and May 2002. It then consolidated a bit, testing the breakout level in June before moving much higher in August. This is exactly how we read a stock chart, and it works the same with a relative strength chart.

Now that you observed that chemicals were definitively outperforming the broad market, you may have wished for a fundamental explanation. Sometimes none is apparent, but in this case, two value drivers emerged. One was the fact that tremendous economic growth in Asia was siphoning off much of the world's chemicals for use in plastics and other industrial applications. And the other, and perhaps more exciting, factor was the fantastic new demand for the chemicals in fertilizer by agricultural companies feeding the boom in the use of corn as a feedstock for ethanol. U.S. farmers were about to plant 90.5 million acres of corn in the spring of 2007, which was the greatest amount since 95.5 million acres were planted in 1944 and a 15 percent increase over 2006. It turns out that corn uses nearly 50 percent more nitrogen per acre than cotton and 22 times more than the amount needed by soybeans. Since corn already accounted for 40 percent of U.S. fertilizer demand, it stood to reason that a big jump in acreage would spur a big jump in chemical fertilizer use.

While all of this became apparent to many investors only in late January 2007, after President Bush announced in his State of the Union speech that his administration would make ethanol production a top government-supported priority, it was clearly already appreciated by value investors looking for cheap cyclical stocks to own, first in 2004 and then more emphatically in the middle of 2006. You have already seen the signals in the relative strength chart in Figure 2-13. Now you can see in Figure 2-14 that there were just as many, if not more, signals concerning the strength of this obscure sector in the chart of the sector itself. Through July 2007, there were at least six opportunities dating back to 2003 to get long specialty chemicals as the sector index either moved above its weekly 13-34 MACD 0 line or crested above an old high after a brief downward thrust to shake out weak hands.

So how to play this sector? Well, ironically, the folks over at exchange-traded fund powerhouse Barclays had closed their chemicals ETF for lack of interest in 2002, just before the titanic move in the group was about to get underway. The ETF had only $19

$DJUSCX (DJ US Specialty Chemicals Index) INDX @ StockCharts.com
6-Jul-2007 Open 310.39 High 315.99 Low 310.21 Close 313.44 Chg +3.11 (+1.00%) ▲

Apart from its relative strength chart, Specialty Chemicals gave repeated buy signals from 2003 to 2007 -- both at weekly MACD 0-line crossings and breakouts to new highs.

Figure 2-14

million in assets, which made it uneconomic to run. (That was probably a good signal for the group all by itself!) So you were forced to look for stocks to play instead. Now, when you moved over to Bigcharts.com to look for some of the specific companies to play, you could see, just as with auto parts, that there were a lot of potential positions. And once again, it was very important that you not become paralyzed by the plethora of choices and just pick one or two horses to ride based on your reading of their individual charts and fundamentals.

If your big idea was to buy specialty chemicals and your research had led you to nitrogen fertilizer, you could hardly do better than finding a chemical maker with "nitrogen" right in its name. Terra Nitrogen (TNH) was a small-cap fertilizer maker based in Iowa that was perhaps best known for its fat 7 percent dividend yield. It showed up in Bigcharts as a strong specialty chemicals contender in October 2006 (see Figure 2-15), with a 21 percent advance from July 2006 during a period when the S&P 500 Index rose just 4 percent. From October 2006 to July 2007, its shares went up another 500 percent, with dividends.

Of course, while Terra Nitrogen turned out to have the very best results among major specialty chemical makers at that time, the results of many of its peers were not too shabby, as Canada-based

Figure 2-15

industry heavyweight Potash Corp. of Saskatchewan (POT) rose 131 percent, Illinois-based midcap CF Industries (CF) rose 270 percent, German powerhouse BASF (BF) rose 74 percent, and Houston-based small cap KMG Chemicals (KMGB) rose 208 percent. The S&P 500 Index, meanwhile, was up a solid but comparatively paltry 15 percent.

For a few years at least, to paraphrase the old DuPont advertising slogan, there really was better living through chemicals.

Relative Strength Example 3: Home Builders and Biotechs

Briefly now I want to show you two groups that gave repeated *sell* signals from mid-2005 to mid-2007—the home builders and biotechs—and a different way to play them.

As you can see in Figure 2-16, the Dow Jones Home Construction Index ($DJUSHB) was a terrific outperformer in the 2003 to mid-2005 period as low interest rates, rising employment, swelling personal income, and an increase in immigration led to a boom in home ownership and residential real estate prices. The home builders started the period as very cheap stocks, with price/earnings multiples in the single digits, and never became really expensive, as earnings growth exploded higher. In 2005, this sweet state of affairs began to unravel when the Federal Reserve began raising interest rates to cool off the economy. Despite initial protests from home construction companies that everything was hunky-dory, smart institutional investors began to sell off their inventory of homebuilders' stocks. The news flow about the homebuilders at first remained positive, and analysts were buoyant on the stocks, encouraging the public to stay in them. But you could clearly observe that a sensational party was actually coming to an end as the group's relative strength

$DJUSHB:$SPX (DJ US Home Const/S&P 500) INDX/INDX © StockCharts.com
6-Jul-2007 **Open** 0.35 **High** 0.36 **Low** 0.35 **Close** 0.36 **Chg** -0.00 (-0.06%) ▼
— $DJUSHB:$SPX (Weekly) 0.36
—MA(13) 0.40
—MA(34) 0.46

Signal 2: Breakdown below prior significant low

Home-building sector offered fantastic relative strength in '03 and '04 then fell apart in late '05. It gave repeated sell signals in '06 and '07.

Signal 3

Aug '06 rally attempt fails to push MACD up through 0

—MACD(13,34,1) -0.043, -0.043, 0.000

Signal 1: Cross down through weekly MACD 0 line

Figure 2-16

petered out. The first clear RS signal, as shown in the chart, came in November 2005 as the weekly 13-34 MACD line fell below 0. A second signal came in April 2006, and after that it was just all downhill for the homebuilders. One brief recovery attempt in the late summer of 2006 was made when the Federal Reserve stopped raising interest rates, but as you can see, the MACD never pierced the 0 line before succumbing to more selling throughout the first half of 2007.

There were at least three ways to play this development. One was to short-sell an exchange-traded fund that tracks the homebuilders, such as the Homebuilders SPDR (XHB). Another was to buy an exchange-traded fund that provides inverse exposure to the homebuilders, such as the Ultra Short Real Estate ProShares (SRS). And another, naturally, was to sell individual stocks short.

At this point, let's stop a moment to observe that you can build a set of sector relative strength charts with exchange-traded funds at StockCharts.com just like the one you created for Dow Jones industry groups. To do so, follow the instructions provided for the Dow Jones sector indexes, but substitute the symbols for ETFs instead. I have provided a massive list of all major ETFs created and marketed by iShares, PowerShares, ProShares, Rydex, and Market Vectors for you in Appendix B.

One obvious advantage of using the ETFs for your relative strength work is that you can leverage your idea that an industry, market cap, or regional group is about to outperform or underperform without the risk that the individual stocks you have chosen might buck the trend. But another advantage comes when you recognize that the largest stocks within most ETFs account for the majority of their movement. And therefore you can zero in on the top stocks of the ETF for maximum return on your point of view.

As an example, consider the situation presented by the biotechs in 2005–2007. As you can see in Figure 2-17, the Biotech iShares (IBB) began to seriously underperform the broad market in the spring of 2006. The IBB:$SPX relative strength line sank sharply below prior significant lows, which constituted a breakdown, and then its weekly 13-34 MACD line fell below 0. If you were looking for short sales then—or simply looking for either stocks to avoid or former winners to clear out of your portfolio for a profit—those were certainly both clear signals that the biotech sector was a great place to look.

IBB:$SPX (Biotech iShares/S&P 500 Large Cap Index) AMEX/INDX ⊛ StockCharts.com
6-Jul-2007   **Op** 0.051 **Hi** 0.052 **Lo** 0.051 **Cl** 0.052 **Vol** 0 **Chg** -0.000 (-0.59%) ▾

Biotech stocks fell into a coma in 2006 and were among the few stock groups failing to advance in the first half of '07.

Signal 1: Biotech iShares RS line sinks below prior significant low

MACD(13,34,1) -0.0013, -0.0013, 0.0000

Signal 2: Weekly MACD 0 line cross

Signal 3: Recovery fails at MACD 0 line

Figure 2-17

To find the biggest stocks within an ETF, visit the Web site ETFInvestmentOutlook.com instead of Bigcharts.com. This site provides all the components of all the major ETFs in easy-to-read lists. What is particularly nice about this site is that it recognizes that most ETFs are market-cap weighted, which means that the largest companies make the greatest contributions to the funds' day-to-day changes.

As a result, if you believe that major institutional investors are going to willy-nilly unload shares in a sector or heavily short an ETF, you will typically get the most bang for your buck if you short that ETF's biggest component. As you can see in Figure 2-18, the

IBB Holdings
Biotechnology Nasdaq iShares

Stock	Symbol	▼ Weight	Sector
Amgen Inc	AMGN	11.5%	Medical-Biomedical/Gene
Gilead Sciences Inc	GILD	7.1%	Therapeutics
Celgene Corp	CELG	5.2%	Medical-Biomedical/Gene
Teva Pharmaceutical-sp ADR	TEVA	4.7%	Medical-Generic Drugs
Biogen Idec Inc	BIIB	3.8%	Medical-Biomedical/Gene
Genzyme Corp	GENZ	3.3%	Medical-Biomedical/Gene

Figure 2-18

site shows that six stocks account for more than a third of the movement of the entire ETF—but one accounts for a whopping 11 percent. That biggie is Amgen (AMGN), and it fell 24 percent from
April 2006 to July 2007, a period when the S&P 500 was up 18 percent and the IBB itself lost 3 percent. It is rare that you can find a
stock to sell with confidence during a bull market, but through the
combination of discovering a sector with poor relative strength and
the determination of that sector's biggest component, a world-beat-
ing short was served up on a platter. And now you know how to find
the next one yourself.

Relative Strength Example 4: Semiconductors

Next let's look at two final ways to look at find stocks to play using
sector relative strength: the breadth tables at ETFInvestmentOut-
look.com and the StockScouter rating system at MSN Money. Our
stalking horse this time will be semiconductors, an industry that was
trying to break out of a 42-month downtrend in July 2007. As you
can see in Figure 2-19, the group, whose largest exchange-traded
fund is Semiconductors Holders (SMH), fell much harder than the
broad market amid the post-millennial bear market. The SMH:$SPX

Figure 2-19

relative strength line shows that the group began to lose favor in the spring of 2000 and did not regain traction until the spring of 2003. At that point, the chips became an outperforming group and remained so for nine months. The chips then sank again relative to the market for another 3½ years before staging a recovery in the summer of 2007. Since industries tend to act in similar ways in market cycle after market cycle, it was fair to surmise that semiconductor stocks might turn out to be outperformers in the second half of 2007, if only for a while — at least long enough for some multiweek trades.

To play this idea, it was certainly possible to just buy the SMH — it is a very liquid security and lets you play your point of view in an absolutely pure way. Another option was to play the idea through ProShares Ultra Semiconductors (USD), a specialty ETF that provides 150 percent of the return of the Dow Jones Semiconductor Index via leverage. But to focus on individual stocks that could deliver the greatest returns and the least volatility, we need to look at individual stocks.

Visit ETFInvestmentOutlook.com and click on the link Price Breadth on the front page. That will take you to the page shown in Figure 2-20. It shows clearly the percentage of each ETF's component stocks that were winners in the past day, and the number that are above a variety of moving averages. You can see that on this day, July 6, 2007, almost 95 percent of the stocks in SMH were advancers, yet only 23 percent were above their 5-day moving average, and just 5.5 percent were above their 20-day moving average. Since we already think that the semiconductors are a recovering industry, it's reassuring to observe that most of the components of the ETF are rising from a depressed condition.

To look for stocks to play in the SMH fund, click its symbol. On the page that comes up, click the Holdings link to view all the

ETF Investment Outlook

Home | Subscribe | Contact Us | About

Price Breadth ETF Rankings (FAQs)

Select Family: — All —   Select Category: — All —   Go >>

* Last updated after market close on Friday, July 6, 2007

Name	Symbol	Advance%	Decline%	AD Net%	5-day SMA	10-day SMA	20-day SMA
Retail HOLDRS	RTH	100.0%	0.0%	100.0%	28.9%	6.7%	5.8%
Homebuilders SPDR	XHB	100.0%	0.0%	100.0%	-5.7%	-24.3%	-17.1%
Gold Miners MV	GDX	97.4%	-2.6%	94.7%	80.0%	15.5%	12.6%
Semiconductors SPDR	XSD	95.7%	-4.4%	91.3%	27.0%	1.7%	10.4%
Semiconductor HOLDRS	SMH	94.7%	-5.3%	89.5%	23.2%	-3.7%	5.5%
Oil & Gas Services PS DY	PXJ	93.3%	-6.7%	86.7%	56.7%	17.3%	28.3%
Semiconductor GS iShares	IGW	90.0%	-10.0%	80.0%	23.2%	-0.4%	8.5%

Figure 2-20

stocks in the fund. In this case, you will see that the top four stocks—Texas Instruments (TXN), Intel (INTC), Applied Materials (AMAT), and Analog Devices (ADI)—made up 54 percent of the entire 19-stock fund. As with the biotech ETF, you should focus on the leaders. In mid-July 2007, TXN made up a whopping 21.4 percent of SMH, so it was the place to start.

And as you can observe in Figure 2-21, so far it was not disappointing, as its price had exceeded its 2002 and 2006 highs, and its 13-34 Weekly MACD had crossed above 0 and was approaching its 2003 momentum high. You could take a position immediately. A breakout above that MACD high later would be seen as a big positive, and a reason to add money to your initial position. Also note

Figure 2-21

that just as sectors tend to perform the same way in cycle after cycle, so do individual stocks within the sector. In this case, Texas Instruments jumped 100 percent from the median of its 2003 range to its top in early 2004. If it were to repeat that performance in 2007, it would go from $28 to around $56. That would still be 47 percent higher than the close at which this chart was made, which shows that even if you catch on to a sector RS move a couple of months after it begins, it can still yield very handsome returns for a short-term trade. Ultimately, semiconductor stocks would trade much lower in 2007 — a change also easily seen in advance on their RS charts.

Relative Strength Example 5: Size

Now I have another set of ways to help you find stocks to play relative strength, and that is via market capitalization and "style" groups. These groups are not as well recognized for their capacity to help you make money as a daily trader as sectors are, which heightens their effectiveness.

Let's start with size. It matters. The late 1990s' bull market, for instance, was all about large-cap stocks. Small caps performed fairly well in 1996 and 1997, but they fell off a cliff relative to big caps in 1998 and only treaded water in 1999. During those four years, as a daily trader, you really needed to stay focused on trading larger companies' stocks for the most part, as you can see in Figure 2-22, which compares the S&P Smallcap 600 to the S&P 500. In 2000, that condition pulled a 180-degree turn, and small caps outperformed, with one nine-month exception in 2002, for the next seven years.

A cycle in which the market has favored small caps over large caps, and vice versa, has stretched for seven years, on average, in the past century, so the prolonged period of strength for the Mighty

$SML:$SPX (S&P 600 SmCap/S&P 500) INDX/INDX   © StockCharts.com
12-Jul-2007 **Open** 0.28 **High** 0.29 **Low** 0.28 **Close** 0.29 **Volume** 0 **Chg** -0.00 (-0.31%) ▾
— $SML:$SPX (Weekly) 0.29
—MA(34) 0.29

Relative strength between
small-caps and large caps has
been dramatic for long
stretches of the past 10 years.

Small
beats large

Large
beats
small

Small
beats large

MACD(13,34,1) 0.001, 0.001, 0.000

13/34 MACD 0-line signals clarify transition zones

Figure 2-22

Mites in the 2000s was not at all unusual. As you can see in Figure 2-22, you can use crosses of the weekly 13-34 MACD 0 line as a guide to help you understand when those transitions are taking place. There will always be periods when the signal is ambiguous, but most of the time the MACD will be either sloping up from the 0 line or sloping down from the 0 line—helping you make a decision about what group of stocks to favor in your research. Note that I say favor, not trade exclusively. There will naturally be exceptions. But if you come down to a choice between two equal-seeming stocks—one large, one small—the market's current preference for size can be your tie-breaking factor.

Of course, you can play size relative strength all by itself if you feel strongly about it. At the start of 2000, there were very few ways to isolate and successfully play the phenomenon of size outperformance, but starting in 2001 a series of exchange-traded funds tracking each of the capitalization categories was launched. The largest and most heavily traded are the Russell 2000 iShares (IWM) for small caps, the S&P 400 Midcap iShares (IJH) for midcaps, and the Russell 1000 iShares (IWB), S&P 500 iShares (IVV), and S&P 500 SPDRs (SPY) for large caps.

Many major hedge fund managers will make a choice to play small caps when they sense the start of a major period of outperformance, buying a huge whack of the IWMs, as they say, to start. Then, as they begin to narrow their focus to individual small caps that they believe will outperform the small-cap indexes, they take profits incrementally on their IWMs and roll the money into specific stocks. This is an effective method of portfolio management, as it puts you in the game and making money on your idea that small caps are the place to be while you are deciding exactly which stock will go up the most.

Now, as if that were not cool enough, starting in 2007 you could supercharge your bet that one of the market-cap groups would outperform the rest by buying ETFs that provided *double* the return of the relevant index. They are listed in Appendix B with the word *ultra* in their names: the ProShares Ultra Smallcap 600 Fund (SAA) provides 200 percent of the return of the S&P 600, while the ProShares Ultra Short Smallcap 600 Fund (SDD) provides 200 percent of the inverse return of the S&P 600. If you feel strongly about your point of view on the direction of a market-cap group, this is the way to go. One caveat: these are new, so trading volume and liquidity are low—just as they were for the regular ETFs at the dawn of their existence.

So to recap: every Monday, as you research relative strength, determine which market-cap groups have an edge at that time. Run RS charts to study small caps relative to midcaps and large caps, mark down the group that is in favor, and place them at the top of your weekly trading worksheet. You can keep an ETF of the group that is in favor—long or short—in your portfolio as an "anchor" holding while you are looking for more high-octane plays.

Relative Strength Example 6: Style + Size

The big valuation buckets, growth and value, often seem too broad to be effective at usefully categorizing stocks. Yet it is remarkable how often one group emerges into favor and leaves its mirror image in the dust. When you take a look at Figure 2-23, you can clearly see that the value half of the S&P 500, which trades independently as the exchange-traded fund IVE, has exhibited a great amount of relative strength relative to the growth half of the S&P 500, which trades as the exchange-traded fund IVW. From April 2003 to July 2007, the value half of the S&P 500 rose 119 percent with dividends, led by massive moves in formerly pokey stocks like AT&T (T) and Conoco Phillips (COP), while the growth half rose just 66 percent. The S&P 500 itself was up 80 percent.

Both style halves of the S&P 500 performed well, in other words, but the market clearly favored value. And it was the same with the value/growth splits for the S&P Midcap 400 and the S&P Smallcap 600. Indeed, the value half of the Midcap 400, symbol IJJ, turned out to be the best cap/style split of all for most of the 2003–2007 period. This is highly relevant information

IVE:IVW (S&P 500 Value iShares/S&P 500 Growth iShares) NYSE/NYSE © StockCharts.com
12-Jul-2007   **Op** 1.174 **Hi** 1.184 **Lo** 1.151 **Cl** 1.184 **Vol** 1 **Chg** -0.001 (-0.10%) ▾
— IVE:IVW (Weekly) 1.184

Value and growth stocks
trade off in favorability over
long periods of time. From
mid-2003 to mid-2007, the
value half of the S&P 500 (IVE)
strongly outperformed the
growth half (IVW).

Figure 2-23

when you are planning your trades each week. When you can
see that value is in favor, you should always give priority to companies in that group. Just as with sectors, you can check out the
largest weightings of the size/style funds at ETFinvestmentout-
look.com and use that list as one of your starting points for select-
ing new trades.

Relative Strength Example 7: Region

The final place to look for relative strength among stocks is across
geographic regions. For much of the 2001–2007 period, the S&P
500—the benchmark index in the United States—was certainly far
from a leader in the world. From January 1, 2002, to July 15, 2007,
the S&P 500 was up 30 percent, while the benchmark exchange-
traded fund representing the markets of the rest of the world, the
iShares MSCI EAFE (EFA), was up 125 percent. (That fund name

looks like an alphabet soup, but all you need to know is that MSCI stands for Morgan Stanley Capital International, which created the index, and EAFE stands for Europe, Australasia, and Far East.) This massive differential was easy to witness in relative strength charts throughout the period, as shown in Figure 2-24, and would have encouraged you to look to the strongest European, Australian, and Asian stocks for at least half of your trades or investments during this period. The names of the stocks in the EFA are listed by weighting at ETFInvestmentOutlook.com, as well as other investment websites like MSN Money and morningstar.com. Again, once you know that they are favored by the market, this list provides an excellent starting point for your Monday morning studies.

Figure 2-24

Of course, there are many specific parts of the world that you can capture today with your trading, via either ETFs or individual stocks, that will help you take further advantage of relative strength insights. You can now buy ETFs tracking just Europe, or individual countries within Europe, or all emerging markets, or just Latin America. I strongly encourage you to study their relative strength versus the S&P 500 as well every week, and make your picks accordingly. You will find all their symbols in Appendix B. You can do extremely well trading the Austrian exchange-traded fund (EWO), for instance, if you come to believe that it will outperform Europe as a whole. Or consider that from 2005 to mid-2007, as an example, the iShares Emerging Markets (EEM) was up 120 percent, the South Korean ETF was up 135 percent, and the iShares Latin America 40 (ILF) was up 200 percent, while the S&P 500 dawdled along at a respectable but leisurely 30 percent.

To drill down to find even livelier bets among individual stocks, ETFInvestmentOutlook.com and other ETS sites list all of the holdings of the funds. Use it the same way as with sectors. In the ILF, for example, all but a handful of the largest companies were available for purchase in the United States in the form of American depositary receipts, or ADRs, which trade just like any common stock. The two ILF leaders, American Movil (AMX) and Vale do Rio (RIO), were up 300 percent and 250 percent, respectively, in the 2005 to mid-2007 span and were easy to spot all along the way via sector and stock relative strength studies.

Picking Stocks via Pattern Recognition

Once you have identified the sectors, market-cap groups, style groups, and regions to focus on for your trades, you are more than halfway home. However, while at least 50 percent of a stock's success comes from its sector, up to 20 percent more comes from its market-cap and valuation group, and at least another 10 percent comes from its region, you've still got to do some good, old-fashioned stock picking to complete that last 20 percent of the deal. I'm going to spend a lot of the rest of the book on this subject, but before going any further, I do want to share with you two chart setups, or patterns, that tend to work very well again and again for daily traders.

There are dozens and dozens of books on technical analysis, so I am not going to spend a lot of time showing you the ins and outs of every chart pattern you might witness. Instead, I want to keep it simple and just urge you to look for two patterns that are the easiest to spot, are the least susceptible to misinterpretation, and work the most reliably. The problem with chart patterns, after all, is that interpretations are subjective and observers are prone to subconscious bias. That is, if you are largely bullish for reasons that have nothing to do with an individual stock, then most patterns will look bullish to you. And by the same token, if you are prone to a negative view of the market, then most patterns will tend to look bearish. You need to recognize this very human tendency and attempt to see each chart independent of your view of the market, a sector, or a company's products.

In the interest of keeping things simple, let's get one thing straight. There are only two things that a stock or an index can do in the future: it can continue to do what it's currently doing, or it can reverse. For that reason, we group all trade setups into "continuation" patterns and "reversal" patterns. The question is: does the current price and volume action suggest that a rising stock or index is going to keep going higher after a brief pause, or does it suggest that a brief pause is actually the start of a major downward reversal?

Very often a stock trades so erratically that it establishes no pattern whatsoever. You can steer clear of these, since there is no way you can establish an edge that will give you a decent shot at buying shares from someone who is making a big mistake by letting them go.

Bull Flags

My favorite continuation pattern is known as a *bull flag,* or *pennant.* These occur when stocks are in an uptrend, and they represent a momentary pause for busy bulls. When you hear someone say that you should buy stocks "on dips," that person is really talking about purchasing stocks that are making bull flags. A great example was presented by Southern Peru Copper (PCU) in the first half of 2007. This was a stock that I recommended regularly to my newsletter subscribers as it made a series of flags en route to rising 120 percent in seven months. This was a stock that had four things going for it at the time: it was (1) a big-cap, (2) high-dividend (3) copper miner (4) in Latin America. You couldn't ask for much better than that in the first half of 2007. It was like walking into a casino and discovering that everyone at the blackjack table next to the south wall was beating the dealer. I mean, why wouldn't you sit down there? Your odds of success are so much better there than anywhere else.

Now that you knew what to buy, you only needed to know when to buy it. And so you needed to keep your eyes peeled for reliable continuation patterns. As you can see in Figure 2-25, PCU pro-

Figure 2-25

vided us with at least five low-risk, high-reward entry points in March, May, June, and July. A bull flag occurs when a stock runs up to a high (that's the flagpole), and then subsequently trades down or sideways into an uptrend line or moving average. You never really know if the pattern will be successful until the stock touches that uptrend or moving average, then rebounds above the trend of the mini-downtrend. Typically there is a five-point A-B-C-D-E pattern, as shown, but don't get hung up on counting waves. Just recognize that once a stock begins trading back up out of that brief pause, that is the safest time to buy it. After all, if it fails at that point, you know exactly where to set a protective stop: just below that rising trend line or moving average. That's because if the stock collapses after momentarily moving up out of the flag, and crosses down through the trend line or moving average, the uptrend is broken and it's time to move on and find another stock.

Reverse Head and Shoulders

A reliable and fairly common reversal pattern is known as the "reverse head and shoulders," or simply as a "double bottom." It is called a reverse head and shoulders because the chart appears to have three parts that kind of look like, well, an upside-down head and shoulders. Let me show you an example with a stock that was recommended successfully in my newsletter in the first half of 2007: ocean bunker fuel provider Aegean Marine Petroleum Network (ANW).

The first part, shown in Figure 2-26 as A, is the left shoulder. It represents the bears' first attempt to knock the stock down. The bulls ultimately win this skirmish, and the stock trades up for some period of time. But then the bears seize another opportunity—typically associated with some negative news event—and push the stock down again to a point that is lower than the first decline, signified by B here. The bears fail to persuade enough shareholders to join their raid on the stock, however, and it trades back up above the left shoulder for a while. Usually the stock will become stymied at the same level at which it was turned back the first time, and so the bears make one last attempt to crush it following another negative news event. But this time, the bulls rally their forces and repel the attack at around the same level as A. That reversal forms the right shoulder (C) and typically saps the bears' spirits. Time after time, once a right shoulder is successfully defended by bulls, the

Figure 2-26

shares will go on to trade much higher. The best time at which to buy the stock for the highest reward is at C, but the safest is at D, when the shares exceed the prior resistance level and push on to new highs, or at E, which represents a test of the D breakout.

There are many other chart patterns that work reliably for traders, but most of them are variations on these two themes. You are looking for either pauses within an uptrend or downtrend, or the failure of either bulls or bears to accomplish their goals. Take dispassionate advantage of both, and you'll regularly have success. Now let's go on to look at more scientific ways of working as a daily trader.

TUESDAY

The Historical Edge

New investors look at the stock ticker on television and see a lot of bright green and red lights, flashing numbers, and four-letter symbols. They hear conversations about the yen-euro ratio, factory utilization rates, core inflation, and energy prices, and it all becomes one big blur. The stock market can appear confusing and erratic even to rocket scientists.

Yet the fact of the matter is that the market is remarkably predictable. To be sure, its movements are less about what has happened in the past than about what investors believe will happen in the future. And because the future is inherently unknowable, day-to-day pricing is as much about human perceptions, hopes, dreams, regrets, and fears as it is about mere reality.

Yet because market movements are the result of an accumulation of human actions, and because humans are hardwired by genetic and evolutionary pressures to do the same things over and over again, a school of investment analysis has emerged that records this repetitive behavior and then looks for predictable patterns.

These analysts could not care less about cash flows, dividend yields, earnings prospects, double bottoms, or bull flags. They care only about how investors have tended to act in the past when certain price actions, earnings reports, economic reports, and turns of the calendar have combined and interacted.

This type of analysis—which lifts investing closer to the status of a science, rather than merely an art—began as the sole province of pioneering hedge fund managers who had the foresight to hire mathematicians and software engineers capable of turning these views into computer code. When done properly, this can be amazingly accurate, so the large firms that initiated these studies piled up profits and locked the secrets away for their eyes only. But then along came the era of low-cost distributed computing. Relatively economical Solaris workstations replaced IBM mainframes, Microsoft SQL databases replaced proprietary hand-crafted software, and the Internet arrived as a means of low-cost distribution. The old model in which a few brainiacs and billionaires were able to husband all this knowledge and keep it away from the rest of investors slipped away.

The big change came when a Texas-based investment analysis firm called Logical Information Machines—which for years had made millions by providing price-and-event-relationship data and analysis software to energy traders at utilities and merchant banks—decided to offer all but its most sophisticated tools to the public. I first came across Logical Information Machines back in the late 1990s, and I have followed the progress of its founder, Tony Kolton, with a keen interest ever since. Tony is your classic broad-shouldered, big-hearted, lightning-quick Chicago trader. He started off in the futures trading pits, trading contracts for 10 years with arms waving before deciding that there had to be a more systematic way to make big money in commodities and stocks. He hooked up with a programmer who began to turn his ideas on seasonality into code in the early 1990s, and an incredible trading tool called the Market Information Machine was born.

Markethistory.com, the commercial Web site operated by Logical Information Machines, allows the average investor to have the same dispassionate historical trade analysis tools used by top quantitative traders in Chicago, Manhattan and London. Its ideas help you to trade stocks only when the probabilities are clearly in your favor. Leveraging the comprehensive database engine behind the Market Information Machine, you can discover trades based on the fact that a stock, index, ETF, or futures contract is facing a price event, earnings date, or calendar day of the week that has proved to be a successful directional predictor in the past—not because you think you can read a chart better than 10,000 other professionals.

One of the real keys to success as a trader, after all, is knowing that something is false when most others believe it is true, or vice versa. Perhaps you have heard the financial industry dictum, "Past performance is no guarantee of future results." Once you discover that this truism is bunk, you can start to make a lot of money. Tom Ronk is one southern California–based trader who leverages this view to give him an edge on the market. While the majority of hedgers expend their resources to arbitrage away risk, he says he uses Markethistory's probability data, in combination with a proprietary pattern-recognition program, to *embrace* risk. A belief that people and companies will act in predictable patterns gives him the confidence to buy or short certain stocks into earnings release dates—events that most pros shun.

In this chapter, I'm going to show you, step by step, how to use these tools to your advantage. Although I am recommending that you devote at least 30 to 60 minutes of research time every Tuesday to this type of analysis, it is a methodology that you can harness every other day of the week as well. If you've settled on two or three stocks to trade using other techniques, you can run them through the analytical engine at Markethistory.com to see which has the most positive seasonal tendencies at the time. The bottom line is that history provides us with solid facts on which to base our trading beliefs, and these facts beat pure momentum or valuation projections. History may have its flaws, but it beats guessing every time.

So now let's get started with Markethistory. My discussion is divided into three parts: using its EarningsEdge database, SeasonalEdge database, and EventEdge database. Some of my explanation is adapted, with permission, from Markethistory's documentation.

EarningsEdge

The primary notion to accept when screening for an earnings-related historical edge is that earnings news does drive stock prices. The market values a company in part based on its record of earning money in the past, but it cares most about a company's future ability to make money. The market takes the pulse of a company's profitability four times per year when quarterly reports are issued, as required by federal securities law.

It's important to note that until 2000, companies would often selectively disclose their earnings projections to their largest shareholders and top brokerage analysts during the quarter. But in October 2000, the Securities and Exchange Commission implemented

Regulation Full Disclosure, which requires publicly traded companies to disclose material information to all investors at the same time. Reg FD, as it is known in the business, was initially slammed by many large investors as an unconstitutional intrusion on free-speech rights, but it very quickly became recognized as a major milestone in the effort to bring communications transparency to the U.S. financial markets.

Reg FD had another unexpected result as well: it turned earnings release dates into events that could sometimes bring about major information dislocations. Since no one but company insiders knows what will be in a release—or in the postrelease comments about future business prospects—there has been a big increase in earnings "surprises," or earnings well above or below analysts' consensus estimates, for many fast-growing companies. So now when earnings information is released, it can very abruptly change a stock's price trend for the better or for the worse. Earnings releases are trend-changing or trend-confirming because the information is so vital to the public's perception of the vitality of that company.

How big are these surprises? Well, it varies by company. Let me give you an example. When it comes to large, slow-growth multinational corporations like General Electric (GE), which are covered by more than a dozen major brokerage analysts, there is typically very little variation between consensus expectations and the actual reported number. In the quarters ending June, September, and December 2006 and March 2007, there was exactly zero variance for GE, in fact. But when you are talking about a livelier company like Apple (AAPL), the picture changes. In the four quarters from June 2006 to March 2007, Apple outperformed consensus expectations by 22.7 percent, 22 percent, 46 percent, and 36 percent, respectively. As shown in Figure 3-1, that was a variance of 10 cents to 36 cents, despite the fact that the consensus was the result of estimates by 19 professional analysts!

Chief financial officers at most companies have become adept at managing their quarterly earnings numbers to present the company in its most favorable light. Without running afoul of Reg FD, they have learned to carefully manage the expectations of the analysts assigned to follow the company so that when earnings are announced, they at a minimum do not disappoint—and quite possibly surprise on the upside. As a result of this expectations-management process, the movements of stock prices in the days and weeks leading up to and following these earnings announcements may follow a predictable pattern. *Most* companies' stock price histories still show random or unpredictable movements around earnings dates. But some seem to repeat a similar pattern quarter after quarter, year after year.

Markethistory's EarningsEdge product is designed to help traders identify companies that have a consistent pattern of positive or negative movement before or after their earnings release dates. It combines a calendar of expected earnings releases with a history of past earnings releases in a way that lets you see whether a pattern exists.

Earnings History	Jun-06	Sep-06	Dec-06	Mar-07
EPS Est	0.44	0.51	0.78	0.64
EPS Actual	0.54	0.62	1.14	0.87
Difference	0.10	0.11	0.36	0.23
Surprise %	22.7%	21.6%	46.2%	35.9%

Figure 3-1

The site has developed a special Edge Index indicator that shows where the edge is sharpest and the strength of the signal. It's all very cutting edge, so to speak, and it's exceptionally helpful to us in planning our daily trading.

Before getting into the details of exactly how you can use this feature, let me give you a real example that worked for me in the winter of 2007. I was following all stocks related to coal mining at the time. Joy Global (JOYG), a maker of large coal-mining equipment based in Milwaukee, Wisconsin, had traded up significantly from its summer lows but had stalled in a four-point range from mid-December to mid-February. On February 20, Terry Bedford, a Toronto hedge fund manager and friend with whom I exchange trading ideas throughout the day, sent me an instant message at 1:46 p.m. eastern time stating, "JOYG is out—volume a little skinny." That meant that the stock was in the process of breaking out of its range but that there wasn't quite as much trading volume as he would normally like to see to signify a true breakout. I liked the idea as a trade right away purely on the basis of the breakout, but first I checked Markethistory.com to see if JOYG had any EarningsEdge or SeasonalEdge at the moment that would help me make a final decision.

I input the ticker symbol as I'm about to show you how to do, and I discovered that around the last 13 earnings release dates, JOYG had shown a "strong bullish edge that peaks 4 days before the announcement and no significant edge after earnings were released." Digging a little further, I discovered that in just the past seven earnings releases, JOYG had also shown a strong bullish edge that peaked four days before an earnings release and a "weak bearish edge" that peaked five days after earnings were released. I relayed that information to Terry, and his response was, "They have that information for every stock? Wow!"

Wow indeed. As shown in Figure 3-2, we both bought the stock on February 20 at around $49.65 and held it until midday on February 23, which was four trading days prior to the announced earnings release date. The sale price was around $54, yielding an 8.7 percent profit in four days. A couple of days later, after we were long gone, the stock collapsed 24 percent with the rest of the market into a March low.

Now that I have your attention, let me show you how to do this. First, you need to subscribe to Markethistory.com. Because of the great value of the site, the subscription price went up tenfold in 2007. To get the EarningsEdge information, you need to take the Silver plan, which costs $149 per month. To get SeasonalEdge and EventEdge, you need to pay $249 per month. The site will give you

JOYG (Joy Global Inc.) Nasdaq GS   © StockCharts.com
30-Mar-2007   **Op** 43.33 **Hi** 44.26 **Lo** 42.51 **Cl** 42.79 **Vol** 2.4M **Chg** -0.60 (-1.38%) ▼
JOYG (Daily)

On 2/20, JOYG breaks above 2-mo. range. EarningsEdge shows history of big moves ending 4 days before earnings release. ...

Sell

Buy

...Purchase on 2/20 and sale on 2/23 yields 8.7% profit.... Shares then collapsed into 2/28 earnings release date (large dot), but we were long gone.

Nov 6   13   20   27 **Dec**   11   18   26 **2007**   16   22   **Feb**   12   20   **Mar**   12   19   26

Figure 3-2

a two-week free trial as part of every subscription, so if you can't figure out how to make it work, you can just quit quickly and you won't
be charged. But honestly, if you can't make this information pay off
by a factor of five in the first month, you probably shouldn't be trading anyway.

When you first log into the site, you will see a list of staff-written
trading recommendations on the home page. Organized and edited
by chief research analyst Gibbons Burke, these are well written and
informative—and you should check them carefully every day. But
for your Tuesday research purposes, click on the EarningsEdge link
in the left sidebar. You will land on a page similar to Figure 3-3. At
the top is a five-month calendar. Clicking on any date takes you to
a page similar to the current one, except forward or backward in
time. You can also navigate forward or backward via the << and >>
arrows. The meat of the page, however, is the table in the middle

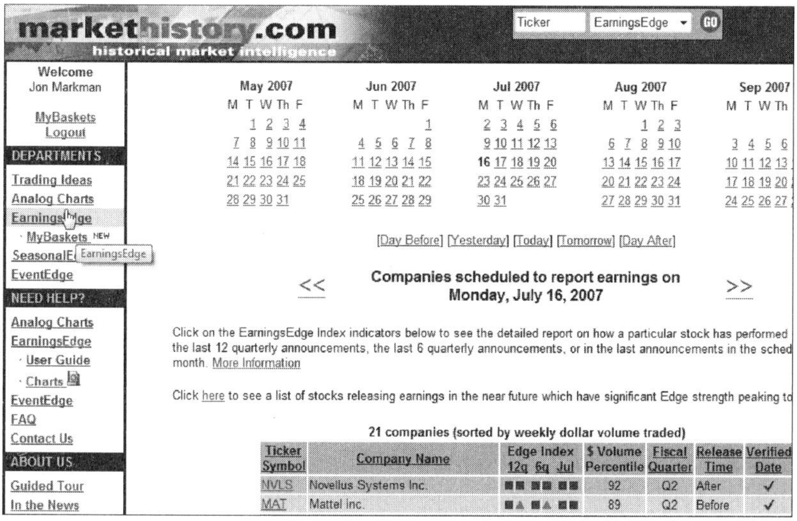

Figure 3-3

that lists all companies scheduled to report earnings on the following trading day and three different views of their past earnings releases: the past twelve quarters, the past six quarters, and earnings releases occurring only in the month the company is next scheduled to report (in this case, July).

The Edge Index indicators provide at a glance what you need to know about each company and the predictability of price changes around its earnings releases. For each of the three different views, there are two Edge Index icons. The one on the left represents the average historical price movement of the stock *before* the earnings announcement, and the one on the right represents the average historical price movement *after* the earnings announcement. The two icons are separated by a vertical yellow line, which represents the earnings announcement date. An upward-pointing green triangle means that the stock has a bullish pattern of movement, while a downward-pointing red triangle indicates a bearish pattern of movement. A blue square indicates that there is no significant edge one way or the other. No icon means that the site does not have historical earnings data for that stock.

Companies are listed in order of importance to the market based on the dollar value of the shares traded in the last five trading days, a figure called the Dollar Volume Percentile. It is calculated by summing the volume for the past five trading days and multiplying it by the average price. Stocks are then ranked on a percentile scale. A stock ranked 95 had a transaction volume in the past five days that exceeded that of 95 percent of the stocks trading. Sorting by this column puts the most "significant" and liquid stocks at the top of the list. You can change the sort order of a list of companies simply by clicking on the column header at the top of the list.

In the case of Novellus Systems (NVLS), which was scheduled to report earnings on July 16, as shown in Figure 3-3, six blue squares show that there has been no valuable predictability around its earnings reports in the past. So you just skip that and go to the next one. The table shows that Mattel (MAT) has had a bullish pattern of postrelease predictability in the past 6 and 12 release dates, although there has been no particular edge in its July releases. If you click the six-release triangle icon, you arrive at the page shown in Figure 3-4.

This page provides a chart showing the historical percent change performance of Mattel over the 31 trading days leading up to and following the past half-dozen earnings release dates as well as a text block of "automatic language" that explains the chart. In this case,

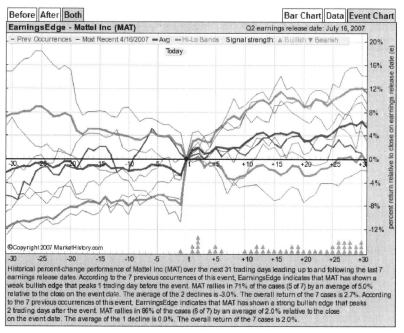

Figure 3-4

EarningsEdge shows that MAT has a weak bullish edge that peaks one trading day before the release date and a strong bullish edge that peaks two days after the release date. Weak in this case means that the prerelease edge has appeared in five of the past seven release dates, and strong means that the postrelease edge has occurred following six of the past seven release dates. That sounds good, but when you read to the bottom of the text, you discover that the average return in those postrelease periods is only 2 percent. It's not worth trading for a 2 percent edge, so you would go on to find better ideas. Before we go on, though, note the triangles at the bottom of the chart. Each one shows a date before or after the earnings announcement on which there has been, on average, a positive price change in the past. The highest stack of triangles is what Markethistory refers to as the peak date, or the one on which you will get the most bang for your buck. (As it turned out, Mattel shares did rise sharply one day ahead of its July 16, 2007, earnings release but fell thereafter in the wake of a series of toy recalls.)

Luckily, Markethistory knows exactly what we are looking for: strong edges that can provide us with big short-term gains. So next scroll down to the middle of the main EarningsEdge page to view a table listing companies with an edge leading into their next earnings release date. Figure 3-5 shows the page on July 14, 2007. It reveals that gold and copper miner Freeport-McMoRan (FCX) and 59 other companies have earnings releases coming up for which there is either a strong positive or negative pre- or postrelease edge. The Type column shows us whether the edge has come over the past six quarters or the past twelve quarters, while the $ Volume Percentile column shows us that the handful of stocks at the top of the list are among the most heavily traded stocks on the board.

Ticker Symbol	Company Name	Edge Index	Type	$ Volume Percentile	Fiscal Quarter	Release Date	Verified Date
FCX	Freeport-McMoRan Copper & Gold I	▲	6q	99	Q2	July 19	✓
IBM	International Business Machines	▲	6q	99	Q2	July 19	
NOV	National Oilwell Varco, Inc.	▲	12q	98	Q2	July 25	✓
NOV	National Oilwell Varco, Inc.	▲	6q	98	Q2	July 25	✓
BRCM	Broadcom Corp.	▲	12q	98	Q2	July 19	✓
LMT	Lockheed Martin Corporation	▲	12q	95	Q2	July 26	
PLD	ProLogis Trust	▲	6q	94	Q2	July 26	✓
MTG	MGIC Investment Corp.	▼	6q	94	Q2	July 19	✓
SO	Southern Company	▲	6q	93	Q2	July 26	✓

Figure 3-5

In the early summer of 2007, you would have already been predisposed to look for trades in basic materials and precious metals as well as energy and technology as a result of the sector relative strength work discussed in Chapter 2. So a review of the EarningsEdge reports for Freeport, IBM (IBM), National Oilwell Varco (NOV), and Broadcom (BRCM) would have been your next task. On this particular day, none of the EarningsEdge reports looked appealing. Either it was too late to take advantage of them, or the edges were too weak, or the potential returns were too small. No problem. This is a frequent occurrence—and it's why effective research takes time. The next step is to click on a date in the calendar at the top of the page that is three to nine weeks in the future. That way, if you find a prerelease EarningsEdge with a strong bullish or bearish edge and a large potential return, you can buy or short the stock immediately and wait to see if it works out. Even better, you can scroll to the bottom of the Earnings Edge page to see a list of companies scheduled to release earnings in the upcoming weeks that exhibit a pattern of movement leading up to the release of earnings. A scan of the page on early September showed just what I was looking for: a couple of companies in favored sectors with green triangles (upward-pointing) in the six-quarter and twelve-quarter categories, as shown in Figure 3-6: aircraft interior manufacturer B/E Aerospace (BEAV) and medical device maker Varian (VARI).

In September, both stocks were in attractive weekly uptrends coming out of an August bottom, trading above their 34-bar moving averages. The uptrend for VARI was fresher, but the uptrend for BEAV was longer. You could trade both, but a look at their EarningsEdge reports revealed a difference.

BEAV showed a strong bullish edge in the prior thirteen quarterly earnings reports, rising an average of 12 percent in the 22 days prior to each. But additionally, it showed a strong bullish edge in all of the past October earnings reports. In each of the past six Octobers, BEAV rallied an average of 12 percent in the period from 19 days prior to the earnings report to the day of the report. The report went on to say that BEAV had risen five of six prior Octobers in the 29 days following its earnings reports by an average of 5 percent. This suggested that if you wanted to trade BEAV, which was scheduled to report on Oct. 29, it was best to start the trade October 3 and sell either the day before the report or 29 trading days after the report, on December 11.

To dig a little deeper into the idea, click the Data tab on top of the chart on the Earnings Edge page and study the table of proba-

BEAV	B/E Aerospace, Inc.	▲	12q	85	Q3	October 30
DPL	DPL Inc.	▲	6q	85	Q3	October 30
GVA	Granite Construction Incorporate	▲	6q	83	Q3	October 24
STO	Statoil ASA	▲	12q	78	Q3	October 29
GPC	Genuine Parts Company	▲	12q	75	Q3	October 18
VARI	Varian Inc	▲	6q	75	Q4	October 30

Figure 3-6

bilistic outcomes. As you can see in Figure 3-7, the page that comes up shows the average returns for the stock at regular intervals after the October earnings release dates of the past.

In the column headed t-29, which stands for "t plus 29" or 29 days after the release date, the average return for BEAV was +5.3 percent. When you look more closely at the data, you can see that in a couple of years the trades started slowly, with negative results in the initial three-day period after the report. But the longer you waited in each of the prior events, the better the returns became. The uniformity of the positive results after three weeks was encouraging. Moreover, the stock was emerging powerfully out of its August bottom, showing a positive momentum shift in a 13-34 MACD 0 line crossover. It had also just traced out two successful bull flags much as it had earlier in the year, and it looked like another flag was just about to bust loose higher. All things considered, you would have to put this down as a great trade prospect for

Before	After	Both						Bar Chart	Data	Event Chart

B/E Aerospace, Inc. (BEAV)
percent-change performance relative to the close on Event Date (t)

Event Date	t	t+3	t+24	t+25	t+26	t+27	t+28	t+29	t+30	t+31
10/05/1995	2.9	-5.6	-3.5	0.0	-4.2	-4.2	-2.8	0.0	-2.8	-2.6
10/22/2003	-5.2	2.2	11.8	13.4	16.1	18.9	14.0	9.8	8.3	12.8
10/27/2004	-1.4	-6.0	14.0	14.3	16.8	13.7	11.0	9.8	8.5	9.6
10/26/2005	5.6	-2.6	-5.9	-3.1	-3.1	0.9	4.6	5.8	8.6	8.8
10/30/2006	4.2	-3.2	3.1	2.6	2.2	1.9	1.3	1.3	2.2	2.1
10/30/2007	5.5	4.4	NaN	NaN	NaN	NaN	NaN	NaN	NaN	NaN
Avg	1.9	-1.8	3.9	5.4	5.6	6.2	5.6	5.3	5.0	6.1
AvgPos	4.5	3.3	9.7	10.1	11.7	8.8	7.7	6.7	6.9	8.3
AvgNeg	-3.3	-4.4	-4.7	-3.1	-3.7	-4.2	-2.8	NaN	-2.8	-2.8
PctPos	66.7	33.3	60.0	60.0	60.0	80.0	80.0	80.0	80.0	80.0
PctNeg	33.3	66.7	40.0	20.0	40.0	20.0	20.0	0.0	20.0	20.0
Maximum	5.6	4.4	14.0	14.3	16.8	18.9	14.0	9.8	8.6	12.8
Minimum	-5.2	-6.0	-5.9	-3.1	-4.2	-4.2	-2.8	0.0	-2.8	-2.8
StdDev	4.3	4.2	8.9	7.9	10.2	9.7	6.9	4.6	5.1	6.3
ZStat	0.4	-0.4	0.4	0.7	0.5	0.6	0.8	1.2	1.0	1.0

Occurences: 6   ©Copyright 2007 MarketHistory.com

Figure 3-7

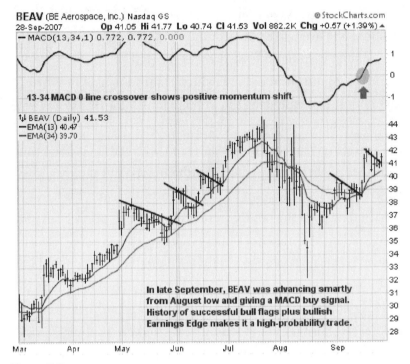

BEAV (BE Aerospace, Inc.) Nasdaq GS   ⓒ StockCharts.com
28-Sep-2007   **Op** 41.05 **Hi** 41.77 **Lo** 40.74 **Cl** 41.53 **Vol** 882.2K **Chg** +0.57 (+1.39%) ▲
— MACD(13,34,1) 0.772, 0.772, 0.000

13-34 MACD 0 line crossover shows positive momentum shift

↑↓ BEAV (Daily) 41.53
—EMA(13) 40.47
—EMA(34) 39.70

In late September, BEAV was advancing smartly
from August low and giving a MACD buy signal.
History of successful bull flags plus bullish
Earnings Edge makes it a high-probability trade.

Mar   Apr   May   Jun   Jul   Aug   Sep

Figure 3-8

the next opening bell. (It turned out that BEAV rose 22 percent over the next month, surpassing historic expectations.)

So how about Varian? That's a slightly different story. In this case, the chart, automatic language, and table showed a relatively undistinguished history over the past 12 announcements but an outstanding performance surrounding just the past six announcements. Its best prerelease trading timeframe was 22 days (positive each of the past seven years for an average 5 percent gain), which meant that we needed to buy it on September 28. Meanwhile, its best postreleease timeframe was 25 days, or December 5 (positive five of the past seven years for an average 11 percent gain). In Figure 3-9,

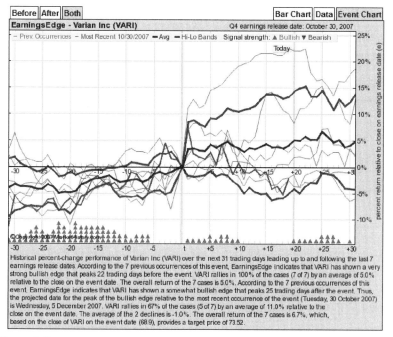

Figure 3-9

note the stack of triangles on the lines marked t-20 and t+25. This meant the optimum time holding period for VARI, presuming you liked it for other reasons as well, was a 45-day span on either side of its third-quarter earnings release in which you could reasonably expect to earn a 16 percent profit.

Furthermore, a look at the Data page for Varian, shown in Figure 3-10, revealed that if you look at just the last six earnings reports, the stock had an unblemished record going back to the first quarter of 2006, and its most recent report had been preceded by a 7 percent gain over 22 days. Considering that the stock was in a very attractive weekly and daily uptrend during a period in which its sector was just coming into favor, this looked like another great trade

| Before | After | Both | | | | | | | | Bar Chart | Data | Event Chart |

Varian Inc (VARI)
percent-change performance relative to the close on Event Date (t)

t-26	t-22	t-21	t-19	t-18	t-17	t-16	t-15	t-14	t	Event Date
8.1	8.1	8.4	8.1	3.0	3.9	4.5	3.3	2.4	4.0	04/26/2006
2.3	5.3	4.3	5.9	2.2	-0.0	-0.4	0.5	-0.0	0.5	07/26/2006
-0.9	1.4	2.5	0.2	0.3	1.7	1.7	1.8	0.9	-2.4	11/01/2006
3.1	4.6	3.2	4.9	3.2	1.7	2.5	4.4	2.9	0.3	01/24/2007
3.4	0.3	-0.0	0.8	2.3	2.3	1.1	-0.1	0.6	1.0	04/25/2007
4.7	7.1	8.4	5.1	5.1	6.4	4.8	3.5	3.9	0.6	07/25/2007
8.5	8.3	6.8	7.1	7.3	4.8	2.4	1.7	2.8	-1.4	10/30/2007
4.2	5.0	4.8	4.6	3.3	3.0	2.4	2.2	1.9	0.4	Avg
5.0	5.0	5.6	4.6	3.3	3.5	2.8	2.5	2.3	1.3	AvgPos
-0.9	NaN	-0.0	NaN	NaN	-0.0	-0.4	-0.1	-0.0	-1.9	AvgNeg
85.7	100.0	85.7	100.0	100.0	85.7	85.7	85.7	85.7	71.4	PctPos
14.3	0.0	14.3	0.0	0.0	14.3	14.3	14.3	14.3	28.6	PctNeg
8.5	8.3	8.4	8.1	7.3	6.4	4.8	4.4	3.9	4.0	Maximum
-0.9	0.3	-0.0	0.2	0.3	-0.0	-0.4	-0.1	-0.0	-2.4	Minimum
3.3	3.2	3.2	3.0	2.3	2.2	1.8	1.6	1.4	2.0	StdDev
1.3	1.6	1.5	1.5	1.5	1.3	1.3	1.3	1.4	0.2	ZStat

Occurences: 7   ©Copyright 2007 MarketHistory.com

Figure 3-10

to put on immediately in late September. Since results will vary from year to year, the best strategy is to focus on achieving the total expected level of return, rather than to merely hold for the entire recommended period. In this case, VARI shares ultimately rose 16 percent in the month following September 28, so Oct. 31 was the best exit date. After all, this is not like a horse race in which your stallion has to cross a finish line in order for you to declare victory. Once you have your profit in hand, take it!

For one last piece of confirming information before trading, it's often worthwhile to do a reality check of a company's fundamentals. A check of the company's Earnings Estimates and Earning Surprises pages at MSN Money revealed that in the next two quarters and full fiscal year, analysts were expecting Varian to report earnings growth of 15 percent, 15 percent, and 20 percent, respectively. Yet a look at the company's Surprises page showed that the consensus estimate had underestimated Varian's quarterly earnings by an average of 12 percent over the past five quarters. So now you need to take out your calculator and figure that if the analysts' consensus fiscal 2008 estimate of $2.77 was off by 12 percent, the company would be on track to actually earn as much as $3.10 over the next year. If that number turned out to be in the ballpark, then Varian trading at $62 was going for a "forward" price/earnings multiple of 20 (62 divided by 3.10). Considering that a growth stock is fairly priced when its price/earnings multiple is 1.5 times its growth rate, and Varian was trading at a P/E that was right in line with its growth rate, the stock looked like a buy on a fundamental basis as well as on an EarningsEdge basis.

The fact that these two trades happened to work out extremely well is not really the point. The key issue is that the use of the EarningsEdge tool put the odds of making a successful trade in your favor, which is all that you can ask for as an active daily trader.

SeasonalEdge

Now let's move on to Markethistory's *SeasonalEdge* feature, which is also incredibly helpful as a means of finding and timing trades on a daily basis. It was actually this feature that originally sparked my interest in the work done by Logical Information Machines, as I had published a lot of original research on the tendencies of stocks and indexes to reliably trade in a similar fashion in certain months of the year. The work I did with indexes and exchange-traded funds was featured as one of the top discoveries of the year in 2002 by the venerable annual publication *Stock Trader's Almanac* and still forms the basis for its seasonal recommendations.

Markethistory takes my work much further in that it provides a systematic list of the top seasonal equity trades on any given day of the year going forward. Whereas my research just looked at how stocks performed in discrete months, Markethistory shows how stocks have tended to perform historically during any given date range. To start, click the SeasonalEdge link in the left sidebar of the home page of the Web site. On the page that comes up, click on the After tab so that you are looking only at SeasonalEdges that occur after the current date. You'll then see a familiar format, with a few notable exceptions. Now instead of having columns relating to how the stock performs before and after earnings release dates, the table shows how stocks have performed over the next 10 to 30 days. By default, stocks are ranked on this page by their Edge Index, which sums up the statistical predictability of the expected return, with the highest numbers (over 100) being best. But I prefer to sort by Percent Return, and then further investigate only the stocks with Edge Index Sums over 90 and Odds of 80 percent or better. The final column shows the number of days in the future over which the SeasonalEdge stretches. In the case of the list for July 16, 2007, shown in Figure 3-11, I was immediately attracted to Teledyne Technologies (TDY). I happened to know that it was in the currently favored aircraft suppliers and industrial electronics industry. Now I could see other factors in its favor: it had an unblemished record of gains over the next 29 days during the past seven years, averaging +13.2 percent. An Edge Index sum score of 166.7 meant that statistically this track record was probably not a fluke. That just has to pique your interest as a daily trader looking for high-probability ideas.

Now if you had clicked on the TDY symbol, you would have seen a chart showing TDY's changes over the past seven years. I prefer going straight to the Data tab at this point to see the actual returns going forward from the current date. A study of this page

	U.S. Stocks with a seasonal edge on Monday, July 16, 2007						

<< **U.S. Stocks with a seasonal edge on Monday, July 16, 2007** >>

Click on the SeasonalEdge Index indicators below to see the detailed report on how a particular stock has performed before and after the the given date in the near future which have significant Edge strength peaking today.

500 U.S. Stocks (sorted by percent return)

Before | After

Ticker Symbol	U.S. Stocks Name	Edge Index		Percent Return	$ Volume Percentile	Odds	Days
		Peak	Sum				
CCMP	Cabot Microelectronics Corporati	▲ 3.3	76.7	15.81	78	86% (6 of 7)	t+25
CGX	Consolidated Graphics Inc	▲ 3.3	86.5	14.93	83	77% (10 of 13)	t+24
ZOLL	Zoll Medical Corporation	▲ 2.7	38.7	13.66	80	73% (11 of 15)	t+25
TDY	Teledyne Technologies	▲ 4.4	166.7	13.21	79	100% (7 of 7)	t+29
MBT	Mobile Telesystems Ojsc Sponsored Adr	▲ 3.6	105.8	11.96	96	100% (7 of 7)	t+27
CERN	Cerner Corp	▲ 2.9	98.4	10.7	89	70% (14 of 20)	t+11
GIL	Gildan Activewear	▲ 5.4	201	10.66	82	100% (9 of 9)	t+27

Figure 3-11

lets you see whether there was a single super-strong period that is making the numbers look good, or whether returns were consistent over that period. In this case, shown in Figure 3-12, we can see that in every case the very first day of the run was negative, but holding for 24 to 29 days yielded gains of 12 to 13 percent on average. And more importantly, we can see that returns were pretty consistent in every period, with excellent 19.2 percent, 8.8 percent, and 26.4 percent returns in the past three years.

The data on this page also help us make two other judgments. You can see that most of the gains for TDY were obtained by the twenty-fourth day, which suggests that if you in fact have earned a 10 to 15 percent return 24 trading days after purchase, which in this case would be August 14, you might as well book it and move on. This page thus also helps us set a target price. Since Teledyne was selling for $48.50 at this time and we're looking for a 13 percent gain, then we can set $54.80 as our target.

And finally, I recommend that you do a reality check on ideas gained from SeasonalEdge probability lists. You already know that

Before	After	Both						Bar Chart	Data	Event Chart

Teledyne Technologies (TDY)   Jul 14, 2007
percent-change performance relative to the close on Event Date (t)

Event Date	t	t+1	t+24	t+25	t+26	t+27	t+28	t+29	t+30	t+31
07/14/2000	-1.1	-0.4	17.6	15.8	14.7	13.7	12.2	16.2	12.9	9.4
07/16/2001	-2.2	-1.8	8.8	9.8	11.4	15.0	12.1	9.9	11.7	13.6
07/16/2002	0.6	-0.5	3.0	4.3	5.7	5.7	4.2	9.3	4.2	-0.5
07/16/2003	1.8	-2.0	1.7	1.6	4.0	1.0	1.6	2.7	2.4	2.4
07/16/2004	-0.1	-1.1	15.9	19.2	19.2	19.0	19.8	19.2	18.3	18.5
07/15/2005	-0.3	-1.4	6.9	7.5	9.7	7.3	8.0	8.8	6.7	9.8
07/14/2006	-0.8	-0.3	31.1	31.2	28.9	29.3	25.7	26.4	25.6	27.3
Avg	-0.3	-1.1	12.1	12.8	13.4	13.0	12.0	13.2	11.7	11.5
AvgPos	1.2	NaN	12.1	12.8	13.4	13.0	12.0	13.2	11.7	13.5
AvgNeg	-0.9	-1.1	NaN	NaN	NaN	NaN	NaN	NaN	NaN	-0.5
PctPos	28.6	0.0	100.0	100.0	100.0	100.0	100.0	100.0	100.0	85.7
PctNeg	71.4	100.0	0.0	0.0	0.0	0.0	0.0	0.0	0.0	14.3
Maximum	1.8	-0.3	31.1	31.2	28.9	29.3	25.7	26.4	25.6	27.3
Minimum	-2.2	-2.0	1.7	1.6	4.0	1.0	1.6	2.7	2.4	-0.5
StdDev	1.3	0.7	10.3	10.2	8.6	9.4	8.5	7.9	8.2	9.5
ZStat	-0.2	-1.5	1.2	1.3	1.6	1.4	1.4	1.7	1.4	1.2

Occurences: 7   ©Copyright 2007 MarketHistory.com

Figure 3-12

Teledyne is in a favored industrial group, which is a big plus. Next, study its chart and its fundamentals as the final steps before a trade. In this case, shown in Figure 3-13, we can see a chart that looks remarkably similar to Joy Global a few months before. Its 13-34 MACD is turning up from near 0, and it appears to be breaking out above a two-month range. The chart is thus another plus for this trade idea.

The final step involves a quick look at the fundamentals. According to figures listed at MSN Money, the $1.7 billion company was due to report earnings on July 26. Analysts' consensus expectations for all of fiscal 2007 and 2008 amounted to growth of 14.6 percent and 13 percent, respectively. However, a look at the list of earnings surprises showed that analysts had been underestimating earnings by a median of 10 percent in the past four quarters. Adding 10 percent to expectations for both years helped me get to an estimate of $3.10 for 2008. If that turned out to be

TDY (Teledyne Technologies) NYSE © StockCharts.com
13-Jul-2007 **Op** 47.82 **Hi** 48.99 **Lo** 47.72 **Cl** 48.53 **Vol** 192.6K **Chg** +0.83 (+1.74%) ▲
— MACD(13,34,1) 0.820, 0.820, 0.000

Rising 13-34 MACD above 0

TDY (Daily) 48.53
— EMA(13) 47.06
— EMA(34) 46.24

TDY appears on the verge of
breakout above 2-month
range ahead of period of
historical seasonal strength.
From probabilistic point of
view, it's a buy.

Set stop
below the
trendline,
around
$45.50.

Figure 3-13

close to the right number, then Teledyne was currently trading at a forward price/earnings multiple of around 15. Since the company typically traded at a multiple of 20 and the industry average was more like 25, we could set a conservative 2008 target for Teledyne of $62 (20 times $3.10), or almost 30 percent higher than the current price. So now we have three positives going for us: a SeasonalEdge, a technical edge, and a valuation edge. The probabilities say that you've got to make this trade with an expectation to hold at least until mid-August.

It turned out that the mid-August credit crisis interrupted the flow of this trade and Teledyne gained only 2 percent by the twenty-ninth day—though once the market recovered it did go on and achieve the full 13 percent gain by late September. Yet the point is not whether this single trade worked out or not. All you can ask for as an active investor is an opportunity to make high-probability trades in which the odds are in your favor. If they don't work out, no sweat. Set a protective stop under or over a trendline or significant moving average to prevent a runaway loss, and move on. Or you can automate the stop process by following the lead of Tom Ronk, the quantitative trader and Markethistory devotee whom I mentioned earlier. His research has led him to program in an initial 5 percent stop loss and 5 percent trailing stop on all stocks over $10, and a 10 percent initial stop and 10 percent trailing stop on all stocks with prices under $10.

I now want to move on to show you a few trades found in SeasonalEdge that were big winners.

Here's a nice, quick example: On June 21, 2007, the editors of Markethistory.com published a note in their Trading Ideas section observing that Enbridge Energy Partners (EEP) had a strong historical tendency to advance 4.6 percent in the next 15 days. The three-week trade starting June 21 had worked in 14 of the past 15 years, and the lone failure had resulted in just a 1.8 percent loss. Now that potential return might not sound like a lot, but if you can earn 4.6 percent on your money every 15 days, you are going to be a very successful trader. Moreover, you could leverage an exceptionally strong tendency in a low-volatility gas pipeline stock by buying call options or selling puts. At the time, the EEP chart was not particularly outstanding, but it was in a favored group at a time when the market was recovering from an early June plunge. As you can see in Figure 3-14, this turned out to be a very successful trade, yielding a quick 9 percent after first suffering a tiny three-day set-back. This example shows that a potential SeasonalEdge return does not have to be huge for you to make money—just high probability.

Another great time to look for SeasonalEdge trades is during sharp, abrupt broad market declines during bull markets. When the market is plunging and people appear to be losing their heads, you just have to keep in mind that the bulls still rule the Street and that when the spasm passes, order will be restored. Order, in this case, means high-probability seasonal trades that have worked for years at a particular time of year and are unlikely to suddenly fail. Just such an opportunity arose in the last week of June 2007. The S&P 500 had slumped by 55 points from an all-time closing high in late May to 1487 in early June. Stocks then recovered for two weeks before slumping again to a lower low of 1484 midday on June 26.

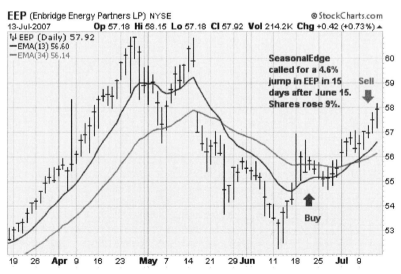

Figure 3-14

During this time, the editors of Markethistory.com published a report calling traders' attention to the strong short-term record of financial services firm American Capital Strategies (ACAS) in the ensuing seven days. The editors noted on June 25 that ACAS had been down with the market over the previous few days, posting a 5.6 percent loss over the prior week. But they observed that over the past nine years, ACAS had seen material strength over the ensuing week heading into July. The stock had recorded a nine-for-nine record over the seven days following June 25, rising an average of 5 percent. I liked this trade immediately because it looked as if ACAS could make a double bottom around the $42 level—the same spot where the bulls had supported it during the February and March sell-offs. You may recall from the end of Chapter 2 that double bottoms, which sometimes come in the form of a reverse head and shoulders pattern, are among the most reliable setups.

You can see in Figure 3-15 how it worked out. Counting seven days took the stock to July 5 because July 4 was a holiday, and the trade netted a quick 6 percent. And this situation is a reminder that, like the Joy Global trade, the SeasonalEdges have an "expire by" date. Don't hang around just to see what happens. In this case, ACAS sank sharply the day after July 5.

The final successful SeasonalEdge example that I want to share with you illustrates a condition in which we find the market at least a few times a year. I'm sure this will sound familiar. The market has been trading down modestly for a few days, and suddenly it just falls over, so that near the end of the day, the Dow Jones Industrials are down almost 200 points. Many of your positions are in the red, and everything looks like a short. But then you remember that the market shows every indication of being a thriving bull, so the

ACAS (American Capital Strategies, Ltd.) Nasdaq GS   © StockCharts.com
13-Jul-2007   **Op** 45.80 **Hi** 46.15 **Lo** 45.50 **Cl** 46.03 **Vol** 1.9M **Chg** +0.31 (+0.68%) ▲

Double/triple bottom vs. February and March levels: A reliable set-up if you think a stock will rebound due to a strong SeasonalEdge.

Figure 3-15

current correction is likely to be transitory. Now what should you buy? Well, you should always have a list of stocks at your workstation that you wish to buy if they reach certain levels. But failing that, a big down day is always a great time to swing over to the SeasonalEdge page at Markethistory and see whether there are any high-probability trades listed.

June 7, 2007, was such a day. As mentioned a moment ago, the market had been trading sideways with a downward bias after reaching a new high in late May, when suddenly the bottom dropped out and the Dow plunged 198 points. If you had visited the SeasonalEdge page on that afternoon, you would have seen the table shown in Figure 3-16. It shows only seasonal trades on the After tab, and it is sorted by Percent Return. You would have skipped Coldwater Creek because retail was not a favored sector and it had a low Edge Index score, CT Communications because it had

Ticker Symbol	U.S. Stocks Name	Edge Index		Percent Return	$ Volume Percentile	Odds	Days
		Peak	Sum				
CWTR	Coldwater Creek Inc.	▲ 3	75.9	17.71	92	100% (10 of 10)	t+20
CTCI	CT Communications Inc	▲ 3.4	104.7	13.89	73	88% (7 of 8)	t+25
HANS	Hansen Natural Corporation	▲ 3.1	33.7	13.34	94	79% (11 of 14)	t+30
SCHN	Schnitzer Steel Industries Inc.	▲ 3	119	12.88	94	85% (11 of 13)	t+20
CKR	CKE Restaurants Inc.	▲ 3.3	110.9	10.91	86	83% (10 of 12)	t+18
KWK	Quicksilver Resources	▲ 2.8	65.1	10.71	91	88% (7 of 8)	t+16
KNDL	Kendle International Inc.	▲ 2.9	42	10.2	90	89% (8 of 9)	t+16
ASVI	ASV Inc.	▲ 3	121.2	9.89	71	75% (9 of 12)	t+16
HC	Hanover Compressor Holding	▲ 3.6	93	8.82	90	89% (8 of 9)	t+14
HLEX	HealthExtras, Inc.	▲ 2.9	45	8.67	81	71% (5 of 7)	t+18
HOG	Harley-Davidson Inc.	▲ 3.3	35.8	7.2	96	80% (16 of 20)	t+27
KNX	Knight Transportation	▲ 4.3	114.3	7.17	82	92% (11 of 12)	t+22

Figure 3-16

recently been bought out, and Hansen Natural because it too was in an unfavorable sector with a very low Edge Index score. Schnitzer Steel, however, was in the favored basic materials sector and steel industry and had a high Edge Index score of 119.

Schnitzer's price chart did not offer an ideal setup, but a glance at its SeasonalEdge data chart showed that while its 13-year record at t+20 was impressive enough, it had also been up in the past six years straight at t+21 following June 7, for an average return of 17.6 percent. Those kinds of numbers have to get your attention. As it turned out, Schnitzer needed all 21 of those days, but ultimately it rose a robust 21 percent by July 9, as shown in Figure 3-17—another fantastic seasonal trade.

All the examples that I have shown so far have been bullish patterns, but as we know all too well, there are plenty of times when you will prefer to trade from the short side of the market. Short trades can present great challenges, but they can also lead to tremendous profits, as they are typically less "crowded" than trades from the long side. So if you have an edge, you will almost certainly be playing the role of a contrarian who has a belief that is different from that of the majority.

Figure 3-17

Tom Ronk points out that stocks decline three times faster than they go up, as fear is exponentially more powerful than greed. That makes sense, right? When a favorite stock is going down, investors feel the pain of loss deeply and sometimes will just sell willy-nilly without regard to all of the stock's positive attributes. This emotional phenomenon is what leads to the sort of selling climaxes described in Chapter 1. A successful short-selling campaign is therefore typically brief and dramatic, as declines happen with a fast and furious flourish.

Now that you know how to work the SeasonalEdge tool from the perspective of individual stocks, let me show you how it works for indexes, exchange-traded funds, commodities, and foreign markets. The concept is exactly the same, but now you are dealing with a different set of instruments. To start, click on the SeasonalEdge link in the left sidebar, and then click on the Exchanges link. You'll see that a new set of menu choices appears: MyBaskets, Indexes, U.S. Stocks, Exchanges, Baskets, ETFs, Europe & Asia, Currencies, Canada, and Futures.

When you click on Indexes and then click on the After tab, you will see all of the major market and industry proxies, such as the S&P 500 (SPX), Nasdaq 100 (NDX), Airline Index (XAL), and Natural Gas Index ($NGA). You can sort these from high to low on historical percentage return following the current date, and then investigate the ones with the highest odds (at least 75 percent) further just as we did with stocks, by clicking on their symbols. This is a great tool to help us with timing the market overall, as well as with timing our approach to stocks within favored sectors and industries. And because many of the indexes have longer histories than individual stocks, there are a greater number of occurrences upon which Markethistory's analytical engine can base its decision.

By the same token, the ETFs section of SeasonalEdge appears on the surface to be an excellent avenue for exploring our timing of those instruments. However, ETFs have been around for only seven or eight years at most, which means that there are very few occurrences upon which to make decisions. And finally, although we won't spend much time with it here, I do want to call your attention to the Futures section of SeasonalEdge as well. Commodities' movements are explained exceptionally well on a seasonal basis, since many of their underlying components—natural gas, gasoline, grains, and the like—are more heavily used or harvested at certain times of the year.

EventEdge

Now that you know how to work the SeasonalEdge feature at Markethistory.com, let's move on to the mother of all probability tools at Markethistory, EventEdge and its cousin, Nitro. These weapons are so powerful for active daily traders that they are pretty much the atomic bomb of short-term investment analysis. Event-Edge is included in the Gold subscription to the site, at $249 per month, but Nitro will cost you $349/month—and in a few moments you'll see why.

Let me start by telling you about a trade that Markethistory recommended early in July 2007. From January through the middle of June, the shares of heavy construction equipment manufacturer Caterpillar (CAT) had staged a dramatic turnaround. As shown in Figure 3-18, the stock had risen almost $25 from a one-year low on improvements in the company's overseas business. Spirits were high. But once the stock reached a new all-time high of $82.89 on June 19, it seemed to hit a wall of resistance. The price fell 9 out of the next 11 days. On the last day of June, the stock jumped $3, and sud-

Figure 3-18

denly all seemed well. But the very next trading day, July 3, the stock suffered its worst setback of the span when a major brokerage analyst issued a sell recommendation. By July 5, shares had hit $77.16— 7 percent off their high during an otherwise strong span for stocks.

You can imagine traders' confusion at this point. Should the stock be shorted following its dramatic run higher to "punish" the late-coming longs, or should it be bought on a return to its 50-day moving average? You could make an educated guess at this point. Or you could turn to the EventEdge tool at Markethistory and find out if this type of action had ever occurred before in the trading of Caterpillar, and if so, what had happened next. The Markethistory editors published a note on July 5 stating that they had asked their EventEdge analytical engine the following question: "What happens when a very big up day is followed by a very big down day in shares of Caterpillar?" The answer: "This unusual event has only been witnessed six other times in the history of CAT. Shareholders stunned by Tuesday's losses should gather hope from the past, as the stock has rallied five of six times over the next week. The typical return for a five day hold is 2.7%." That turned out to be prescient advice, as bulls roared in on their D5 tractors to push the stock up 9 percent over the next five days, a huge short-term gain.

So how did the Markethistory analysts do that? This setup and execution shows the genius of EventEdge. There's no guesswork involved, only probabilities. So let me back up a moment and explain what's going on. Traditional technical analysis holds that the history of price action helps define and shape future events— e.g., if investors have supported a stock on light-volume pullbacks to the 50-day exponential moving average, they are likely to do so again. Traditional technical analysis looks naively at a small range of price and volume data and has little capacity to sort though, prioritize, and integrate a variety of simultaneously occurring events into a single, consistent prediction. Moreover, technical analysis does not assign probabilities to those predictions, and much of a trader's expectations are ultimately based on guesswork. Though technical analysts prefer to call their efforts a combination of research, experience, and instinct, at the end of the day, most of their decisions come from the gut.

EventEdge, on the other hand, is a trade discovery tool that takes guessing out of the picture. Its efforts can be broken down into three tasks:

- **Observation.** EventEdge crisply describes the current trading situation in a given stock, index, or futures contract and all the key events that have occurred in the last five trading days. It shows you where that instrument is in its current trend, reports on other relevant market and index action, and describes economic and calendar events that occurred in the last five trading days that might be relevant.
- **Selection.** EventEdge then lets you select which of the factual events, trend conditions, and seasonal factors you consider to be the most important at the time, and then query Markethistory's database, without any programming knowledge, to discover how the stock or security has gone on to perform. In other words, EventEdge lets you easily create a complex historical query based on what is true and relevant right now, and see what tends to happen next.
- **Detection.** EventEdge charts show everything you need to know about the history of that event, and whether it represents

a tradable edge. You'll see very quickly how many times the current confluence of event has occurred in the past, whether it was bullish or bearish, how the security has performed after the event, whether there was consistency in that performance, and whether the edge should be considered reliable.

EventEdge starts with charts similar to the ones you have already seen. As always, you can click on the Data tab to see the underlying data used to draw the chart and the statistics on all the events. In another useful touch, you can click on the Bar Charts tab to see each separate event on a historical chart. And finally, just to kick the whole thing into overdrive, you can use EventEdge to scan the entire market for various combinations of historically meaningful events among key baskets of stocks, such as all components of the Dow Jones Industrials 30 or the Nasdaq 100. Or you can ask Event-Edge to scan for meaningful events in "custom" baskets of stocks you design yourself, which might include your own or a client's portfolio, or all the stocks in certain sector indexes.

There are two ways to get started using EventEdge. The first is to use the market or basket scan in a search for potentially profitable trading opportunities. You can find this table by clicking on the EventEdge link in the Departments list on the left-hand side of the Markethistory.com Web page. In this particular case, we're going to take a look at U.S. stock baskets, as shown in Figure 3-19. The site has prepopulated the page with scans against the Dow 30, S&P 500, Nasdaq 100, Midcap 400, Smallcap 600, and Russell 1000, which together incorporate every stock with enough volume to care about and, more importantly, enough of a historical record to make judgments about.

		Events triggered on or before Friday, July 13, 2007					
Welcome Jon Markman	**Event Definitions**	Dow30 Fri	S&P500 Fri	Nasdaq100 Fri	S&P400 Fri	S&P600 Fri	Russell1000 Fri
MyBaskets Logout	Up extra big ❷		1	1	3	3	4
DEPARTMENTS	Up very big ❷		8	2	14	10	26
Trading Ideas	Up big ❷	4	69	10	49	55	148
Analog Charts	Up ❷	17	287	54	229	285	568
EarningsEdge	Unchanged from the previous day ❷		9		4	19	15
SeasonalEdge	Down ❷	13	204	46	167	296	340
EventEdge	Down big ❷	1	22	7	22	40	41
· MyBaskets NEW	Down very big ❷		4	1	3	4	7
· Indexes	Down extra big ❷		1		1	1	1
· U.S. Stocks	Cross above upper bollinger band ❷	1	22	5	21	22	52
· Companies	Close above upper bollinger band ❷	9	72	20	49	67	131
· Baskets	Close below lower bollinger band ❷		3		9	11	6
· Europe & Asia	Cross below lower bollinger band ❷		2		5	5	4
· Canada	High crosses above all-time high ❷	1	13	5	13	16	27
· Currencies · Futures	High higher than all-time high ❷	5	47	11	42	31	95

Figure 3-19

As you can see, for each event listed on that page—and there are many more that are not shown in this illustration—the scan page will tell you how many stocks in each market had that event occur on the current date. If you click on a number next to an event, it will display a list of the stocks in that market that had that event occur on the most recent event date. In this case, I clicked on "8" below S&P 500 on the line "Up very big" to see which stocks made major positive moves on a rather lackluster day for the broad market. EventEdge then provides a page listing all the S&P 500 stocks that met that criterion on July 13. They included homebuilders Centex Corp. (CTX), KB Home (KBH), and Lennar (LEN); utility Dynegy (DYN); payroll processor Paychex (PAYX).

It would be reasonable to choose a homebuilder for further study because it was interesting to see three companies in a poorly performing industry up so much in one day. Could the big up day signal the start of a run of better prices? To find out, EventEdge next provided the page shown in Figure 3-20 for Centex. The page is populated with more than 150 technical and calendar events that were true about that stock on that day and the previous five days, as well as more than 150 other factors that you might consider to have relevance, such as the fact that the Housing Starts report was due in three days, that a major Retail Sales report had come in higher than expected that day, that the S&P 500 had been down big three days before, that oil was up big that day, that it was the thirteenth of July, that there was a new moon, and so on. The five columns of events on each side proceed in time from left to right, with the rightmost column denoted as t, or the current event date. The four columns to its left are t-4, which is four trading days before t, t-3, and so on. The actual date each column represents is included in its header.

To study the potential of the stock going forward, you must click the boxes of as many events as you believe are relevant without narrowing the list to such an extent that there would be fewer than

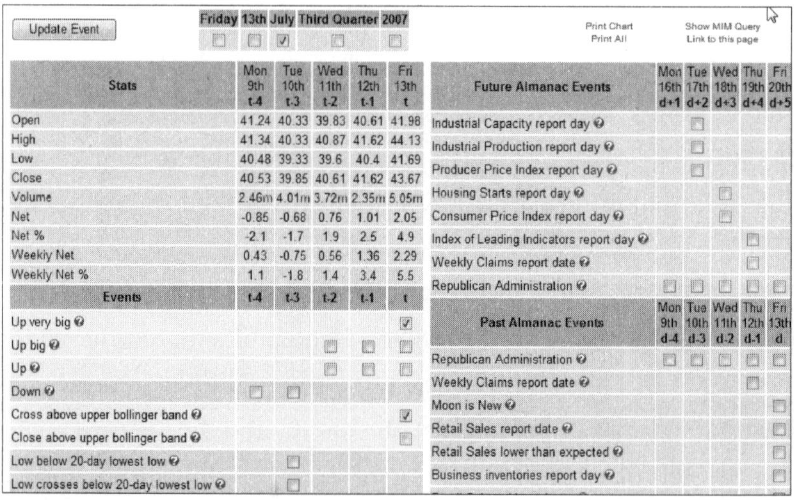
Update Event

Friday	13th	July	Third Quarter	2007
☐	☐	☑	☐	☐

Print Chart
Print All
Show MIM Query
Link to this page

Stats	Mon 9th t-4	Tue 10th t-3	Wed 11th t-2	Thu 12th t-1	Fri 13th t
Open	41.24	40.33	39.83	40.61	41.98
High	41.34	40.33	40.87	41.62	44.13
Low	40.48	39.33	39.6	40.4	41.69
Close	40.53	39.85	40.61	41.62	43.67
Volume	2.46m	4.01m	3.72m	2.35m	5.05m
Net	-0.85	-0.68	0.76	1.01	2.05
Net %	-2.1	-1.7	1.9	2.5	4.9
Weekly Net	0.43	-0.75	0.56	1.36	2.29
Weekly Net %	1.1	-1.8	1.4	3.4	5.5
Events	**t-4**	**t-3**	**t-2**	**t-1**	**t**
Up very big					☑
Up big			☐	☐	☐
Up			☐	☐	☐
Down	☐	☐			
Cross above upper bollinger band					☑
Close above upper bollinger band					☐
Low below 20-day lowest low		☐			
Low crosses below 20-day lowest low		☐			

Future Almanac Events	Mon 16th d+1	Tue 17th d+2	Wed 18th d+3	Thu 19th d+4	Fri 20th d+5
Industrial Capacity report day		☐			
Industrial Production report day		☐			
Producer Price Index report day		☐			
Housing Starts report day			☐		
Consumer Price Index report day			☐		
Index of Leading Indicators report day				☐	
Weekly Claims report date				☐	
Republican Administration	☐	☐	☐	☐	☐
Past Almanac Events	**Mon 9th d-4**	**Tue 10th d-3**	**Wed 11th d-2**	**Thu 12th d-1**	**Fri 13th d**
Republican Administration	☐	☐	☐	☐	☐
Weekly Claims report date				☐	
Moon is New					☐
Retail Sales report date					☐
Retail Sales lower than expected					☐
Business inventories report day					☐

Figure 3-20

around eight occurrences. Then click Update Event to see how the stock has performed in the past under those circumstances. Most of the technical events are repetitive—for instance, if a stock is above its 20-day moving average, it's probably above its 50-day moving average, as well as near the top of its Bollinger Band—but once you get the hang of making refinements to your query and seeing how they interact, you can create event profiles that are just narrow enough to give you a sense as to whether there is a tradable edge.

A chart with automatic text similar to the charts we've seen before is generated once you hit the Update Event button, and, as always, you can see the Data table for the query. In this case, I refined the query to determine what has happened when Centex has experienced a big up day in July and has crossed above its upper Bollinger Band, a technical event that is usually considered short-term bearish because it indicates that a stock is short-term "overbought." EventEdge reported that Centex has been down eight of eight times by an average of –7.3 percent over the next 13 days in those conditions, a very bearish edge. To see a chart of Centex in each of those situations, you can click on the Bar Chart tab, as shown in Figure 3-21, and then use the drop-down menu at the bottom of the chart to choose the prepopulated dates. In this case, on July 18, 2001, it shows what Centex looked like when conditions were the same six years ago just before the stock swooned 7.3 percent in 13 days. As you can imagine, this is incredibly powerful intelligence and should help you make more trades on a daily basis with more confidence. (It turned out that Centex went on to lose 16 percent over the next 13 days, concluding August 1, 2007.)

The most common and useful refinement is to determine if the stock is in an uptrend or a downtrend by checking the boxes signi-

Figure 3-21

fying that it is above (or below) its 50- and 200-day moving averages. An index or stock might register as bearish over the past 15
years for a month after a particular date, but if you just look at its
performance when it was in an established uptrend on that date,
the prognosis can change completely.

Now that you have seen the power of this tool, you are probably
wondering if you can harness its power for any stock, index, ETF,
or futures contract—not just the ones that appear in a scan. And,
of course, the answer is yes. If you are interested in seeing an Event-
Edge report for any particular security or index, you can simply
type its symbol in the search box at the top of the
Markethistory.com Web site, choose EventEdge from the drop-
down menu, and click Go. This will produce a page showing the
EventEdge report for that instrument. Since no events so far have

been specified, the report at first just shows a chart displaying a simple seasonal view of the instrument's historical performance after the current date. You can add refinements from there to make discoveries that will help you decide whether to make a daily trade. For instance, you could type in the symbol for a stock we studied earlier, Teledyne, to see if there is anything more to be learned about whether it is an appropriate trade at present. When I input TDY on July 16, 2007, and put checks in the boxes that allowed me to refine the seasonal search by narrowing the observations to just those occurrences when the price had been down three and four days prior to the present date, EventEdge reported that this condition had been met three times in the past, and in each case the stock was up by 20 percent in 42 days. You wouldn't trade solely on that information, as there were too few occurrences, but it would give you confidence that you were on the right track with the stock at present.

You will recall that I said that you could run EventEdge against all of the stocks in a custom-made basket, not just the indexes. This is an awesome feature of the site. Let's say that you have determined that you are interested in trading the basic materials sector because of your finding that it is experiencing strong relative strength compared with the broad market, and now you want to see if there are any SeasonalEdge, EarningsEdge, or EventEdge reasons to buy any of those stocks at present. First, you need to create a basket. Click on the My Baskets link in the left sidebar. Then click on the Add Basket link on the page that comes up, and in the box that follows, type in the symbols of all the stocks in the XLB SPDR, which is all the basic materials stocks in the S&P 500. You can get the names from ETFInvestmentoutlook.com, as described in Chapter 2. When you're done, your MyBaskets page will look like Figure 3-22.

Now, as you can see, the site lists all the EarningsEdge, Seasonal-Edge, and EventEdge data available about the stocks on your custom list. And if you click on one of the blue links at the top of the table, such as SeasonalEdge, you will be taken to a page that provides a full rundown of all the information available about your list in that area. In this case, you will note that chemical maker Monsanto (MON) has 12-quarter, 6-quarter, and October bullish edges lasting 30 days after its October 10 earnings release. And furthermore, a click on its SeasonalEdge link shows that it was in a bullish calendar posture at the moment as well, with a six-for-six record of rising an average of 7 percent over the next 30 days. All in all, it looked like a good candidate to buy now and hold until mid-

User Basket (2)	#		
Semis ETF	18	✎	✕
XLB Spdr	26	✎	✕
Add Basket or Subscriptions			

XLB Spdr
Analogs(An) - EarningsEdge(Ea) - SeasonalEdge(Se) - EventEdge(Ev) - Stories(St)

Ticker	Company	Analog	Earn	Season	Events	Stories
AA	Alcoa Inc.	2▲ 2▼	07/09: ■ ■	■	Ev	▼
APD	Air Products & Chemicals Inc.	1▲ 3▼	07/25: ■ ▲	■	Ev	
ASH	Ashland Inc.	3▲ 1▼	07/25: ■ ■	■	Ev	St
ATI	Allegheny Technologies		07/25: ▲ ■	■	Ev	
BLL	Ball Corporation	3▲ 0▼	07/26: ■ ▲	▲	Ev	St
BMS	Bemis Co Inc		07/31: ■ ■	■	Ev	St
DOW	Dow Chemical Corp.		07/26: ■ ■	■	Ev	St
ECL	Ecolab Inc.		07/24: ■ ■	■	Ev	St
EMN	Eastman Chemical		07/26: ■ ■	■	Ev	▲
FCX	Freeport-McMoRan Copper & Gold I	2▲ 3▼	07/19: ■ ■	■	Ev	St
IFF	International Flavors & Fragranc	0▲ 1▼	08/07: ■ ■	■	Ev	
IP	International Paper	0▲ 1▼	08/02: ■ ■	■	Ev	St
MON	Monsanto Co.	2▲ 1▼	10/10: ▲ ▲	Se	Ev	St

Figure 3-22

November, or perhaps leverage with November call options. (And Monsanto did go on to gain 35 percent by mid-November.)

Nitro

There is one final feature at Markethistory that you need to know about, and that is Nitro. As its name and subscription cost imply, it is a supercharged trading weapon that sort of turns all the other remarkable functionality of the site inside out. Its pages show only the most predictably reliable EventEdge data for all stocks, indexes, ETFs, and futures contracts, or just the stocks in major indexes or your custom baskets. It helps you move very quickly to the best ideas at any given time. You can spend less time scanning and more time setting up your trades.

On July 13, 2007, the main Nitro page listed about 500 ideas ranked by Edge Total score, which is a measure of the strongest, most consistent, and most reliable trading edges. These generally are the ones that have happened over the longest period of time rather than merely in spikes of apparent predictability. Because we're not interested in futures contracts, indexes, or ETFs for the most part, click on the U.S. Stocks link, and then, on the page that follows, click on the Exchanges link. The page that comes up lists all U.S. stocks and their Nitro edges, although if you wish, you can zoom in further to look only at stocks listed on the New York Stock Exchange, Nasdaq, or Amex.

On July 13, 2007, there were more than 500 entries on the page. But at the top, as sorted by Edge Total score, you can see in Figure 3-23 that there were seven entries for the commercial real estate firm CB Richard Ellis (CBG) alone, as well as two for Latin American wireless communications provider NII Holdings (NIHD) and two for oil services giant Schlumberger (SLB). Clusters of results for a particular stock tend to be a positive, so the next step is to click on the CBG symbol next to the Event with the greatest number of occurrences, which was the third, with 34.

That leads to the now-familiar EventEdge page, which tells us that in 84 percent of the cases in which CBG shares had experienced a high higher than the previous all-time high, they had gone on to rally another 11 percent over the next 31 days. You don't need to refine an all-time high with any trend or Bollinger Band checkmarks, since a new all-time high is the king of all trend indicators. Instead, you could try to narrow down the signal by seeing how the stock did when the S&P 500, Nasdaq, and Dow Jones Industrials were all up and bonds were down on the day of the signal. It turns out that there were fewer occurrences of this combination, but the

EventEdge Nitro Scans

Fri. 13 July ▾

Ticker Symbol	Company Name	#	Z-Stat Index Peak	T-Score Index Peak	Edge Total	$ Volume Percentile	Event
CBG	CB Richard Ellis Group Inc.	8	▲ 3.5	▲ 9.9	600	96	AllTimeHighCross, Friday
ENR	Energizer Holdings Inc	8	▲ 3.2	▲ 8.7	569	95	UnusualVolGain, AboveSMA200
CBG	CB Richard Ellis Group Inc.	34	▲ 1.1	▲ 6.3	554	96	AllTimeHigh
CBG	CB Richard Ellis Group Inc.	31	▲ 1.1	▲ 6.3	496	96	AllTimeHighCross
CYT	Cytec Industries	17	▲ 1.3	▲ 5.4	491	87	AllTimeHigh, 3rd Quarter
CBG	CB Richard Ellis Group Inc.	8	▲ 2.3	▲ 6.6	444	96	AllTimeHigh, 3rd Quarter
CBG	CB Richard Ellis Group Inc.	8	▲ 2.3	▲ 6.6	444	96	AllTimeHighCross, 3rd Quarter
NIHD	NII Holdings Inc	8	▲ 2.1	▲ 5.9	441	96	AllTimeHigh, 3rd Quarter
FE	FirstEnergy Corp.	8	▲ 2.9	▲ 8.1	438	96	CrossAboveSMA100, Friday
MOV	Movado Group Inc.	21	▲ 1.2	▲ 5.7	431	71	CrossBelowSMA50, Friday
LBTYA	Liberty Global Inc. CL A	17	▲ 1.1	▲ 4.4	375	94	AllTimeHigh, AboveSMA200
NIHD	NII Holdings Inc	46	▲ 0.9	▲ 5.9	373	96	AllTimeHighCross
CBG	CB Richard Ellis Group Inc.	11	▲ 2.1	▲ 7	365	96	TrendDayUp, 3rd Quarter
SNDK	SanDisk Corp.	13	▲ 1.7	▲ 6.1	364	99	UpBigVL5day, AboveSMA200, Friday
SLB	Schlumberger Ltd	13	▲ 1.4	▲ 4.9	339	99	AllTimeHigh, AboveSMA200, July
SLB	Schlumberger Ltd	13	▲ 1.4	▲ 4.9	339	99	AllTimeHigh, July
CBG	CB Richard Ellis Group Inc.	21	▲ 1	▲ 4.6	316	96	AllTimeHigh, AboveSMA200

Figure 3-23

result was about the same. All in all, with CB Richard Ellis shares just emerging from five months of consolidation, the stock looked good to go.

On this particular day, it turned out that the NII Holdings trade looked just as good, if not better. I clicked on its AllTimeHighCross line on the Nitro page, since that had occurred 46 times. Event-Edge then reported that in 82 percent of the cases following dates on which the shares had crossed to an all-time high, NIHD had been up by an average of 21 percent over the next 45 days. When I narrowed the search down to just all-time high crosses in July, the software told me that this trade had worked the past four times straight for an average 46-day gain of 29 percent. Every other sensible iteration of the idea was strongly bullish, so combined with the fact that Latin American stocks in general were also in favor, again this looked like a sensible trade.

And finally, how about Schlumberger, which also popped up on Nitro in a blaze of glory? A click on its AllTimeHigh, AboveSMA200, July line revealed, through EventEdge, that the stock had been up 12 of 12 times in these conditions over the next 37 trading days, for an average of 6.7 percent. Trying one refinement to this idea—adding the condition that the Dow had been "down big" three days before—just confirmed the signal's strength. With that condition, Schlumberger had been up in five of five cases by an average of 6.6 percent over the next 28 days. A check of the Data tab showed that these had occurred in 1997, 1980, 1979, 1972, and 1971, which is not terribly important but just goes to show the depth of the data processed by the site's little database elves.

So how do we choose among these three ideas? I put all three of them on a single chart at Stockcharts.com, shown in Figure 3-24, to see how they had all performed in the past six months and to zero in on the chart for NII Holdings, which had the highest potential return if the past were to become prologue. As a daily trader, this is a great problem to have. The choice? Because energy stocks were by far more favored by the market than real estate or technology stocks, Schlumberger looked like the way to go. It was also

Figure 3-24

the relative strength leader among the three, yet a chart that was not overly extended. (It turned out that Schlumberger did go on to gain 23 percent three months later, while NII Holdings and CB Richard Ellis both declined.)

Well, that should keep you busy for a while. Really, in many ways, Markethistory.com can provide you with enough powerful ideas every day to keep you from being distracted by sexier but less provably compelling positions. Yet I am compelled to tell you about a few more ways to find unusual multiweek and multimonth trades to put on every day.

four

WEDNESDAY

Spin-offs, Splitters, Sneakers, and Starters

Now that you have learned how to make fact-based, high-probability purchases of well-grounded stocks based on the historical record, it's time to take an escalator to another floor of the casino and learn how to throw loaded dice, both on the market's least loved, most misunderstood, and often most ignored foundlings and on its most hyped and anticipated newborns. I'm talking about spin-offs, reverse splits, and bankruptcy "sneakers," along with the fresh starters known as initial public offerings (IPOs). This is a world inhabited by the strange and the dubious, the infamous and the notorious, the wannabes and the not-quite-there-yets. Yet it's also a world of hidden talents, unpolished gems, and riches that have been intentionally smeared with dung to throw treasure hunters off the scent. We are throwing off our lab coats, you might say, and entering the smoky realm of cynical speculation.

The beauty of studying and buying stocks with no pedigree, no history, and no following is that most investors believe that these stocks have no future. And the beautiful thing about such opinions is that they are wrong about three-quarters of the time. There's nothing I like better than to mull the purchase of a stock for which expectations are zero because the upside is essentially infinite. If you have a set of methods that help you sift the good 75 percent from the bad 25 percent, you've definitely got a tradable edge.

I'm going to propose that you spend your Wednesday afternoons scanning the market for these kinds of seemingly crazy stocks and using a few rule-based technical and fundamental techniques to separate the gold from the gunk. In this chapter, I'll discuss each category and explain why it merits your attention and your trading dollars. And then I'm going to dive right into practical matters and show you numerous examples of each from the recent past, and explain how you could have found them. Fortunately, there are so many of these kinds of stocks pushed out into the market every month that they can keep you flush with new ideas every day of the week.

Spin-offs

Spin-offs, otherwise known as spin-outs, are created either when a large company decides that one of its divisions would do better on its own or when new tax laws or regulations make cutting one or more divisions loose financially sensible. They typically are born when a conglomerate that was once busy buying up every small and midsized company in sight finally realizes that it's really hard to get all the pieces to work together. The conglomerate, typically suffering a stagnant stock price, complains bitterly that investors don't appreciate all the efforts and sacrifices it has made in order to get big and accelerate revenue growth. Its CEO tells anyone who will listen that the stock is not being properly valued. He pleads with the investment community to put such-and-such a price on his firm's various parts, add them all up, and then set a premium on top of that to applaud the lovely synergy of it all. But the market fails to listen, and the conglomerate's stock remains stagnant or worse. At some point, management decides that it's time to hire a consulting firm like McKinsey & Co., or an investment bank like Goldman Sachs, to recommend ways to break off those underappreciated little pieces and see if the parent can achieve a higher price as a more svelte, more easily understood entity. And what about the spun-off company? Oh, that old thing? Whatever. It's on its own now: good luck, see you later, sister.

These spin-offs are really orphans that have been thrown out into the big, bad world with little more than the clothes on their backs. They might get a few downwardly mobile executives from the larger entity, some intellectual property, a few brand names, and a few buildings. But very often they are also encumbered with as much debt as the former parent can get away with shedding, as well as being given the worst real estate and perhaps a long-running class-action lawsuit. When you pick over the documentation of spin-offs, you often find that they have become a dumping ground for the larger company's lagging personnel, unexceptional products, and loser strategies. They are where the previous management team's great ideas go to die.

Now, as you can well imagine, most investors are not very interested in this sort of corporate debris. The typical spun-off company is in a boring industry that's not believed to be core to the parent's fast-growing mission. The usual method of expulsion from the mother ship is to send the new shares to shareholders of the parent according to some ratio that only a stat-happy banker could love, such as 0.64 to 1. And because these ejections are often done without ceremony—following a widely ignored press release and proxy vote—those spun-off shares just sort of show up in the investment portfolios of the parent's shareholders one day. As you can imagine, the response is usually more along the lines of, "What the heck is this?" than, "Thank you very much!" Someone who owns 1,000 shares of the parent will usually get a seemingly random number of shares in the spin-off, such as 127 or 482—a figure that is known in the industry as an *odd lot*. Most investors don't want odd amounts of stock in their account, and they especially don't want shares of what looks like jettisoned financial junk. So they sell the shares in the first month or two.

These unthinking sales by uninterested parties usually put a lot of pressure on the new stock, and for the first few weeks or months it tends to go either down or sideways. It's rare to see any marketing of the shares by the brokerage community—there are no road shows to drum up interest among institutional investors, no "strong buy" recommendations from the research staff, no portfolio managers going on financial TV talk shows to hype the stock. There's just a company—often with a made-up name like Covidien or Idearc that only marketing consultants and trademark attorneys could love—floating aimlessly in the market netherworld without a tether or a path.

Well, by now you have probably figured out that this is not exactly 100 percent true. I've painted the darkest picture for you because there are some Wall Street investors who live and breathe spin-offs and spend hours determining which of them might have value. And I want you to be one of them. Trust me: many spin-offs may look homely on the outside, but are actually amazing entities with great but underappreciated assets, big hearts, chips on their shoulders, and a lot to prove. Just like ordinary investors who sell stocks at their lows, big companies often tire of divisions just as they're about to turn around. Often those executives that the parent firm thought it was throwing overboard actually prove to be quite adept at steering their new companies around all the obstacles that the market throws at them. Many of them are highly incentivized by pay and option packages to get the stock moving in the right direction quickly. And sometimes the new managers are former heads of the entity when it was independent and have a self-righteous fire in their bellies to prove to the parent firm that it was wrong when it tossed them out like yesterday's newspaper.

Although the odds seem to be stacked against spin-offs, quite a lot of academic research suggests that they tend to outperform their ex-parents and the broad market. A seminal study of 25 years of market history by three Penn State professors found that spin-offs beat the S&P 500 Index by 10 percent per year in their first three years. A report by McKinsey in 1999 likewise showed that spin-offs materially outperformed the market when the parent company had annual sales greater than $200 million. The study of spin-offs launched from 1988 to 1998 showed a return of 27 percent, compared with 17 percent for the broad market.[1] As an independent investor looking for trading ideas, the main weapon in your quiver when you approach spin-off stocks must be patience. No matter how attractive a spin-off looks on the surface, you must wait for it to trade for a few weeks to pick up its trading rhythm. You need to hold off as those odd-lotters and the ebb tide of investment sentiment play their part of the game. And then, when the time is right, you must pounce. Occasionally you will wish to pounce right away, like a hawk that finds prey just a moment after leaving its nest, and I'll show you a few examples of those as well. But usually patience is golden. Now let's look at several of these as they happened in the real world.

Idearc

The dot-com revolution in the late 1990s was all about the future of telecommunications stocks, and companies promising the sun and the moon ran up to tremendous heights. Then the bust came along, of course, and hundreds of rocket ships crashed back to earth. The telecom giants rose and fell just like their punier brethren, and by late 2005 the cobbled-together Baby Bell known as Verizon (VZ) had sunk to $25, near its all-time low. Many of management's once-hot ideas didn't look so smart anymore, so the company looked down its long list of humdrum units for ones that it could sell. One that fit the bill perfectly was a subsidiary that provided Yellow Pages to Verizon customers. What could possibly be less appropriate for the digital age than big, fat paperback books of phone listings that had to be delivered to customers one by one? After all the paperwork was completed, the unit was spun off as a new public company with the odd name Idearc (IAR) at a ratio of 1 share for every 20 shares of Verizon. So if you had held 750 shares of Verizon for years, as of mid-November 2006 you were also the confused owner of 37 shares of IAR.

As you can see in Figure 4-1, the spin-off was launched in the mid-$20s and immediately tried to go higher. But now you can observe the virtue of patience. IAR shares failed at $29, then came back to their starting price and traded in the $26.50 to $27.50 area for three weeks. When a stock jumps, falls, and then stabilizes like

Figure 4-1

that at a meaningful level, your job as a market predator is to determine whether it is time to pounce. In this case, the stock touched the $26.25 area six times, suggesting that major institutional investors had determined that that level was the floor. This might turn out later not to be true, so when you decide to take a position like this, you should start out with only a quarter to half of the funds you would normally expect to allocate to a risky idea.

The next step: apply the rest of your funds to the stock when it exceeds its post-spin-off high on a close. In this case, that happened at $29.25. At that point, everyone who wanted to sell their odd lots has probably done so, and all current holders are winners. That means that there is no overhead resistance — no reservoir of bitter, longtime losers who are just waiting for a chance to unload their shares. At this point, spin-offs and IPOs can really motor, and you will typically see the greatest opportunity for price appreciation.

IAR went from $29 to $35 in a month—a 21 percent gain. Spin-offs typically have a lot of staying power once they get going, so you should not be too anxious to sell. In this case, you could wait for a break of the trendline, as shown in Figure 4-1, or a drop below the daily MACD 13-34 0 line, which happened at around the same point. Either way, this play on the shares of a seemingly boring entity provided a huge gain in a short period.

Genworth

In 2003, financial and industrial conglomerate General Electric (GE) came under a lot of pressure to do something about its stagnant stock price and confusing financial structure. Its shares were down 40 percent from their highs and hovered listlessly around levels first reached five years before. Financial engineers working for new chief executive Jeff Immelt huddled and came up with a plan to spin off 30 percent of the company's life and mortgage insurance business as a separate entity named Genworth. The new $9.8 billion firm would start life with 15 million customers, $100 billion in assets, and $935 million in annual profits, but more importantly, the share sale would raise around $3.3 billion for GE and dramatically cut the parent's debt load. At the time, *BusinessWeek* called the spin-off "one of the largest and quietest stock deals of the year," and noted that investors were wondering why the business was being "kicked out of the GE family." The magazine observed that while the business was a solid performer for an insurance company, it just wasn't performing up to GE standards, and the new CEO was anxious to use the proceeds to invest in sexier, faster-growing wind power, medical technology, and commercial finance operations.

As you can see, this was all very typical for a spin-off: a business that was believed to be boring was shoved out of a conglomerate for reasons that appeared to have less to do with fundamentals than with the pursuit of a new CEO's strategy. The sale took place on May 24, 2004, and the shares immediately traded down by 3 percent. Analyst David Menlow of IPOfinancial.com captured the sentiment of the time perfectly when he told a reporter, "If GE doesn't want it, why should anyone else get excited about it?"

So what happened next? Well, that decline the first day was the low of the next three years, as the stock rocketed out of the box and basically did not stop gaining altitude for the next two years, rising 90 percent over a span of time in which the Financial Sector SPDR (XLF) rose 40 percent and both the S&P 500 Index and General Electric rose 35 percent. The negative sentiment surrounding this spin-off provided a tremendous opportunity for investors.

From a trader's point of view, this example provides a great illustration of the notion that when a spin-off trades above its opening price in the two weeks after launch, begin a position with half of the funds that you would normally put into a full position. Then wait for the stock to experience its first material setback. This will usually happen within a month or two or three. Typically the stock will make a low that's higher than its launch price, and then begin to regain altitude. Apply the remainder of your funds at that breakout point. As you can see in Figure 4-2, in the case of Genworth, that came in October at around $23. From then on, the spin-off is a hold until its chart breaks down, either by falling below an uptrend line or by falling below a significant moving average. By following these guidelines, a trader would have made around 70 percent in Genworth, from $20 to $34.

GNW (Genworth Financial Inc.) NYSE   © StockCharts.com
20-Jul-2007   **Op** 34.33 **Hi** 34.61 **Lo** 31.94 **Cl** 32.24 **Vol** 18.2M **Chg** -2.09 (-6.09%) ▼

GNW (Weekly)

GAME PLAN
FOR GNW
SPIN-OFF

3. Sell on break of uptrend ...

4. ... or first break
of 50-week MA

2. Add on breakout following test of the
breakout and setting of higher low.

1. Buy breakout above
spin-out price in third week.

Jul Oct **05** Apr Jul Oct **06** Apr Jul Oct **07** Apr Jul

Figure 4-2

Coach

No discussion of spin-offs of the 2000s would be complete without a look at the king of them all: the expulsion of luxury leather goods retailer Coach (COH) from the moribund conglomerate Sara Lee (SLE). At the time of the spin-off, Sara Lee was in the midst of a three-year slide in which its shares had fallen by more than 50 percent. Shareholders were after the company to do something, and chief executive Henry Silverman obliged, telling reporters that he believed that the spin-off of Coach would "facilitate a clearer understanding and fairer market valuation" of the business. He turned out to be right about Coach, although spinning it off never did much for Sara Lee shares. From the day that Coach was launched as a separate company in September 2000 through July 2007, the stock advanced a whopping 1,900 percent, crushing the performance of its ex-parent, which rose 14 percent, and the broad market, which was up 1 percent.

The stock fell almost immediately upon its launch into the teeth of the millennial bear market, but it recovered quickly and exceeded its launch price by late October. Afterward, the stock established a pattern of higher lows and higher highs that permitted patient—not trigger-happy—spin-off traders an opportunity to make as much as 20 times their money before its uptrend fell apart in mid-2006, as shown in Figure 4-3. The trading of this stock gives you an idea of how far a spin-off can go. Few of them will ever return 1,900 percent in seven years, but the possibility is always there when the right confluence of negative sentiment meets growth-oriented management and market opportunity.

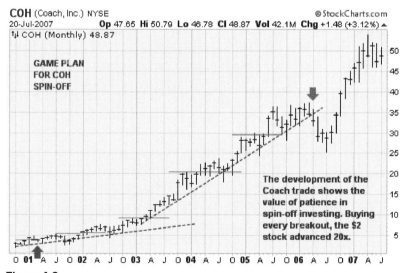

Figure 4-3

Ameriprise Financial

After the success of the Genworth spinoff, you would think that a spin-off from another major financial conglomerate would be met with open arms. And yet you would be wrong. For when American Express (AXP) announced plans to expel its Minnesota-based brokerage service and focus on its credit card business, the market gave a great, big collective yawn. Like Genworth, Ameriprise was a major company on its own, with over $400 billion under management by more than 12,000 financial advisors. The business was large, but its returns were just not what American Express believed were suitable. It shoved the company out the door on September 30, 2005, without retaining any shares.

By now, you probably know what happened next. Because there was very little publicity about this deal, many people who received one share of Ameriprise for every five shares of American Express they owned dumped them right away. The stock fell from $37.50 to $32 in less than a month. Just when things were getting ugly, however, the stock stabilized and began heading north. As you can see in Figure 4-4, the safest time to buy came in November, when the shares exceeded their IPO price at around $37.75. After that, the shares stormed higher, with material volatility, until they broke their uptrend in May 2006 at around $45. On this first foray, your profit was 19 percent.

A few months later, once the entire market had stabilized in mid-summer of 2006, you got a chance to buy the stock back at $40 when it showed definite signs of stabilizing at $40—the same place at which institutional investors had supported the stock in February of that year, as well as in late 2005. From that point onward, the stock advanced steadily to its July 2007 level of around $65. Open profits

AMP (Ameriprise Financial Inc.) NYSE   © StockCharts.com
20-Jul-2007   **Op** 66.34 **Hi** 66.34 **Lo** 62.94 **Cl** 63.20 **Vol** 2.5M **Chg** -3.15 (-4.75%) ▼

GAME PLAN
FOR AMP
SPIN-OFF

2. Sell trendline break.

4. Buy breakout above
2006 high.

3. Buy quadruple bottom vs. Dec.
'05, Feb '06 and June '06 lows.

1. Buy breakout above IPO price.

Figure 4-4

at that point were 63 percent. Once again, it did not take a lot of genius to obtain this kind of return—just cunning, the audacity to go against the crowd for a short while, and the ability to stick with your belief in the value of spin-offs during a few bouts of volatility.

Chipotle Mexican Grill

Restaurants have recorded an underwhelming record as public companies, with only a handful of them ever achieving great success. After you've listed McDonald's (MCD), Starbucks (SBUX), Yum! Brands (YUM), Panera Bread (PNRA), and Brinker International (EAT), the list gets pretty thin. It takes a new chain concept with something really amazing in its special sauce to get investors' attention.

Chipotle Mexican Grill (CMG) was the brainchild of a young San Francisco chef who was enamored of a specialty of the *taque-*

rias in that town's Mission District: aluminum-foil-wrapped burritos that combined naturally grown meat, lettuce, beans, cheese, sour cream, and salsa in a 13-inch flour tortilla. Founder/chief executive Steve Ellis launched his chain in San Francisco in 1993 and accepted a minority investment from McDonald's in 1997 to fuel expansion. In 1999, McDonald's upped its investment to a controlling share, and by 2005 it owned 92 percent of a popular "fast casual" chain that had spread its company-owned stores to nearly 500 locations. Around that time, McDonald's was looking for cash to fuel its own growth, and it decided to spin the company off as a separately traded entity. Originally, the plan was to sell 6.3 million shares at $15.50 to $17.50, but hunger for the shares was greater than expected, and by the time the company went public on January 23, 2006, the offer was $22. And then it doubled on its first day. But the story doesn't end there.

The new IPO traded sideways for a couple of months after its big opening, then offered at least six more entry points over the next year and a half en route to another 150 percent move higher. As you can see in Figure 4-5, traders had an opportunity to buy on a triple bottom in early March 2006, a breakout in late March 2006, and another breakout in May 2006. A trendline break could have been sold in July 2006, but then more opportunities arose when the stock stabilized by October of that year, and every return to its rising trendline offered another buying opportunity. In May 2007, after an earnings report that shocked the Street with its strength, the stock broke out again to a new all-time high, which, as we have seen, can be a powerful buy signal for IPOs at around this stage in their lives. Although the price looked high at $75 on that breakout, the shares went on to break $135 by December.

CMG (Chipotle Mexican Grill Inc.) NYSE © StockCharts.com
24-Aug-2007 **Op** 101.81 **Hi** 103.72 **Lo** 100.53 **Cl** 102.91 **Vol** 171.7K **Chg** +1.54 (+1.52%) ▲
⑴ CMG (Daily) 102.91

GAME PLAN FOR
CMG SPIN-OFF

2. Sell
trendline
break

1. Buy
new-high
breakout

4. Buy
breakout to
new high

3. Buy triple bottom/stabilization,
then add on trendline touches.

Figure 4-5

One special opportunity to buy the shares came in the autumn of 2006, when McDonald's announced that it had begun an offer to shareholders to exchange McDonald's shares for Chipotle shares. The offer was completed in a tax-free swap on October 13, and that moment at which McDonald's fully divested itself of Chipotle shares turned out to be another great time to pick up the stock, as there was no further possible overhang from its former parent's potential sales. To be sure, Chipotle's tremendous strengths as a purveyor of quickly served, high-quality meals in attractive locations and a business structure that provides high returns on capital were most important to the stock's success. But as traders we live for these sorts of strong IPOs that are disbelieved at the start of their runs, as they can make us a lot of money as institutions slowly but surely take large stakes.

HanesBrands

After achieving fantastic success with the spin-off of Coach in 2000, investors begged Sara Lee Corp. to divest more of its brands. In September 2006, the company obliged by spinning off its popular Hanes, Champion, Playtex, Bali, barely there, and Wonderbra lines into a separate company called HanesBrands, Inc. Headquartered in Winston-Salem, North Carolina, the company would employ 50,000 in the design and manufacturing of undergarments, casual wear, and active wear for men and women.

The shares opened with a big 6 percent boost on their first day of trading amid a strong market, then leveled off for a few days. As you can see in Figure 4-6, the first opportunity for active traders came in the middle of October, when shares moved powerfully above the $22.75 level to a new high at $24.50. The stock backslid at that point, falling back to $22, but it would not have violated any

HBI (HanesBrands, Inc.) NYSE · © StockCharts.com
29-Aug-2007 · **Op** 28.25 **Hi** 29.09 **Lo** 28.13 **Cl** 29.02 **Vol** 449.8K **Chg** +0.98 (+3.50%) ▲

HBI (Daily) 29.02

HBI SPIN-OFF
GAME PLAN

Buy first breakout in Oct. '06, then
breakouts in Jan. '07 and Feb. '07
before selling on break of uptrend
in May '07 for 17% gain.

Figure 4-6

protective stops placed at the $21 original breakout level. The shares traded back up to the $24.50 level a couple of times before breaking out again at $25, the next entry or add point. The pattern repeated itself several times, setting up a nice rising trend line that lasted well into April 2007. A break of that trendline, shown on the chart in May, effectively ended the IPO trade in the stock, but not before a trader would have netted a nice 17 percent on the original purchase price.

The earnings news about HanesBrands was decidedly negative during virtually this entire period, but the investment community wanted to get hold of the shares while they didn't look so hot. The success of Coach was a powerful incentive, but so was the potential of owning so many great apparel brands in a single company. By August 2007, a new set of executives had really started to turn the company around, and it was on track to post 17 percent earnings growth over the next couple of years. It's a great exemplar of the notion that IPOs don't have to be sexy to be lucrative, and you don't need to risk taking them right away. Buy on the first couple of breakouts with a protective stop, and hang on for a nice ride higher on a wave of informed buying against a wall of worry.

Embarq

In mid-May 2006, Sprint-Nextel spun off its local telephone division as an independent, non-Bell telecommunications company with 20,000 employees. Industry observers scoffed at the prospects for the new company, observing that its business was under assault from numerous competitors. At a time when rivals AT&T and Verizon were investing a lot of money in fiber-optic infrastructure to support wireline video in some of their markets, and wireless communications were all the rage, Embarq was seen as a dead-end company with no plans to invest in the future at all.

This was a classic example of a situation where neither the institutional nor the individual investor community seemed to think much of the company's chances. Not only did EQ come public during a rough stretch in the broad market, but most of its parent's shareholders thought of themselves as wireless investors. Most shareholders had zero interest in owning a local phone company with seemingly few growth prospects. Said a *Forbes* magazine article about the stock received by Sprint-Nextel shareholders in the 1-for-20 dividend: "With revenue and subscriber numbers expected to fall, who wants to keep them?"[2] The result was predictable: the shares fell immediately, as investors dumped them out of their accounts almost as soon as they dropped in. So the stock was heavily discounted and mispriced before most people even knew it existed.

The new company did have one thing going for it: Standard & Poor's announced that Embarq would replace Applied Micro Circuits in the S&P 500 Index, so there was at least one ready group of buyers: index fund investors, who absolutely had to own it, regardless of their point of view. And it turned out that there was a lot more going for it as well, as wireline delivers tremendous cash flows and is far from dead.

As you can see in Figure 4-7, after the initial round of selling was complete, the stock sprang to a new high in August as the broad market recovered, offering a sensible entry point on this mispriced and misunderstood company. Over the next year, repeated breakouts and returns to a newly established uptrend line provided more

EQ SPIN-OFF
GAME PLAN

Embarq stumbled out of
the gate in its IPO, but
buying its first and
successive breakouts
yielded a 35%-plus gain.

Figure 4-7

opportunities to add or take a new position. By the time the shares
had fallen definitively down through their trendline, buyers of the
original breakout were up 37 percent.

I think you get the picture by now. Spin-offs are truly among the
Rodney Dangerfields of the finance world, stocks that just can't get
no respect. That lack of respect provides just the right atmosphere
for risk-taking active investors who are capable of buying these
stocks technically on breakouts and trendline touches. There are
no calendars of spin-offs, so the best way to get a headsup is to start
a free Google news alert. Visit http://google.com/alerts. In the
Search Terms dialog box type in "spin-off"; set Type to "news"; set
frequency to "once a week"; and submit your e-mail address. Then
you will get e-mail from Google Alerts containing news items about
future business spin-offs once a week. Now let's look at some more
stocks like these in similar but different categories.

Reverse Splits

When a whole lot of bad things happen to a public company over a period of time, whether through stupid strategic decisions or a widespread revulsion for its industry, its stock price can dwindle to a very small number. During the worst of the dot-com crash of 2000–2002, it was not uncommon to see stocks that had once traded at more than $100 decline to less than $5, or even $1.

It's obviously quite embarrassing for chief investors on an emotional level to have their stock sink to such depths, but there are important investment implications as well. Even if a company has cleaned up its act, finally made its widgets work, or nailed the contracts that were in the offing for a long time, it may find that it is hard to persuade investors to come back once its shares trade for less than $5. Many mutual funds, indeed, have rules hardwired into their trading covenants that exclude the ownership of stocks priced at less than $5. A price below half a sawbuck, or worse, below $3, is a scarlet letter. It's very hard to get brokerages interested in providing research on the stock, it's hard to go on financial television and promote all the great things you've done lately, and it's hard to encourage ownership by the big institutions that provide all the liquidity in the market. If a company is serious about getting back into the good graces of investors, an extremely low price is an obstacle that must be surmounted.

So what's the best way to lift your stock price, other than announcing eight straight quarters of 50 percent growth in earnings per share (which really, if you think about it, would just take too long)? The answer is a little trick called the *reverse split*. It's essentially the same as a regular split, in which a successful company with a high stock price cuts its price in half and doubles the number of shares outstanding—except in reverse. A company reduces the number of shares outstanding, which has the effect of boosting the share price. While a typical regular split is done at a 2:1 or 3:2 ratio, the typical reverse split is much larger, in the 1:10 or 1:20 area. The total market capitalization of the company remains the same; only the number of shares and the price change.

Reverse splits are typically considered to be a bad sign because investors know that they're a subterfuge, an attempt to make a stock look more valuable when in fact nothing has changed. Investors know that companies might do a reverse split to avoid being delisted from an exchange and will typically give those companies a wide berth.

But it turns out, once again, that reality may be more complicated. Very often, by the time a company launches a reverse split, it really has figured out how to change its fortunes for the better. The reverse split may be timed to coincide with the launch of an entirely new business strategy or product line, the hiring of a new executive team, or other major events in a company's life cycle. While these changes are sometimes completely bogus, other times they really are quite positive. Thus from time to time a reverse split occurs at a point where there is maximum pessimism about a company and its shares, and yet it is truly about to set off on a new voyage that will genuinely increase revenue, earnings, and cash flow in a material way. In other words, sometimes the moment of a reverse split is a marker that some outsiders continue to see as a sign of total toxicity, but that insiders, savvy independent researchers, and value-focused contrarians might determine is actually a giant, flashing neon sign that says, "Buy now."

Here are a few other reasons to look at reverse splits in a positive light:

1. **Major incremental EPS power.** When stocks do a reverse split, the number of their shares outstanding obviously goes way down. This can make it look as if a stock has greatly improved its earnings strength. For example, if earnings increase 10 percent while the number of shares has fallen by 50 percent, as in the case of a simple 1:2 reverse split, then reported EPS magically doubles to +20 percent.

2. **The odd-lot fallacy.** Most reverse splits result in holders owning odd-lot share positions, a condition we discussed a few moments ago. For example, if you owned 300 shares of a stock and it splits 1:7, you would now have 42.8 shares of the stock, an odd number. Many people do not want an odd number of shares, so they sell the position immediately. This creates a short period of nonfundamental weakness immediately after the split.

3. **Livelier stock action.** It is easier for a stock to move higher when there are fewer shares outstanding. As an example, Microsoft rarely moves more than $1 these days because there are more than 10 billion shares outstanding; it takes a ton of buying to move the needle. In contrast, a stock with just 5 to 10 million shares outstanding can be pushed around very easily, yielding more opportunities to benefit from the volatility.

I'm not going to talk about all the fundamental financial features to study en route to determining the strength of a company that has performed a reverse split. As traders, we figure that all that will show up in the price action of the stock. So let's take a look at a few of these companies.

Avis Budget Group Inc.

One of the real boom-and-bust stocks of the mid-1990s was a conglomerate of leading consumer services brands called Cendant. It was a combination of a 20-year-old direct-mail affinity-marketing firm called CUC International and the nation's largest owner of hotel franchises and real estate brokerages, Hospitality Franchise Systems. Its executives were celebrated for their genius at assembling a new kind of conglomerate with many ways to generate synergy between units, and its shares were nearly as hot at the time as those of Internet prima donnas Yahoo! and Amazon.com. But then disaster struck: the company's big CUC International unit was accused of accounting fraud, and the entire company suffered, plunging more than $10 billion in market value. Then, just as it was emerging from that mess in 2001, the firm was hit by the travel recession caused by the September 11 terrorist attacks. Shares recovered in 2003 with the rest of the market and then traded listlessly in a narrow range for a couple of years.

The company's executives came to believe that they needed to do something drastic to change their fortunes, and they turned to their investment bankers for a new plan. The big idea: spin off the firm's big travel, hotel, and real estate units as separate companies, and retain only its Avis and Budget rental car businesses. Then rename the company Avis Budget Group, perform a 1-for-20 reverse split, slap on some lipstick, and claim that the new entity was highly focused on generating cash flow.

The split and renaming occurred on September 6, 2006, and, as you can see in Figure 4-8, the shares stabilized fairly quickly. The stock fell to $18 a few times, but it stabilized there before bounding above the downtrend that had been in place since the spring. That was the place to establish a position. There was certainly a big risk in buying the stock at multiyear lows then, but the price was firming up in the wake of a reverse split, which you now know can be a positive event in the right circumstances. When the shares broke out to a postsplit high in November, you had a new opportunity to add to the position. Another opportunity to add to the position occurred in January 2007, upon the breakout above the summer highs. And finally, a signal to sell and take profits came six months later, when shares sank beneath their new uptrend in June. From top to bottom, the trade on this reverse split was roughly 40 to 55 percent, from around $19 to around $30. That's a nice reward

Figure 4-8

for the risk of trading in a stock that most other investors were avoiding like an auto accident.

Foster Wheeler

Shares of heavy construction company Foster Wheeler plunged by around 99 percent from 1997 through the middle of 2004 as the company was hit by one financial calamity after another, from asbestos claims to a severe credit crunch. For a while it was on the brink of filing for bankruptcy, but it was ultimately bailed out by a surge in demand for its ability to build large oil and gas processing facilities, natural gas liquefaction plants, power generation plans, and chemical plants. Not too long after it was reorganized for the umpteenth time, executives announced a 1-for-20 reverse split. It occurred on November 30, 2004, and the stock price shot up to close the week at $14, which sounded a heck of a lot better than its previous price, which was under a buck.

There's usually a lot of selling soon after a reverse split, as you know by now, because of the odd-lot phenomenon. Also, a reverse split is sometimes seen as the last resort of a desperate company, and many investors just stay away from the shares on principle. But many other times, the reverse split is accomplished at the end of a lengthy and successful reorganization and marks the beginning of a new era for a stock. That certainly turned out to be the case for Foster Wheeler, as its stock shot up 700 percent from that point through August 2007, with just a few brief pauses to catch its breath.

Active daily traders had numerous chances to get aboard the stock as it advanced powerfully under the spell of all the things that work in favor of reverse splitters. Looking at Figure 4-9, you can see that the initial selling spree following FWLT's debut in the $14 area was

FWLT (Foster Wheeler Corp.) Nasdaq GS   © StockCharts.com
29-Aug-2007   **Op** 114.13 **Hi** 116.00 **Lo** 109.58 **Cl** 114.65 **Vol** 4.8M **Chg** +0.55 (+0.48%) ▲

FWLT (Weekly) 114.65
···MA(75) 62.09

FWLT REVERSE
SPLIT GAME PLAN

Weekly bars for FWLT show 6 low-risk
entries since the Nov. '04 reverse split:
moves above 75-week MA, several
tests of support and two breakouts.
Total return: 700%+

Figure 4-9

quickly contained, and the first entry came a month later, following the waning of odd-lot selling. The next entry came on a move
above the 75-week, or about 1.5-year, moving average, which tends
to set good boundaries for positive and negative phases for stocks
such as this. Subsequent adds or new purchases would be made on
touches of this support or breakouts above prior recovery highs. In
short order, FWLT went from goat to hero, with its beaten-up cohort
of old investors kicking and screaming the whole way.

MicroStrategy

Controversial business intelligence software maker MicroStrategy
(MSTR) provided ample long and short trading opportunities from
its inception as a public company in the late 1990s through the
mid-2000s. In its first incarnation, it was one of the original stock
rockets of the dot-com era, advancing in price by nearly 10 times

from 1998 to 2000 as sales and earnings were reportedly growing at an incredible pace. In 2000, however, journalists began to question the accounting practices of founder and chief executive Mark Saylor. The shares plunged 61 percent in a single day in March that year after the company acknowledged that its revenue recognition techniques had indeed been overly aggressive, and the stock went on to lose 98 percent of its value over the next two years.

Unlike a lot of other dot-com companies, however, Micro-Strategy did make real software that was bought by real customers. Its relational database software helps companies analyze and monitor their businesses, and it's apparently pretty good. After a series of restatements, reorganizations, and the resolution of SEC probes, the company announced a 1:10 reverse split that took effect on July 30, 2002. Now if ever there were a company with a record of inflicting inhuman pain on its shareholders, this is the one—so you can imagine that its announcement of a reverse split didn't exactly set the world on fire. And come on, how many people are in the market for a 48-cent stock in the middle of the worst bear market that investors had endured in a decade? Yet Micro-Strategy was actually in its third straight quarter of profitability, and business was looking up. This was another great setup for a reverse split to succeed: a hated stock in a terrible market that disguised improving fundamentals.

So as we have seen with other reverse splits, the timing turned out to be brilliant. With the split coinciding with a real revival of the company's growth prospects, not to mention what turned out to be the final throes of the millennial bear market, MicroStrategy shares began to rise from the postsplit $4.50 level almost immediately after the split, and went on to advance by 678 percent over one year and 2,500 percent over the next 4½ years before falling apart again in mid-2007.

In Figure 4-10, which displays weekly bars, you can see that the shares broke their long-term downtrend in mid-August 2002, which provided the first entry point for a "probe" position, perhaps 10 to 25 percent of the capital that you might ultimately wish to devote to this trade. Successful traders need validation of an idea such as this, and the first test came after a multiweek slide in September ended in a positive "key" reversal week in October—a pattern in which the high of one week is higher than the previous week's high, the low is higher than the previous week's low, and the close is above the previous week's close. Subsequent new entry points came in mid-October, when the stock exceeded its August high, and then more emphatically in early 2003, when shares repeatedly traded up before returning to touch a newly established uptrend.

Figure 4-10

Mind you, all this time the bears were continuing to short the stock, certain that it would fail again—and as they covered repeatedly, they just added more fuel to the advance. The new weekly uptrend line (dashes) was not violated until March 2004. At that point, the stock had risen 400 percent. It was ultimately headed much higher before crashing anew in mid-2007, but this 18-month journey illustrates the path of a successful reverse splitter. The stock was ridiculed and attacked by its critics, but its proponents in the institutional investment community obviously had more firepower, as shown clearly by the shares' steady progress.

Now, of course, reverse splits don't always work, so as an active trader, you cannot blindly buy a reverse split. You should naturally avoid all reverse splits on penny stocks, and, in fact, avoid any reverse split that starts out at less than $10. You also need to look for the technical signs that the reverse split is having its intended effect. Start a position only on the usual signals that we have discussed, such as the break of a downtrend; add with confidence following new signals, such as new recovery highs or retreats to a new uptrend; and sell on a firm decline below that the weekly uptrend. Stay objective, and don't expect them all to work—but treat each one as if it could be the biggest trade of your career.

Bankruptcies

Speaking of companies with a lot of bad mojo, you can't get much worse than those whose ill-fated business plans, strategic missteps, or lousy timing have resulted in the corporate equivalent of the death penalty: bankruptcy. A public company, just like an individual, will do everything in its power to avoid this fate. But sometimes it is left with no choice. Typically this happens at the end of a long road of sorrow, with creditors clamoring for checks, employees paralyzed with fear about their jobs, customers withdrawing over fear that deliveries won't be made, and suppliers cutting ties over the fear that they won't be paid.

At the point of maximum pain, a company can file to be liquidated and permanently extinguished under Chapter 7 of the U.S. Bankruptcy Code, or it can file to reorganize under the protection of Chapter 11 of the code. We don't care about the former, because companies that do that are goners. The latter, however, get what amounts to a stay of execution. A bankruptcy court trustee distributes assets according to a set of formulas, then permits relief from other debts and contracts so that the company can make a new start. Very often, equity shareholders end up with nothing, as their rights are the first to be terminated, while holders of secured credit, collateral, and senior bonds will get as much as 50 cents on the dollar. The system is in many ways too lenient to the executives of badly run companies, as they are pretty much let off the hook for their misdeeds. That just goes to show what great lobbyists they have.

After the lawyers and trustees get their share of the assets and the wailing dies down, it's time to talk about the company's emerging from bankruptcy as a new entity. The old equity is usually canceled, making prebankruptcy stock completely worthless, and new equity is issued. (Old bonds are very often kept in force, which makes them very valuable if you play your cards right—but that's a subject for another book.) It's at this point that the company issues a press release stating a date on which the new equity will begin trading. I call these stocks "sneakers" because they sort of slink back into trade.

Now the best thing about companies that emerge from bankruptcy is that they have typically made so many shareholders mad that their old constituency won't give them a new look. No matter that massive contractual obligations like unwieldy labor costs have been wiped away with the stroke of a pen. Most of the company's prior fan base is itself wiped out, and will only scowl at the newly issued shares. Moreover, unless the company is a megacap like Texaco—which declared bankruptcy in 1987 in the wake of a super-costly, botched attempt to block the merger of two rivals—it will not be covered by brokerage analysts for quite some time. After all, how many brokers really want to recommend a formerly bankrupt company to their mainstream account holders? Not too many. These companies need to get back on their feet, acquiring customers and suppliers and making their quarterly numbers, before most professionals will even look at them again.

For the most part, this is the right plan. A whole lot of post-bankruptcy stocks start out their new lives by trading right back down into the abyss. After United Airlines (UAUA) emerged from bankruptcy in January 2006, its shares debuted at $43 and in six months were cut in half. The same thing happened to Northwest Airlines (NWA) a year later: its new shares debuted postbankruptcy at around $24 in May 2007 and quickly plunged to $14 by mid-August, three months later. Too bad . . . so sad.

But once again, as active traders looking for great short-term and intermediate-term plays, we aren't expecting every postbankruptcy stock to work out. We are looking for only the ones that emerge into this atmosphere of total skepticism with a solid new business plan and reduced debt and that, most importantly, begin to trade technically just like a great IPO. In other words, the fact that the stock has closed the door on an ugly past helps us only in the sense that this won't be a "crowded" trade if we decide to take it, as these companies have so many ill-wishers in the investment community that are ready to immediately beat them up with aggressive short selling. That's Step 1. Step 2 is a new trading pattern that displays the patterns of accumulation I have described in the past: rising volume, new highs, and regular consolidations to a new uptrend.

Mirant Corp.

One great example of a postbankruptcy success came from an unlikely source: merchant power producer Mirant (MIR). The company was initially spun off from old-line utility Southern Co. (SO), but it was swept up in the dragnet that crushed Enron and was forced to declare bankruptcy on July 14, 2003. For the next 2½ years, attorneys and company executives worked with creditors to restructure debt and contacts, and the company was permitted to reemerge with new equity on January 3, 2006. At the same time, prior bondholders and preferred stockholders were given warrants, which are like long-term call options, to purchase the stock as well.

As you can see in Figure 4-11, the shares began trading at $24, and despite one brief flurry up to $28, they range-traded between $27.50 and $24 for the next seven months. Now, you know from my previous discussions that once a floor has been established on a new equity—whether that new equity is a spin-off, a reverse split or an IPO—that floor tends to be tested numerous times. This is a process that amounts to "price discovery," as bears try to see how far they can push the stock down and bulls who believe that they have a firm idea of the real fundamental value of the company repeatedly buy at a certain level to defend their point of view. That bottom isn't easy

MIR (Mirant Corp.) NYSE — @ StockCharts.com
31-Aug-2007 — Op 40.25 Hi 40.61 Lo 38.23 Cl 38.97 Vol 10.1M Chg -1.67 (-4.11%) ▼
↑↓ MIR (Weekly) 38.97
— EMA(30) 39.87

MIR was both a spin-off and a post-bankruptcy play. Safest entry: On one of multiple bottoms in mid-'06. Add on Aug '06 breakout, then add on tests of breakout and trendline touches through early 2007. Sell on trendline breaks in June or July '07 for 90%+ gain.

MACD(12,26,9) 0.138, 1.155, -1.018

Figure 4-11

to see at first, but once a single level has been tested three or four times, an independent trader can start to assume that it will stick.

In the case of MIR, the $24.50 level was tested eight times without violation on a weekly close over the first five months alone, so by the time it came back to that area in mid-May, it was certainly time for intrepid traders to give this much-hated stock a try. The level was tested three more times after the point at which I have set the first "buy" arrow, and it was tested a couple more times after that. Once again, your initial purchase in the case of postbankruptcy stocks should be done with only 10 to 50 percent of the capital you expect to ultimately put into the play.

The next purchase for an active trader of MIR would have been after the shares emerged from their trading range, which occurred in August. You should know by now that a breakout has the potential to keep going, but it's more than likely that the stock is going to come back and test the breakout level, and that occurred after four straight weeks of decline in mid-September. It's important not to get discouraged by this behavior, because you know it's coming. Your next trade is at the test of the breakout level, in the area of the third arrow. And then you wait and watch and hope that your new position acts like other great postbankruptcy or spin-off plays and quickly establishes a new uptrend, with regular rises and consolidations. If you have more capital left to expend on this trade, add again at each return to the uptrend line, as shown with arrows in January through early April 2007.

By mid-April of that year, the stock had become too extended to chase. You could have added again in June, but by then the stock had begun to move sideways and lose momentum, as shown in the lower clip of the chart in the 12-26-9 MACD. It makes sense as a trader that you should sell your entire position on the first firm cross of the MACD, which occurred at the point at which the stock broke the weekly uptrend for the first time. All told, the postbankruptcy shares of MIR followed a pattern typical of much-reviled equities that eventually find a following among both value buyers and momentum traders and offered a return of up to 90 percent over a 12-month span in which the broad market was up by around 15 percent.

Armstrong World Industries

Like many companies that used asbestos in its manufacturing processes, flooring manufacturer Armstrong World Industries (AWI) was hit hard by class-action lawsuits and entered bankruptcy to obtain protection from crippling court losses in December 2000. The company spent the next six years sorting out its obligations and lobbying for relief in Congress, and finally reemerged as a public company in October 2006. This was a difficult time for any company that depended on the homebuilding and remodeling market, as the sector had already entered a recession as a result of high mortgage interest rates and a rising tide of foreclosures. So the stock really suffered from a double-whammy: its old shareholders had been blown up, and it had no natural constituencies of potential new shareholders, since it was entering into a very shaky business environment.

By now you know that this is an ideal climate in which a contrarian-minded active trader can work, and that certainly turned out to be the case here—at least for a while. As you can see in Figure 4-12, Armstrong World started its new life with a huge one-day gain that immediately dissipated. Shares dropped from a peak of $42.50 to a low of $35 in November before rallying. Unlike MIR at a similar point in its new life, the shares never formed a base or trading range, so there was no opportunity for a safe entry point in the $30s. However, like many of the other IPOs and spin-offs we've seen, the stock did finally exceed its prior high of $42.50 with a breakout in mid-January 2007, and that became the first opportunity for a reasonably secure entry. Traders got a quick $2.50 on this much-bewailed stock and then saw their opportunity to add to their position on the typical test of the breakout in early February. The only other reasonable chance to add came on a consolidation in March. By the end of the month, however, the newly established uptrend was deteriorating amid a slowdown in momentum, and smart traders would have sold.

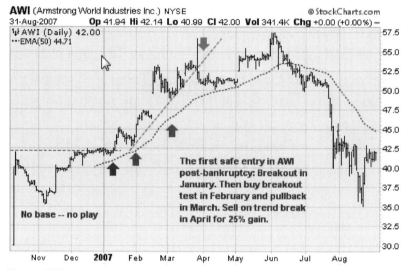

Figure 4-12

Although AWI involved a fairly short-lived trade in a postbankruptcy stock, it still illustrates the nice low-risk chances that emerge when a company that has been on the scrap heap returns to the playing arena. Only a small handful have what it takes to persevere as splendidly as a Mirant, but if you string together a couple of AWIs every year, you can really prosper as an active trader.

Silicon Graphics Inc.

One of the most hard-luck companies on the planet during the mid-2000s was also one of the most innovative: Silicon Graphics Inc. (SGI), a maker of super-high-performance computer hardware and software that was absolutely vital to the Hollywood revolution in special effects as well as to scientists exploring the edge of physics, defense intelligence analysts exploring enemy connections, and business intelligence analysts exploring complex store traffic patterns. Many of the most brilliant minds in Silicon Valley worked at SGI during its time in the sun, but ultimately the shift to distributed computing left its products looking too expensive compared to the competition.

After years of management changes and restructurings, the company finally filed for Chapter 11 bankruptcy protection on May 8, 2006. Over the next six months, it sold real estate, wormed out of some onerous contracts, and shed personnel, then reemerged in October of the same year. After its years in the tank, investors did not think much of its chances, and for the first two months SGIC shares languished, sinking from $20 to a low of $17.50. None of the analysts who had crowed about the company's products just a few years before felt comfortable recommending it to customers. It was another classic postbankruptcy hard-luck case. But then in December, the company's fortunes began to turn around, as it was able to report new contracts with the U.S. Defense Department, international broadcasters, and university researchers, and it looked as if earnings would finally begin to perk up.

As you can see in Figure 4-13, no reasonable entry points for active traders emerged when the stock began trading in October, and after its initial turnaround in November it did not base, or trade sideways, long enough to establish a floor of value. The first of our usual patterns emerged in mid-December, when shares shot up above the initial October price in a breakout. That was the spot at which active traders could start an initial one-quarter position. The half-month brought consolidation below the breakout point, which was aggravating but not devastating, and in any event the decline came to a halt at the 34-day exponential moving average, which is typical of a nascent momentum move.

SGIC (Silicon Graphics Inc.) NYSE © StockCharts.com
31-Aug-2007 **Op** 25.32 **Hi** 25.32 **Lo** 23.81 **Cl** 24.38 **Vol** 8,949 **Chg** -1.10 (-4.32%) ▼

SGIC provided two entries post-bankruptcy: A Dec. '06 breakout and a Jan. '07 breakout. After that, shares screamed higher for a month with only a brief consolidation. Sell point came on momentum shift in Feb. '06.

Figure 4-13

In mid-January, the shares bolted higher again after new reports of strong system sales, providing another point at which active traders could add to positions on a sensational second breakout. After that, shares screamed higher for nearly a month in a frantic bout of short covering and news, as word got around that SGIC had hired a new chief executive who appeared capable of taking the company into a new era of success. Only the briefest of consolidations emerged, so there were no low-risk new entry points until buying power dried up at the end of the month. By the start of March, shares were moving sluggishly sideways. Although that might have looked like a normal consolidation, the 12-26-9 MACD was showing a different story, as momentum had definitely shifted downward from an extremely overbought condition. Whether you sold in mid-February or early March, the result was the same: a profit of around 40 percent in less than 2½ months.

Sears Holdings Corp.

All of the ideas in this section so far have been rock solid, but the reigning monarch of postbankruptcy plays is probably Sears Holdings Corp. (SHLD). The fact that the company's current name is Sears is a bit of misdirection, because this stock started life as the lowly, bedraggled, much-vilified discount department store Kmart. Bear with me, because the tale is a bit complicated. Despite its standing as the third-largest discount retailer in the nation, Kmart filed for bankruptcy in January 2002 after a dizzying plunge in sales and confidence. Hundreds of employees were fired, and shares held by loyal employees and customers were voided of value. The company had fantastic real estate assets to go along with its widely known name, and its bonds were scooped up for pennies on the dollar by Connecticut-based hedge fund manager Edward Lampert.

The financier-turned-retailer took a controlling interest in the firm and took it public again in April 2003 amid a blistering chorus of criticism and skepticism from former creditors. That just happened to be the start of a brand-new bull market in stocks, but the new shares traded sideways, establishing an excellent base, for their first three months. As shown in Figure 4-14, the first really solid entry point for active traders came on—what else?— a breakout off that base in June of that year. Shares then traded sideways with an upward bias until a test of the breakout in December. The next great entry point came in March 2004 on the next breakout, and

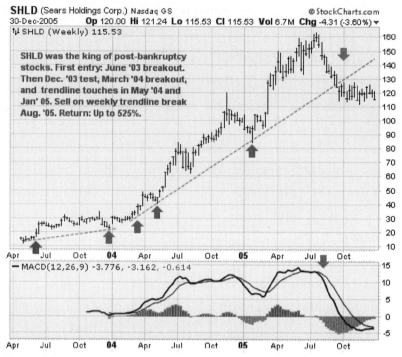

Figure 4-14

another came in May on a test of the new uptrend. After that, the stock was clearly under powerful accumulation by both value-oriented and momentum funds, as it did not consolidate back to the uptrend of its weekly bars for another nine months.

In November 2004, Kmart announced that it would buy its archrival Sears Roebuck in an $11.4 billion deal and take its more popular name. Again, the media and investors initially reacted negatively to the idea, and the shares traded down to $85 from $100. It was no coincidence, you can be sure, that $85 just happened to represent a touch of the uptrend, and buyers of that decline were rewarded with a move of $70 over the next six months. Over the summer of 2005, shares lost momentum from a highly overbought condition, and the weekly 12-26-9 MACD confirmed the action with a definitive sell signal. The final break of the uptrend did not occur until the early autumn of 2005, but whether traders sold in August or September, their gain from the initial breakout was upwards of 500 percent, which ain't too shabby for a position in a beaten-up, down-at-the-heels discount retailer. Once again, you should note that the trading methodology never varies: buy break-outs and consolidations on either a daily or a weekly chart, and don't sell until you get a definitive break of the uptrend or a severe loss of momentum from an oversold condition.

Initial Public Offerings

Ah, youth! So carefree, a time when everything is fresh and clear. Ambition and dreams run wild, and each day dawns brimming with possibility. That is the condition in which companies find themselves when they first approach the public equity markets with shares for sale. They raise money through initial public offer-ings, or IPOs, for a variety of reasons. The most commonly listed excuse is "general corporate purposes," which is vague enough to cover anything. Very often the money is used to expand factories or sales staffs, fund research, acquire other companies, or provide an opportunity for the founders to cash out a portion of their investments.

Whatever their purpose, most IPOs begin a swift, sure trek to the netherworld of broken promises and abandoned dreams. Many aca-demic studies show that the vast majority of new public companies stumble badly in their first few years, missing revenue and sales goals and failing to capture the interest of either institutional or retail investors. If you are looking for great short-selling opportunities, the recent IPO rosters are a great place to start.

Of course, quite a few IPOs do succeed, and quite brilliantly. Let's spend a few moments now looking at a few recent examples, and how active traders could have played them from the long side just as we have seen with spin-offs (which are a variety of IPO), reverse splitters, and postbankruptcy sneakers.

Danaos Corp.

Ask half a dozen experts for the motive force behind the globalization of trade and you'll get half a dozen erudite answers, as the issue is delightfully complex. But I would suggest that a lot of the credit can be given to the humble standardized shipping container—those 40-foot-long boxes you see on the decks of oceangoing ships, railcar flatbeds, and truck trailers. Without agreement among the world's manufacturing and freight-forwarding giants on the size and shape of a common box, getting iPods and chairs and auto parts from Shanghai to Seattle and Scotland would be crazy-expensive, not to mention a huge hassle.

Shipping those containers seems like an easy task, but the ability to do so is actually something that is in great demand and low supply. To give you an idea of how constricted the supply of all those containers has been this year, consider that the Baltic Exchange's dry-freight index—a composite of prices for shipping all sorts of "dry" things, such as commodities and containers—rose a whopping 40 percent in the first half of 2007 alone. One of the reasons for the surge is that port congestion has been terrible, keeping ships in harbors longer than shippers would like and running up the bills. In addition, there has been a scant supply of ships coming on line. The *Financial Times* reported that at Newcastle, Australia, a key port in the world supply chain, queuing for loads reached a historic high of 72 vessels in April 2007, compared with an average of 26 throughout 2006. That keeps a lot of ships off the high seas, increasing their demand and rates.

For many years there was no satisfactory way to play the rise of container shipping, as most of the carriers are private, government-owned, or small parts of large international conglomerates. But in 2005 and 2006, two companies that give investors a chance to directly participate came public: Seaspan (SSW), based in Vancouver, Canada, and Danaos Corp. (DAC), based in Athens, Greece. I want to focus on Danaos because it traded so well from a technical point of view.

Keep in mind that virtually every company that hits the market with an IPO has a great story to tell: they are all in full PR mode, and they are attempting to spin their dreams into gold. That is why it is so important to watch the technicals instead, as the trading patterns rarely lie. In the case of DAC, as you can see in Figure 4-15, the shares traded down for the first month, offering no opportunities from the long side. But in mid-November, the shares popped to a new post-IPO high, offering the first reasonable entry point. From there, the shares climbed steadily in an ideal stair-step pattern of advance and consolidation along a well-established trend line, offering numerous opportunities to add to an initial stake. The first major sell signal came in mid-August amid a marketwide swoon when the daily bars slipped below their uptrend. A sale at that point netted upwards of 70 percent from mid-November. Now that's what I call clear sailing.

DAC (Danaos Corp.) NYSE   @ StockCharts.com
31-Aug-2007   **Op** 35.00 **Hi** 35.00 **Lo** 34.66 **Cl** 34.85 **Vol** 40.0K **Chg** +0.00 (+0.00%) −

DAC traded down for a month after its
IPO. First buying opportunity: Mid-Nov
'06 breakout to new high. Then add on
trendline/MA touches in March, June
and July '07. Sell on trendline break in
Aug. '07 for 70% gain.

Figure 4-15

First Solar Inc.

In the second half of 2006, alternative energy stocks were quite the
rage, and a number of companies selling solar solutions came public. First Solar (FSLR) designs and makes modules that leverage
thin-film semiconductor technology to turn sunlight into electricity. The company used the proceeds of its IPO to fuel an expansion of its Arizona plants and add manufacturing facilities in Ohio
and Germany. Analysts consider FSLR to be the price, value, and
technology leader among its peers in an emerging market that benefits from both industrial and retail demand as well as government
subsidies. As you can see in Figure 4-16, the stock traded higher
immediately out of its initial public offering in mid-December
2007, which is fairly rare. The least risky first trade came on the
advance to a new high a few days after the IPO, and, as you can
observe, the attractive stair-step pattern of consolidations followed

FSLR (First Solar Inc.) Nasdaq GM
31-Aug-2007   Op 102.60 Hi 104.90 Lo 100.52 Cl 103.74 Vol 3.5M Chg +1.25 (+1.22%) ▲

FSLR jumped higher out of the gate, offering first entry on gap higher in Dec. '06. Chances to add came on trendline/MA touches in Feb. through June '07. Sell signal was oversold MACD break or trendline break in summer. Gain: +250%

Figure 4-16

by moves to new highs offered ample opportunities to add to your initial stake.

Because the first move in the stock provided incredibly strong momentum, the MACD traded downward from March to June 2007 even though shares were advancing at a fairly brisk pace. That was not a nonconfirmation of strength or a sell signal, however. The sell signal came after the shares had climbed to an extremely over-bought level, above 10 in the MACD clip, and then petered out again in a sideways pattern with a downward bias. A sale at the break shown at the first down arrow would have netted a nearly 300 percent profit in the stock from the first purchase. But even waiting for a firm break of the daily-bar uptrend in August still netted a 250 percent gain for early risk takers.

I have shown you two IPOs out of the more than 200 stocks that debuted in U.S. markets in 2006 and 2007. I could have shown you another 10 or 20 that were equally attractive, such as Mindray Medical International (MR), Aegean Marine Petroleum Network (ANW), Atlas Energy (ATN) and New Oriental Education & Technology Group (EDU). All of these exhibited exactly the same characteristics as DAC and FSLR: modest starts followed by positive, clear-cut patterns of accumulation and consolidation within an uptrend. That means, of course, that upwards of 175 other IPOs traded either flat, down, or way down. To trade the many losers from the short side, take all of the previous recommendations and do the reverse: sell short on breakdowns, and add to your short positions on advances back to resistance. In summary, you definitely need to choose carefully when you put your money to work as an active trader in the IPO arena. Yet this also means that because there is plenty of action in these names, they can provide you with highly volatile long and short opportunities every day of the week, if that's how you wish to trade.

Finding and Monitoring IPOs

So how do you find these ideas and keep track of them? One straightforward methodology is similar to the technique that I showed you in Chapter 2 for monitoring the relative strength of sectors and exchange-traded funds, although obviously with some major differences. Here's what you do.

Visit the Renaissance Capital Web site IPOhome.com (http://www.ipohome.com) and click on the link in the lower left corner titled IPO Top Performers. That will bring you to a page (http://www.ipohome.com/marketwatch/performance.asp?sort=offer &order=DESC) that gives IPOs that listed in the past 12 months in descending order by aftermarket return, as shown in Figure 4-17. In September 2007, the page listed 240 IPOs. Print the page, then visit StockCharts.com.

At StockCharts.com, which you should have a subscription to by now, click on the SharpCharts link in the left navigation bar of the home page, then click on Your Favorite Charts on the page that appears, and finally click on the Create New List link in the middle of that new page. A dialog box will pop up asking you to name the new list, so type in something like New IPOs. In the middle of the new page that appears, look for the Favorites title bar. Under that, you'll see a text box labeled Many. In that space, type all the stock symbols found on the IPOhome.com page that you printed, with each symbol followed by a comma and a space. This could take 30 minutes, but it's worth the hassle. After you've typed the first half dozen, the page will look like Figure 4-18, but you should go ahead and type in all 225+ symbols.

Top Performing IPOs (Last 12 Months)

		Top Performing IPOs (Last 12 Months)						
Company Name	Symbol	Date	Underwriter	Offer Price	First Day Close Price	Current Price	Total Return	Aftermarket Return
First Solar	FSLR	11/16/2006	Credit Suisse	$20.00	$24.74	$103.74	418.7%	319.3%
Riverbed Technology	RVBD	9/20/2006	Goldman Sachs	$9.75	$15.30	$44.40	355.4%	190.2%
New Oriental Education	EDU	9/6/2006	Credit Suisse	$15.00	$20.88	$52.95	253.0%	153.6%
Mindray Medical International	MR	9/25/2006	Goldman Sachs	$13.50	$17.55	$35.49	162.9%	102.2%

Figure 4-17

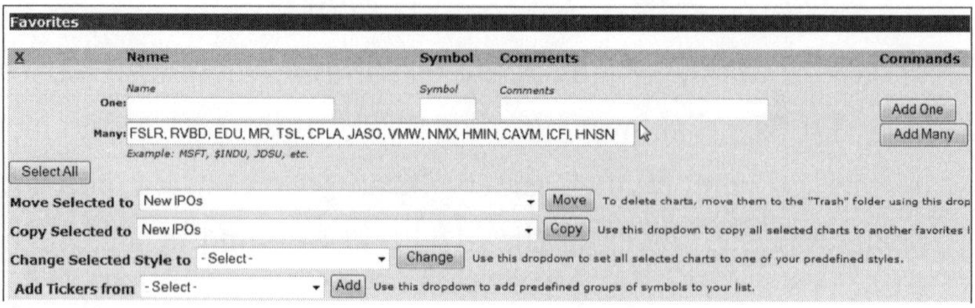

Figure 4-18

Next, click the Add Many button, and you will see a long page listing all the symbols you typed in. Finally, change the drop-down box in the middle of the top of the page from Edit to 10 Per Page. Then you will finally see charts of all of the past year's IPOs. Click the Next button at the top of each page to see each group of 10, listed alphabetically. To use a chart style different from the default, go back to Edit mode, click Select All at the bottom of the page that appears, then touch the drop-down menu next to the label Change Selected Style to and choose an alternative chart style that you may have created at StockCharts. These might include styles that allow you to look at daily bars, weekly bars, or monthly bars with a variety of moving averages and/or technical indicators such as MACD or RSI.

Although this takes a while to set up, you can now quickly spin through 250 IPOs (and spin-offs) by scanning 25 pages with 10 charts each, looking for the patterns that have augured successful trading in the past. To look through the list even faster, choose the CandleGlance view instead of 10 Per Page. On the page that appears, choose One Year for Duration and choose MACD (or something else of your choice) for an Indicator. Now you can scan through the list even faster, as there are 30 smaller charts on each page; I've shown a part of one CandleGlance page in Figure 4-19.

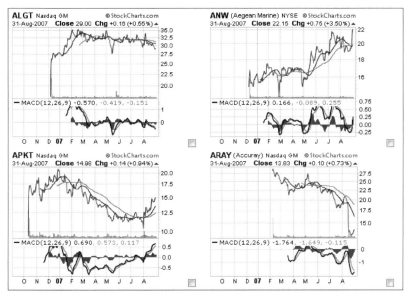

Figure 4-19

Once you get the hang of it, you can sprint through these seven pages in just a few minutes every Wednesday afternoon in your hunt for tradable patterns.

Two months after you create your first group of 250 IPOs at StockCharts to examine, return to IPOhome.com and click on the home page link titled Recent IPO Pricings. On that page, you will find IPOs that have been listed in just the past 60 days. Print out the list, then go to your list of IPOs at StockCharts.com, enter the Edit mode, type in all the new names on the same line under Favorites that you previously used, and click Add Many again. This will add all the new IPOs to your list. Repeat every two months.

That should keep you going for a while. In fact, I'll repeat my comment from an earlier chapter: if you can't find enough ideas—long and short—among the spin-offs, splitters, sneakers, and starters to keep you busy every day of your trading career, you should really take up another profession or hobby. The markets provide dozens of money-making avenues every day; pick one and run.

1. Patricia L. Anslinger, Steven J. Klepper, Somu Subramaniam, "Breaking Up Is Good to Do," The McKinsey Quarterly 1999 Number 1; http://www.kellogg.northwestern.edu/faculty/thompsnt/htm/emp-corp-restruc/brup99.pdf
2. http://www.forbes.com/2006/05/04/sprint-nextel-embarq_cx_df_0505 sprint.html "Can Embarq Take Off?" by Dan Frommer, *Forbes*, May 5, 2006.

THURSDAY

Model Behavior

Now that you have gotten a glimpse of the Wild West of spin-offs and reverse splits for an exciting, profitable midweek break, I urge you to turn your attention for an hour on Thursday afternoons back to methodologies that have been tested and proven to work. We're talking here about investment models—often called *quantitative models*—of market behavior.

To accomplish this mission, we'll spend a fair amount of time looking at the StockScouter stock-rating system at the Web site MSN Money. A bit of background first, though. I signed on as managing editor and columnist at the Web's most popular financial portal at the dawn of the modern Internet era in 1997, and I used the tools created by ace coders there to build powerful price-forecasting models based on earnings, revenue, and price momentum. The models were fairly naïve, as quants would put it, but they worked very well during that go-go era for stocks, helping investors to systematically find stocks that would rise 50 to 100 percent or more each year. That was nice while it lasted—but it didn't last real long, in retrospect. Not too long after the bear market began in 2000, it became clear that many of the formerly successful methods of picking stocks using growth and momentum criteria alone (not just mine, but also the venerable systems created by Value Line and Zachs) were no longer working. And at the same time, a variety of scandals had stained the credibility of traditional fundamental investment analysts at brokerages.

As a result, I determined that it was time to develop a brand-new type of stock-rating system, one that for the first time would include the avoidance of risk and volatility as a key factor, rather than merely focus on potential return. Normally, you see, fund managers take risk into consideration strictly at the portfolio level by diversifying their holdings among sectors and asset classes. But my idea was to try to take risk into account way down at the individual equity position level. The system debuted in June 2001 and has been incredibly successful, as its benchmark portfolio has trounced the broad market by a factor of 7. That portfolio—which buys and sells 50 top-rated stocks each month—rose 250.3 percent through October 2007, compared with +34.4 percent for the S&P 500 Index. In my previous book, *Swing Trading*, I showed readers how to take advantage of the system with 50-stock portfolios held over six months. Now I want to explain how to exploit StockScouter for trading 10-stock portfolios over shorter periods. Because when you just choose the top 10 stocks each month, the system's record since its inception ramps up to 384 percent from June 2001 to October 2007, or 11 times better than the market, with only slightly more risk.

I also want to briefly explain another model that I developed and have given the rather innocuous name of Core Select. It is a method of trading only those stocks that have been up in 9 or 10 of the past 10 years, where the maximum calendar-year loss for that single possible down year was less than 9 percent. This is another quantitative methodology that can provide you with awesome stocks to trade on a daily and weekly basis, as you'll see in a few minutes.

StockScouter

My team designed the StockScouter rating system to help individual investors quickly analyze and assess a stock's potential for outperforming the broad market. Working closely with Gradient Analytics, an independent research firm at the cutting edge of financial engineering for institutional money managers, we identified statistically predictive traits that affect the performance of successful U.S. securities and developed a systematic way to help discover, research, hold, and sell those securities.

StockScouter, like similar systems that cost Wall Street pros hundreds of thousands of dollars a year, depends on mathematics, software, an innovative mix of measurements, and historical testing to attempt to forecast the short- and long-term outlook for all U.S. companies that have traded on the three major exchanges for at least the past six months. In mid-2007, that represented a universe of about 5,500 stocks.

In rating the outlook for stocks from strong to poor on a 10-point scale, StockScouter does not make subjective judgments. Instead, it compares the fundamental and technical qualities of individual companies and their stocks to benchmarks that have proved to be statistically predictive of stock performance in the past. It then assigns an expected six-month return to each stock based on this statistical profile and balances that return against expected volatility.

This ratio of expected return to expected volatility, or risk, yields a stock's final overall rating.

The balance of expected reward with expected risk is a key concept that sets StockScouter apart from other stock-rating systems. Stocks with high expected future returns will see their ratings reduced if the volatility of those returns is also expected to be high. Thus an ideal stock in this system is expected to move briskly and *directly* to a higher price, rather than simply briskly.

StockScouter is not perfect; no predictive rating system could be. But its models have been thoroughly tested to the highest professional standards. Used alone or in conjunction with the other stock research tools that we've discussed, it will help you make more thoughtful choices by reducing the number of stocks you should consider trading on any given day to a smart group of 10.

StockScouter rates each stock in its coverage universe on a scale of 1 to 10, with 10 being the best. Ratings are scored on a bell curve. This means that there are fewer stocks with a rating of 10 than with a rating of 9 and fewer stocks with a rating of 9 than with a rating of 8; likewise, there are more stocks with a rating of 2 than with a rating of 1 and more stocks with a rating of 3 than with a rating of 2. Stocks thus bunch up in the middle, with the result that stocks rated 4 to 7 are expected to perform in line with the market. The ratings are recalculated and updated daily to reflect the most current technical, fundamental, ownership, and valuation data. After using the system for the past six years, I ignore all stocks with ratings of 7 and under. I focus only on stocks rated 8, 9, or 10—and mostly just on those rated 9 or 10.

Before moving on to methodologies for using the models, let me tell you a little more about how the system arrives at its scores.

StockScouter ratings are derived from the Gradient research team's analysis of four key factors that reflect either a company's fundamental quality or investors' ardor for its shares. The system rates factor performance on a five-point scale from A to F, just as you'd see on a report card. Here are the four factors and some of their key subfactors.

1. **Fundamentals.** This factor assesses a company's past earnings growth, its estimated future earnings growth, and its capacity to beat brokerage analysts' consensus estimate. To receive a high grade, a company generally must grow reasonably fast, beat analysts' growth estimates, and be expected by analysts to grow its earnings at a solid pace in the future. However, a powerful recent earnings surprise or a big boost in estimates by an experienced analyst can also boost the grade of a stock with otherwise seemingly lackluster fundamentals.

2. **Ownership.** This factor assesses whether a stock is under accumulation by executives and board members. To receive a high grade, a stock generally must be under accumulation by high-ranking executives or board members in significant quantities, or at least not be the subject of heavy insider selling.

3. **Valuation.** This factor assesses whether a stock's price is high or low relative to its current level of sales, earnings, and expected earnings growth. It's counterintuitive, but our research showed that big companies' shares should be slightly more expensive than their peers to receive a high grade. Meanwhile, as you'd expect, small companies' shares must be much cheaper than their peers to receive a high grade.

4. **Technical.** This factor assesses whether a stock's price trend is positive or negative. To receive a high grade, a stock's price must generally be rising at an accelerating rate over the medium and short term. However, a stock with a very low price relative to its 10-week trend can receive a high grade if the system believes that it is likely to rebound from an extremely oversold level

StockScouter does not simply average these subfactors to yield a factor grade. Instead, the subfactors are assigned different weights that vary with a stock's size and sector. Likewise, factor grades are not simply added or averaged to yield a final overall rating. They are also weighted according to a proprietary methodology developed by the financial engineers at Gradient Analytics.

After all of the factors and their constituent subfactors have been measured and weighted, StockScouter awards each stock a core rating. That core rating is then balanced against the standard deviation, or volatility, of the stock's return over the past 12 months to yield the final overall rating. It's convenient to think of the overall rating as the balance between expected return and expected risk. A stock with high expected return and high expected risk will generally receive a lower rating than a stock with modest expected return and very low expected risk. An investor managing a portfolio with guidance from the StockScouter system would attempt to stay invested in stocks that are rated 8 to 10 at the time of the pick for a period of as much as six months; changes in the rating postpick over those six months are immaterial.

Now, of course, we know that there is more to price performance than an individual stock's merits—much more. So StockScouter also assesses three market preferences that tend to boost or hinder securities' performance over one- to six-month periods. Our studies showed that stocks with favorable market preferences tend to yield the strongest performance for as long as those preferences are in favor. Think of these as tailwinds if they are in a stock's favor, or as headwinds if they are not, just as we discussed in Chapter 2. These are updated in the StockScouter database weekly. The market preferences are:

- **Sector.** The universe of stocks is sliced into 12 industrial sectors, such as technology or health care, by their federal identification code. Generally, investors prefer a third or less of these sectors at any given time. Those sectors are called "in favor." The rest are either out of favor or in a no-man's-land labeled "neutral." Widely accepted academic and professional research indicates that as much as 60 percent of a stock's performance derives from the strength or weakness of its sector.

- **Market cap.** The stock universe is divided into four market capitalization categories. Roughly the top 400 stocks by market cap are labeled "large," the next 1,000 are "mid," the next 2,500 are "small," and the rest are "micro." Generally, investors prefer only one or two groups at a time. We call stocks in those groups "in favor." The rest are either out of favor or neutral.

- **Style.** The universe is divided into two investment styles by price/sales ratio. High-priced stocks are categorized as part of the "growth" style of investing, while low-priced stocks are categorized as being in the "value" style. Generally, investors prefer one style or the other for periods lasting a year or more. We rate each in favor, out of favor, or neutral.

Our research showed that the best stocks to own over one- to six-month periods are those that are rated 8, 9, or 10 and are members of at least one or two, but preferably three, categories preferred by the market. In the short term, our system would prefer a stock rated 8 or 9 with three in-favor tailwinds over a stock rated 10 with just one in-favor tailwind. When no sectors, market caps, or style are rated in favor, the system prefers stocks with neutral tailwinds. (Note: Stocks are sorted into sector, market cap, and style categories monthly to maintain stability, but market preferences are updated weekly to maintain freshness.)

The Gradient team extensively tested 10-stock portfolios managed according to these rules against data from 20 years of market history. In cases where a tiebreaker was required to choose between stocks with identical ratings and market preferences, the team programmatically chose those with the lowest expected risk. Additionally, any stock that fell 20 percent from the initial purchase price at the close of a trading day was dumped from the portfolio, and the five-year T-bill interest rate was substituted in its place (after accounting for the 20 percent loss).

How to Use the System

So how can you use this system to make a fortune as an active trader? There are several ways, and fortunately none of them involves running a 50-stock portfolio with monthly rebalances. The first thing you need to do is open a trading account at Foliofn.com, an online brokerage that is the best in the business at allowing you to trade "baskets" of stocks inexpensively and efficiently. Foliofn.com sells trading subscriptions rather than charging commissions—starting at $29 per month for unlimited trades—and makes it really easy to buy and sell groups of stocks rather than individual stocks.

You will also need to navigate the MSN Money Web site to find the StockScouter Top 10, or learn how to use the Screener at MSN Money to run the list of stocks at the start of every month yourself. For the greatest convenience, you can save yourself some trouble and subscribe to my advisory service, called Strategic Advantage, to learn the names of the top-rated stocks at the start of every month.

If all this sounds too good to be true and you want to stop reading now, I can't blame you. But that would be unfortunate, because this advice has worked really well for six years, through hell and high water. Or at least through boom, bust, war, recession, flood, hurricane, and credit crisis. If you follow it in a low-cost trading account, particularly one in which gains compound tax-free, then there is a distinct chance—though not a guarantee, of course—that you can make serious, life-changing money.

Now, the problem is that you have to be ready not just to buy the 10 new stocks at times when you think this is a terrible idea, but also to be ready to sell them when you love them so much that you can't bear the thought. You are almost certainly going to have misgivings about the top-ranked stocks sometimes, not to mention the notion of putting your hard-earned money into the emotionless hands of a system.

Trust me on this. Even though I came up with the idea for StockScouter and have marveled at its success every day since, I still sometimes look at the top-ranked stocks and go, "Naaah!" Its built-in flexibility, backed by hundreds of hours of testing, has helped

StockScouter make many seemingly odd choices over the years that have turned out brilliantly. As an example, during the bear market years of 2001 and 2002, the system churned out one profitable portfolio after another because it was focused on small-cap regional banks and real estate investment trusts at a time when most people continued to be fixated on the possibility that their rapidly deteriorating large-cap tech stocks would turn around. Those regional banks were huge winners, while most of the techs never recovered.

The numbers don't lie. If you had followed the six-month-hold system on the 10 top-ranked stocks from January 2001 through August 2007, you'd be up 25.9 percent per year since, on average, versus a gain of 4.0 percent per year in the Standard & Poor's 500 Index ($SPX) and 6.1 percent in the Nasdaq Composite Index ($COMP). That kind of return more than triples your money over six years. If you started with $100,000 in 2001, you'd end up with roughly $488,000 by September 2007, compared with only $112,500 if you were strictly in an S&P 500 Index fund, as shown in Table 5-1.

Table 5-1   Triple Your Money in Six Years*

Year	SS 10 Chg	SS $100,000	S&P 500 Chg	S&P 500 $100,00
2001	13.80%	$113,819.06	−13.00%	$86,957.31
2002	17.00%	$133,155.85	−23.40%	$66,638.89
2003	82.70%	$243,212.75	26.40%	$84,218.50
2004	21.20%	$294,884.92	9.00%	$91,792.65
2005	20.40%	$355,020.49	3.00%	$94,547.37
2006	19.50%	$424,273.79	13.60%	$107,424.18
2007†	15.00%	$487,914.86	4.80%	$112,580.54
Cum. Ret.	388%		12.58%	

*Starts with $100,000 on January 2, 2001, with equal-dollar investments in SS 10, then is rebalanced and reinvested every six months in the new top 10.
†Through August 31.

Of course, there's a catch. As many of you know, these kinds of returns are more ideal than real because in the world of creating quantitative investment models, there is no trading-price slippage, bid/ask spread, or other difficulties in obtaining the exact quote listed in the market's historical record. In the real world, if 10,000 people try to buy a top-ranked small-cap stock that trades less than 100,000 shares per day and is quoted at $10.20, any given individual might actually have to pay $10.40, $10.65, or $10.80 to start a position, as the price will be driven up by demand. The same goes for sales at the end of the period. Returns are also reduced by commissions, and, if the stocks are held in anything but a tax-free retirement account, the government is going to want its cut—robbing you of the ability to actually reinvest all the proceeds every six months. So maybe in the real world you wouldn't be up 3.4 times your original investment at the end of six years. Maybe the "real" number is a gain of only 2½ or 3 times your money. No biggie. StockScouter's top-10 strategy has still blown away the market since its launch and shows no signs of wearing out.

What's the magic recipe, and why am I willing to share it with you? It's nothing more than the strategy first described in 2001 in my MSN Money column as well as in my book *Swing Trading*. The only difference is this: further refinements in testing allow us to go for 10 stocks rather than the 50 originally recommended, and you can hold them either for one month or for overlapping groups of six months each if you want to trade more actively. And finally, you can just use the 10 top stocks as a great mini-universe of names to trade using swing techniques.

Remember that I said that the system picked odd little banks and REITs in 2000 to 2002 to great success? Well, its focus on strong-trending sectors and market-cap groups really kicked into high gear during 2003, producing that 83 percent gain you see in Table 5-1—more than three times the excellent advance of the broad market. What you may not recall about that year is how difficult it was to buy stocks in January 2003 amid a steep decline in both public confidence and share values as a result of the looming crisis in Iraq. It's times like that that make a systematic approach so valuable.

I'm not worried about explaining how to exploit StockScouter portfolios because I know that most people won't have the discipline to execute the strategy and will kick out stocks with which they are unfamiliar. It's just human nature. If you decide that you want to give it a try anyway, remember that success in the market often demands that you do things that feel uncomfortable. Consider the courage that you would have had to have if you were following the plan of rebalancing every six months and you had to buy new stocks on July 1, 2006, during a scary plunge in prices. Many pundits were predicting a return of the bear market. Yet StockScouter's top 10 produced a return of around 16.9 percent, led by FTD Group (FTD) and Claire's Stores (CLE), which were up 30 percent apiece over the next six months.

Or if you were following the monthly method, how about rebalancing on March 1, 2007, after the market had just plunged by 4 percent amid fears that growth in China was about to fall apart? It was a tough time for many to buy stocks, yet that 10-stock portfolio went on to gain 13.7 percent over the next six months. It was paced by Creditcorp (BAP), a Peruvian bank, up 30 percent, and chip maker Cypress Semiconductor (CY), up 40 percent. Or how about on August 1, 2007, after the market had just plunged 5 percent in a month? The portfolio built on that date went on to gain 9.5 percent in just a month and a half, led by tremendous recoveries in GPS device vendor Garmin (GRMN), up 36 percent; oilfield services provider Oceaneering (OII), up 35 percent; and oilfield reservoir mapper Core Labs (CLB), up 20 percent.

Since this is a trading book, I want to show you now the most active way to use StockScouter systematically, and along the way you'll see how to dive down a little further and use the model for picking individual stocks to play for just days or weeks.

Creating the StockScouter 10 List

The most reliable way of getting the StockScouter top-rated list every month, as I said, is by subscribing to my *Strategic Advantage* newsletter. I create a special version of it on the last day of every month, send it out to subscribers via e-mail in a "Flash" report, and report on its progress during the month. But if you want to get the list on your own, there are a couple of ways. One is to visit the Top 10 Picks page at MSN Money, located at this link: http://moneycentral.msn.com/investor/StockRating/srstopstocksresultsaspx?sco=49. On September 22, 2007, the page resembled Figure 5-1.

Top-rated stocks							
Symbol	Company name	Overall rating	Core rating	Price	Market cap market prefs	Sector market prefs	Growth vs. value market prefs
FCX	FREEPORT MCMORAN COPPER & GOLD INC	10	10	108.67	In favor	In favor	Neutral
RIO	CIA VALE DO RIO DOCE	9	9	30.45	In favor	In favor	Neutral
NEM	NEWMONT MINING CORP NEW	9	8	47.56	In favor	In favor	Neutral
ABX	BARRICK GOLD CORP	8	8	40.06	In favor	In favor	Neutral
VZ	VERIZON COMMUNICATIONS INC	8	8	44.38	In favor	In favor	Neutral
AAPL	APPLE INC	10	10	144.15	In favor	Neutral	Neutral
CSCO	CISCO SYSTEMS INC	10	10	32.30	In favor	Neutral	Neutral
JNPR	JUNIPER NETWORKS INC	10	10	35.91	In favor	Neutral	Neutral
LEH	LEHMAN BROTHERS HOLDINGS INC	10	10	62.70	In favor	Neutral	Neutral
NOK	NOKIA CORP	10	10	37.05	In favor	Neutral	Neutral

Figure 5-1

To start a 10-stock "basket" trade with these 10 stocks, visit your account at Foliofn.com, type in the amount of money you wish to spread among the 10 stocks, click the Submit button, and you're good to go. Pretty simple. If you wished to put $20,000 into these 10 stocks, for instance, Foliofn.com's software would purchase $2,000 of each. That would buy you 18 shares of Freeport McMoRan (FCX), 65 shares of Vale do Rio Doce (RIO), 42 shares of Newmont Mining (NEM), and so on.

If you wish to trade the StockScouter 10 system actively, then decide how much you wish to invest in this strategy over six months. Let's say it's $120,000, just to use round numbers. You will become fully invested in that amount over the course of the six months, but not all at once. Start by putting the first $20,000 into the first set of stocks, as noted previously. Then put the rest of the money into either a money market fund or a broad, low-cost exchange-traded index fund such as Vanguard FTSE All-World ex-US (VEU). To create a new StockScouter portfolio each succeeding month, take the money out of the money market or index fund. This strategy allows you to stay fully invested in the market while progressively adding more return (and risk) as the months progress.

After you've done this for six months, you will have all your money in the StockScouter strategy. On the seventh month, sell all of the stocks that you bought the first month, and use those proceeds to buy the next month's 10. At the start of the eighth month, sell the stocks bought in the second month and use the proceeds to buy that month's 10. Repeat until rich. This method produced average annual gains of 22.1 percent from January 2001 through August 2007 versus average annual gains of 3.3 percent for the S&P

500, including +12.4 percent in 2001 (vs. –13 percent for the broad market), +61 percent in 2003 (vs. 26.4 percent for the market) and +23 percent in 2005 (vs. 3 percent for the market).

To create the list of 10 on your own, or to tweak it if you are devilishly inclined to meddle with success, visit this page at the MSN Money Web site: http://moneycentral.msn.com/investor/controls/cabx.asp. Follow the instructions to download the MSN Money Investment Toolbox. Then, on the site's Investing home page, at http://money.msn.com/investor, click on the Stock Screener link on the left navigation bar. That sends you to the Deluxe Screener page. There you can use a series of criteria to narrow the thousands of stocks in the MSN Money database down to just 10 to consider.

Touch the first Field Name box in the Screener, and you will see a fly-out menu with 14 choices. Choose StockScouter Rating, and then in the next menu that appears, slide your mouse over to Ratings and click. That sets StockScouter Rating as your first criterion. Next, click the Operator box to the right and choose the >= symbol. Then in the Value column, type in the number 8. Next, go to the second row of the Screener and this time, after choosing StockScouter Rating in the first Field Name box, click on Return Expectation. Set the operator to >= again, and in the Value box choose Very High. Next, in the third row, choose StockScouter Rating/Market Cap Market Preferences. This time, choose Display only as the operator, and you will not need to put anything in the Value column. Then in the next two lines, repeat the last instruction, except for the Field Name choose StockScouter Rating/Sector Market Preference and then StockScouter Rating/Growth vs. Value Market Preference. In the upper right corner of the page, change the number in the Return Top Matches to 100 instead of the default, which is 25. Then click Run Search. When you're all done, the Screener will look like Figure 5-2.

Next, click on File in the top menu bar of Screener, and on the drop-down menu that appears, choose Export/Results to Excel. The Screener will then send the results of your screen to an Excel file and open the resulting worksheet for you. On that sheet, sort the columns first by Market Cap Market Preferences, and highlight all the In Favor choices with the software's text highlighting tool. Then do the same for Sector Market Preferences and Growth vs. Value Market Preferences. Make your top 10 out of the stocks that have the most highlighted In Favor market preferences. It's best when all three columns are highlighted; the next best is when two are highlighted; and if there is only one column highlighted, just choose the top 10 listed. If all the market preferences are Neutral, then just take the top 10 exported stocks. And finally, in a circumstance such as the one that appears in Figure 5-3, when there are, say, three stocks with two columns highlighted and the rest with

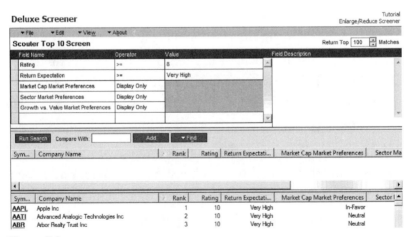

Figure 5-2

only one column highlighted, take all the ones with two high-lighted first, and then divide the rest between the two remaining highlighted groups.

On July 22, the system generated 3 stocks in two favored groups; 7 in which only Sectors were in favor, and 16 in which only Market Caps were favored. I have marked my "accepted" choices of the latter two groups with boldface: the first four of Sector and the first three of Market Cap. Don't get too hung up on the differences between them. At this point in the analytical process, the StockScouter system considers all of these stocks to be roughly equivalent in terms of their likelihood to advance over the next six months. Eliminate all stocks that trade less than 30,000 shares per day on average, and you are good to go. You will notice that the final 10 chosen this way differs from the ones listed on the Top 10 page at the MSN Money Web site. That's OK. The system considers their differences to be minor. Pick one set of 10, buy them, and you're good.

By now you probably want to know what stocks the system picked over the past seven years. I could show them all to you, but

Symbol	Company Name	Rating	Return Expectation	Market Cap Market Preferences	Sector Market Preferences
FCX	Freeport McMoRan Copper & Gold	10	Very High	**In-Favor**	**In-Favor**
OTE	Hellenic Telecom Depository Receipt	10	Very High	**In-Favor**	**In-Favor**
PEG	Public Srvce Ent Ord Shs	10	Very High	**In-Favor**	**In-Favor**
BG	Bunge Ord Shs	10	Very High	Neutral	**In-Favor**
CMP	Compass Minerals International Inc	10	Very High	Neutral	**In-Favor**
HSC	Harsco Corp	10	Very High	Neutral	**In-Favor**
KALU	Kaiser Aluminum Corp	10	Very High	Neutral	**In-Favor**
KGC	KINROSS GOLD CORP	10	Very High	Neutral	In-Favor
MERC	Mercer International Inc	10	Very High	Neutral	In-Favor
PCH	Potlatch Corp (Holding Co)	10	Very High	Neutral	In-Favor
AAPL	Apple Inc	10	Very High	**In-Favor**	Neutral
ADI	Analog Devices Inc	10	Very High	**In-Favor**	Neutral
AXP	American Express Co	10	Very High	**In-Favor**	Neutral
CME	CME Group Inc	10	Very High	In-Favor	Neutral
COP	ConocoPhillips	10	Very High	In-Favor	Neutral
CSCO	Cisco Systems Inc	10	Very High	In-Favor	Neutral
JNPR	Juniper Networks Inc	10	Very High	In-Favor	Neutral
KLAC	KLA Tencor Corp	10	Very High	In-Favor	Neutral
LEH	Lehman Brothers Holdings Ord Shs	10	Very High	In-Favor	Neutral

Figure 5-3

it's a pretty repetitive story. Over and over, StockScouter picks some stocks that are obvious and some that are unusual, and most of them just seem to work out, with a few clunkers thrown in just to keep us on our toes. To give you a close-up view with recent examples, I'll now show you the stocks the system picked in the first nine months of 2007—a period of much teeth-gnashing and brow-furrowing over residential real estate values, home construction, retail, and credit derivatives. In some cases, I'll also try to explain the fundamentals and the business, social, or cultural change going on behind the scenes that made the picks work.

If ever there were a difficult period in the market, it was this one. Yet the results were simply awesome. The hidden hand that guides StockScouter unemotionally steered investors completely away from the market's problem areas and focused primarily on telecom, foreign stocks, technology, and energy. In the first three tables that follow, the Chg column is the stock's raw price change from the date of the set's inception to the close of trading six months later; for the rest, it's through the close of September 22 (the date this chapter was written). Dividends were not included even though they add a very material amount of money to many of the picks.

January 2007 StockScouter Top 10

The StockScouter selections for January 2007 are shown in Table 5-2.

The year 2007 started with investors in an optimistic mood, but shares got off on the wrong foot. Pundits were already complaining about the crisis in home-building and financial stocks, although the worst of the crisis was on the distant horizon. Without a compass, it was difficult, as usual, to figure out which way to go. But that is why deploying StockScouter is so useful. Its elves do all the

Table 5-2 January 2007

StockScouter 10	Ticker	SS	Cost	Last	Chg*
Philippine Long Distance Tel	PHI	10	$49.64	$57.20	15.23%
Mobile Telesystems	MBT	10	$50.38	$60.57	20.23%
Atlantic Tele-Network	ATNI	10	$28.60	$28.64	0.14%
CT Communications	CTCI	10	$23.48	$30.51	29.94%
Millicom International	MICC	10	$61.98	$91.64	47.85%
AGL Resources	ATG	9	$39.23	$40.48	3.19%
DTE Energy	DTE	9	$48.61	$48.22	-0.80%
PG&E	PCG	9	$47.62	$45.30	-4.87%
CenterPnt Energy	CNP	9	$16.67	$17.40	4.38%
Sempra Energy	SRE	9	$56.33	$59.23	5.15%
AVERAGE					12.04%
S&P 500 Index	$INX		1,418.30	1,503.35	6.00%

* Through June 29, 2007.

heavy analytical lifting. In January, the system was heavily focused on foreign telecommunications companies, wireless communications companies, and utilities. The one thing they all had in common was high dividend yields. Philippine Long Distance Tel (PHI), the first pick, generates a 7 percent one-year yield; Mobile Telesystems (MBT), a Russian cellular phone company, generates a 2.5 percent yield; and AGL Resources (ATG), an Atlanta natural gas distributor, generates a 4.3 percent yield.

Would you have put together a portfolio like this on your own, without StockScouter? Probably not, as it would be considered too undiversified by any standard, with five utilities and five telecoms. But diversification is for sissies. When we're out for risk-balanced return, a focused approach on leaders is our game. In this case, the StockScouter Top 10 delivered a 12 percent return in six months, which was double the U.S. market's gain. Yet still you have to wonder what the system was seeing.

We'll get more deeply into trading themes and "ecosystems" in the next chapter. But for now I just want to point out that although wireless communication was by no means new to anyone in January 2007, its ubiquity certainly was in many ways. Think about it. When you get in your car, you reach for it. When you're at work, you take a break to have a moment alone with it. When you get into an elevator, you fondle it. Cigarettes? A cup of coffee? Nope, it's the third most addictive substance in modern life, the cell phone. And by 2007 it was becoming more difficult for many people to curb their longing to hug it more tightly than most of their personal relationships.

With its shiny surfaces, its sleek and satisfying touch, its mysteries, and its air of sophistication, the cell phone connects us to the world, even as it disconnects us from people three feet away. In just the past couple of years, the cell phone has challenged individuals, employers, manufacturers, and therapists in ways that its inventors in the late 1940s never imagined.

The costs, of course, are becoming ever more evident, and I don't mean just the monthly bill. The overuse of cell phones has become a social problem for tens of thousands of people from Moscow, Russia, to Moscow, Idaho, which is not very different from other harmful addictions: an obstacle to one-on-one personal contact and an escape from reality. That sounds extreme, but we've all witnessed the evidence: the guy at a restaurant who talks on the phone through an entire meal, ignoring his kids around the table; the woman who yaks on the phone in the car, ignoring her husband; the teen who text-messages all the way home from school, avoiding contact with kids all around him.

Is it just rude, or is it pathological? And pardon my own manners, but either way StockScouter sniffed out an investment angle.

Jim Williams, an industrial sociologist whom you'll meet more formally in the next chapter, notes that cell phone addiction is part of a set of symptoms in a widening gulf of personal isolation. He cites a study by Duke University researchers that found that one-quarter of Americans say that they have no one with whom to discuss their most important personal business. Despite the growing use of phones, e-mail, and instant messaging, in other words, Williams says studies show that we don't have as many pals as our parents did. "Just as more information has led to less wisdom, more acquaintances via the Internet and cell phones have produced fewer friends," he says.

If the mobile phone has truly had these effects, it's because it has become incredibly pervasive. Consider that, as recently as 1987, there were only 1 million cell phones in use. By 2007, something like 200 million Americans carried them. Almost three-quarters of American households have at least one, and many have three to five. About half of teens aged 13 to 16 have one. They far outnumber wired phones in the United States. Most emerging countries in Asia and Africa have skipped right over wired phones and gone straight into the wireless age. Naturally, India and China are the two fastest-growing markets: nearly 6 million people signed up for cellular service in India in August alone; the one-month total in China was around 5 million.

In Spain, where a population of 41 million people has more than 35 million cell phones, authorities complain that obsessive-compulsive behavior has afflicted teenagers disproportionately. Newspapers are filled with stories of young users spending so much class time making calls, receiving text messages, and surfing the Web that they flunk out. A Spanish wire service reports that up to

15 percent of Spanish teens sleep with their mobile phones to make sure they can answer messages overnight. And to pay bills approaching $1,000 a month, some have turned to crime. Over in Australia, a researcher at Queensland University concluded that cellular addiction stems from the fact that many users consider the cell phone to be both a "security blanket" and safety device that has improved their sense of self-worth and thus became obsessive in their perceived need to be near one. Maybe that's why more than 300 million phones were sold in 2007 with digital cameras fitted inside—which is far more than the number of stand-alone digital cameras sold.

If you think that an uptake this rapid and extensive has something more going for it than mere usefulness and security, you're right. A sales job of historic proportions has helped, as cellular companies have invested vast sums of money in Madison Avenue techniques to persuade us to hook up. More money is spent on marketing cell phones, in fact, than on marketing any other object in America, including cars, tobacco, and laundry detergent. A study in *Advertising Age* reported that the top three "megabrands" of advertising in 2005 were Verizon Communications, AT&T, and Sprint Nextel, with a total of $6.5 billion spent between them that year. The only other advertisers that were in the same league were General Motors, Ford, and Procter & Gamble. The result was a steady increase in spending, both in the United States and abroad, on cellular service per month. The average American's monthly cellular bill in 2006 was around $49.30, or nearly $600 per year—and that was the figure that fueled record revenue gains for providers.

So that is the fundamental business and cultural change that actually underlay the StockScouter picks in January. As a systematic active trader, you may not have known it, but it was there nonetheless, lurking in the stocks' valuation, trading patterns, insider activity, and earnings growth. And this was even more true overseas: huge markets in the Philippines, Africa, Latin America, and Russia were years behind the United States and Europe, but were trying to catch up in a hurry.

Check out the chart of top-rated Philippine Long Distance Telephone, which despite its name is primarily a wireless company. As you can see in Figure 5-4, its three-year weekly chart at the end of 2006 had the ideal look that we have seen in previous chapters. Price momentum had shifted insistently enough that the stock was hugging its 9-week moving average rather than its 34-week or 13-week moving average. We could easily have decided to buy this stock as a result of appreciating its sector and regional relative strength, but the fact that it rose to the top of the StockScouter rank-

Figure 5-4

ings made it a no-brainer. The shares gained 15 percent over the next six months, more than double the return on the U.S. market. As you can see, even if you had not wished to trade the StockScouter 10 as a system, it would have led you in this case to a perfect swing-trading candidate advancing out of a bull flag.

February 2007 StockScouter Top 10

The StockScouter selections for February 2007 are shown in Table 5-3.

In February, StockScouter retained some interest in foreign and domestic telecommunications, choosing stocks like Mahanagar Telephone (MTE) of India, but shifted most of its focus to commodities and foreign trade. Now you can see that StockScouter does not get emotionally locked into any one theme. It just sifts through the numbers to figure out what's going to work best next. In this case, it figured out that South Korean steelmaker Posco

Table 5-3   February 2007

StockScouter 10	Ticker	SS	Cost	Last	Chg*
Mahanagar Telephone	MTE	10	$7.46	$7.31	−2.01%
Liberty Media Interactive	LINTA	9	$24.06	$20.95	−12.93%
Liberty Media Capital	LCAPA	8	$101.67	$114.45	12.57%
Ashland	ASH	8	$69.12	$61.06	−11.66%
Posco	PKX	8	$86.84	$142.45	64.04%
Alcoa	AA	10	$31.80	$38.20	20.13%
Ryanair Hldgs	RYAAY	10	$43.57	$41.49	−4.77%
Lan Airlines ADR Rep 1	LFL	10	$11.82	$16.01	35.48%
Celanese	CE	10	$26.02	$37.50	44.12%
Genco Shipping & Trading	GNK	10	$30.87	$56.33	82.47%
AVERAGE					**22.74%**
S&P 500 Index	$INX		1,455.27	1,455.27	1.18%

* Through July 31, 2007.

(PKX), U.S. aluminum producer Alcoa (AA), chemical producer Celanese (CE), Chilean air carrier Lan Airlines (LFL), and Greek dry-bulk ocean fleet owner Genco Shipping & Trading (GNK) had the best prospects going forward. And it was right again, netting 22.7 percent for the group over the next six months, compared with a gain of just 1.2 percent for the U.S. market.

StockScouter was particularly smart about Genco, having made it a 10 and a top pick starting in the summer of 2006. What was it picking up on? Again, although the system came at the company from a strictly quantitative standpoint, there were deep fundamental strengths in the idea. The company was the brainchild of Greek shipping magnate Peter Georgiopoulos. If you've ever owned any of the oil tanker stocks, you may recognize that name, as he was the founder and chairman of General Maritime, which went public at $10 in 2001, promptly fell to $2.35 toward the end of 2002, and then advanced more than tenfold to $32 in 2007. Georgiopoulos, who spent the early part of his career with the junk bond kings of Drexel Burnham Lambert, saw the mom-and-pop oil tanker business, which was out of favor at the time, as one that was ripe for consolidation and business streamlining. His success at building a profitable $1.4 billion company out of other companies' spare parts has become legendary. General Maritime now floats around 60 of its own tankers.

Georgiopoulos aimed to do the same with Genco, and it took a similar path. The shares went public at $15 in mid-2005, promptly fell to $12.85 by the end of the year, and then took off in a steady upward arc, touching $65 by September 2007. The key to the company's success over the rest of this quarter, and the next year, was China and India's accelerating demand for iron ore, coal, and grain. While that sounded like a tired theme to some investors by February 2007, it was still an undeniable phenomenon. By mid-2007, the urban population of China had reached over 600 million people, or 47 percent of the overall population, compared with 23.9 percent before the reforms of 1978. That was an urban migration of historic proportions that required a massive improvement of civic infrastructure and had generated enormous consumer demand. Spending by urban residents in China now constitutes more than 60 percent of all spending in the country. In other words, dry-bulk shippers' primary role in the world economy today is to move raw iron ore, coal, and grain from Brazil, Australia, Indonesia, and Africa to China so that country's manufacturers can make steel for roads, airports, and factories and feed a population that has left inefficient, understaffed farms behind.

The ships usually return empty, by the way. China may be a big country with a lot of resources, but the iron content of its native ore is inferior to that of ore dug out of the ground elsewhere, its coal mines are inefficient and hazardous, and multiyear drought has impaired its crops. Researchers say it's cheaper for China to close down its dangerous coal mines and just float low-cost, high-energy boxes of rocks from Australia—and that's where Genco fits in. Georgiopoulos's original strategy was to buy 16 relatively new ships from a Chinese fleet owner. At the time, long-term charter rates were high, so he put 15 of them out on one- and two-year contracts to raw materials providers such as Cargill and BHP Billiton (BHP). That proved to be a smart strategy, as rates declined not long after.

There are lots of public dry-bulk shipping companies, but in 2006 and 2007 Genco stood out for its ability to put boats out on two-year charters that provided stability for big dividend payouts, while still retaining some exposure to the high and rising spot market. Another feature of its conservative approach: Genco started with a $450 million, 10-year revolving credit facility at LIBOR plus 95 basis points, which it could draw down for ship acquisitions. That allowed the company to finance its growth without having to dilute shareholders' equity by selling more shares. General Maritime used the same strategy, allowing it to grow to a 50-ship fleet from 16 without issuing new shares, a nice feat.

Shipping companies essentially add value by buying and financing ships at good prices, then chartering them out at high rates. StockScouter managed to figure out that this was a pretty good business plan. In Figure 5-5, you can see what Genco looked like on the eve of the day that it was picked for the February Top 10 list. From that point on, Genco shares rose higher

Figure 5-5

and higher as its management announced repeated purchases of seemingly inexpensive large vessels and put them out on time charters at higher and higher rates. You probably see the correlation now. The rates surprised analysts so much that that they were forced to repeatedly raise their estimates and revise their price targets higher. By midyear, the company had 94 percent of its ships on charter for 2007 and 60 percent of its ships chartered for 2008, which gave it full support for its dividend plus exposure to higher shipping rates down the road. Since StockScouter picked up on this in its uncanny way, traders made 82 percent on the stock in just six months.

March 2007 StockScouter Top 10

The StockScouter selections for March 2007 are shown in Table 5-4.

In March 2007, StockScouter switched its point of view around completely to favor technology and financial stocks. It had silently moved on from companies that bought communications equipment to the companies that made the equipment. Medium-sized wireless and wireline telecom gear makers Harris Corp. (HRS), Amphenol (APH), and Cypress Semiconductor (CY) found favor, as did industrial distributor MSC Industrial (MSM) and antivirus software maker McAfee (MFE). Meanwhile, the financial sector also rose to the top of the heap, giving Peruvian bank Creditcorp (BAP) a chance to shine. This was the group of names you had to buy, following the 10-stock system in the face of a sharp downturn in the market—the first major shock of 2007. Risk takers were rewarded, as the group rose by 10.2 percent over the next six months, or twice the rate of the broad market.

Table 5-4 March 2007

StockScouter 10	Ticker	SS	Cost	Last	Chg*
Harris Corp.	HRS	10	$50.37	$60.83	20.77%
Amphenol Corp.	APH	10	$33.92	$36.11	6.47%
MSC Industrial Direct	MSM	10	$45.47	$51.80	13.92%
BMC Software	BMC	10	$32.00	$30.62	−4.31%
Microchip Technology	MCHP	10	$37.49	$38.52	2.75%
Cypress Semiconductor	CY	10	$19.98	$25.04	25.33%
Raymond James Financial	RJF	10	$31.41	$32.79	4.39%
Hutchinson Technology	HTCH	10	$23.52	$23.01	−2.17%
Credicorp Ltd.	BAP	10	$50.43	$61.35	21.65%
McAfee	MFE	10	$31.65	$35.75	12.95%
AVERAGE					**10.18%**
S&P 500 Index	$INX		1,406.22	1,473.99	4.82%

* Through August 31, 2007.

April 2007 StockScouter Top 10

The StockScouter selections for April 2007 are shown in Table 5-5.

In April, you can see that the model retained its interest in utilities and telecommunications, but now shifted its attention to energy for the first time in the year. What's fascinating to me is that the model appears to have picked up on the fact that crude oil had returned to favor after nine months of decline and sideways action. As you can see in Figure 5-6, crude oil traded up to $79 per barrel in mid-2006, then crashed to the low $50s by the start of 2007. All of that time, energy stocks did not surface in the 10-stock model. However, in April, the price of crude surpassed its 50-week moving average for the first time, a level that had served as support in the past. The model added five large-cap oil and gas stocks that month—and they did well over the ensuing six months as the price of a barrel of crude oil shot up to the low $80s. Once again, this shows that

Table 5-5   April 2007

StockScouter 10	Ticker	SS	Cost	Last	Chg*
Mirant	MIR	9	$40.94	$41.32	0.93%
DCP Midstream Partners LP	DPM	9	$39.09	$44.89	14.84%
Aqua America	WTR	8	$22.31	$23.87	6.99%
Consolidated Comm.	CNSL	8	$19.88	$18.90	−4.93%
Occidental Petroleum	OXY	10	$50.30	$64.41	28.05%
Unit Corp.	UNT	10	$51.50	$50.54	−1.86%
Statoil A	STO	10	$27.74	$34.62	24.80%
Dynegy Class A	DYN	10	$9.47	$8.86	−6.44%
Imperial Oil	IMO	10	$37.58	$50.14	33.42%
Partner Comm.	PTNR	10	$14.75	$16.01	8.54%
AVERAGE					**10.43%**
S&P 500 Index	$INX		1,420.86	1,525.75	7.38%

* Through September 21, 2007.

without any explicit programming that tells it to look for changes in commodity prices, the model senses change and acts on its own.

It's interesting that the model offered a pretty eclectic group of energy names, including international driller and chemical refiner Occidental Petroleum (OXY), Oklahoma-based gas driller Unit Corp. (UNT), Canada-based integrated energy giant Imperial Oil (IMO), and Norway-based integrated energy giant Statoil (STO). What was StockScouter thinking in its little algorithmic brain? Well, nothing, really. It's just arithmetic. But if you had created the portfolio yourself following a week of deep thinking, you would have leaned on another China-related argument.

Consider some perspective offered around this time by veteran global macro analyst Dennis Gartman. He noted that through the early 1990s, China was energy-independent, producing enough crude oil from its huge Daqing oil field to meet domestic demand and even export a little to allies. In 1985, it produced 2.7 million

StockScouter added energy stocks in April when crude oil rose back above its 50-week EMA. Good timing.

Figure 5-6

barrels of oil a day and consumed 2 million. By 1995, though, China's economic growth had risen to the point where it needed to begin importing oil; that year, production was around 3 million barrels per day, but demand was 3.2 million. By 2000, demand had risen to 4.4 million barrels. And by 2005, although domestic production had risen to 3.7 million barrels per day, demand had grown to 7 million. So if you run the math, you'll see that production rose 37 percent from 1985 to 2005, but demand rose 250 percent.

China now brings in all that oil from Angola, Saudi Arabia, Iran, Canada, Russia, Oman, Congo, Yemen, and Venezuela. Think for a moment about all that oil previously bound for Europe and the United States that is now being diverted to China. Now think about all the other fast-growing Eastern European, South Asian, and Central American countries that need crude oil and gas to fuel their swelling middle-class lifestyles. Right in front of us is a living page ripped from future history books. And as traders, we had a unique opportunity to take advantage of it automatically through the StockScouter model.

May 2007 StockScouter Top 10

The StockScouter selections for May 2007 are shown in Table 5-6.

In May, the model tripped into new territory by adding some retail, media, and transportation to its technology and energy positions. This change hadn't worked out so well after five months, as character-based products and media provider Marvel Entertainment (MVL) tripped and teen clothing vendor Abercrombie & Fitch (ANF) drifted sideways. No harm was done, though, as the portfolio was merely flat while the broad market rose 3 percent. You can't win 'em all. Nor should you expect to. The interesting thing about the underperformance of this group is that May 1 was probably the easiest time of the year to start a new portfolio, at least from

Table 5-6 May 2007

StockScouter 10	Ticker	SS	Cost	Last	Chg*
Abercrombie & Fitch Co.	ANF	10	$83.39	$79.83	−4.27%
Cabot Oil & Gas Corp.	COG	10	$36.88	$36.54	−0.92%
Fastenal Co.	FAST	10	$41.65	$44.87	7.73%
Heartland Express	HTLD	10	$13.08	$14.86	13.61%
Intuit	INTU	10	$29.11	$29.70	2.03%
National Semiconductor	NSM	10	$26.72	$26.43	−1.09%
Tidewater	TDW	10	$66.26	$67.00	1.12%
Marvel Entertainment	MVL	10	$29.60	$22.76	−23.11%
Choice Hotels International	CHH	10	$38.58	$39.03	1.17%
AVX Corp	AVX	10	$16.52	$16.00	−3.15%
AVERAGE					**−0.69%**
S&P 500 Index	$INX		1,482.37	1,525.75	2.93%

* Through September 21, 2007.

a psychological point of view. Stocks had fully recovered from their March swoon, and April had featured a nice, steady upward move without fireworks. It just goes to show again that it's typically best to start portfolios when you feel the least comfortable and, vice versa, to be cautious when you feel the most invincible.

June 2007 StockScouter Top 10

The StockScouter selections for June 2007 are shown in Table 5-7.

In June, the model decided that retail and entertainment hadn't been such a hot idea and switched back to energy and technology. That worked well during a very difficult period in the market, as the group rose 7.45 percent over the next four months, compared with a flat spot in the broad market. Apple (AAPL) was the big winner on the tech side, as the release of its new iPhone, as well as new Macintosh and iPod models, pushed expectations of earnings growth higher.

Table 5-7 June 2007

StockScouter 10	Ticker	SS	Cost	Last	Chg*
BMC Software	BMC	10	$31.85	$31.50	−1.10%
ENSCO International	ESV	10	$61.52	$56.79	−7.69%
Analog Devices	ADI	10	$35.70	$36.60	2.52%
Apple Inc.	AAPL	10	$118.77	$144.15	21.37%
Cohu Inc.	COHU	10	$20.61	$20.32	−1.41%
Harris Corp.	HRS	10	$49.65	$58.05	16.92%
Intuit Inc.	INTU	10	$30.53	$29.70	−2.72%
FMC Technologies	FTI	10	$37.88	$56.74	49.79%
Overseas Shipholding	OSG	10	$79.31	$75.74	−4.50%
Pride International	PDE	10	$35.90	$36.39	1.36%
AVERAGE					**7.45%**
S&P 500 Index	$INX		1,530.62	1,525.75	−0.32%

* Through September 21, 2007.

But another star in June was FMC Technologies (FTI), an underappreciated provider of construction services to the oil and gas industry. This was a very old-school company that was the subject of a passage in a famous book by Philip A. Fisher called *Common Stocks, Uncommon Profits*. The growth-at-a-reasonable-price pioneer wrote about how he made a fortune in FMC by buying it during an earnings setback and then holding it for 30 years. What's particularly interesting in this case is that the model chose FMC Technologies at a point when it was making a new all-time high, as shown in Figure 5-7, which is often a difficult time for many investors to buy a stock. It feels like all the money has been made already, and you're a sucker for coming in late. But once again, the model did a great job of figuring out that earnings, revenue, and cash flow were just about to ramp up again for this maker of subsea platforms for energy exploration companies, and four months

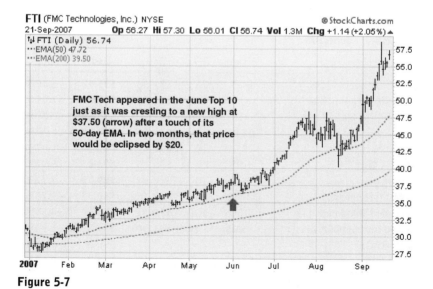

Figure 5-7

later it had zoomed almost 50 percent higher to repeated all-time highs. This goes to show, again, that you shouldn't be put off from buying StockScouter 10 stocks at either new highs or new lows, as the model tends to get at least enough of its 10 names right to help push you toward your fortune.

July 2007 StockScouter Top 10

The StockScouter selections for July 2007 are shown in Table 5-8.

If ever there were a time to buy stocks that would ultimately make you strike your forehead and yell out a loud, Homer Simpson–inflected "Doh!" it would be July 2007. The market had been crankin' since late March, and spirits were high. And then all of a sudden, in the middle of the month, the roof started caving in as investors began to worry about subprime mortgages, a worldwide credit crunch ensued, and upside-down global macro hedge fund managers started selling positions left and right.

Table 5-8 July 2007

StockScouter 10	Ticker	SS	Cost	Last	Chg*
Cal Dive International	DVR	10	$16.50	$15.47	−6.24%
Norsk Hydro ADR	NHY	9	$38.00	$43.26	13.84%
United Micro	UMC	9	$3.52	$3.53	0.28%
BreitBurn Energy LP	BBEP	8	$33.99	$33.54	−1.32%
Petroleum Development	PETD	8	$48.47	$44.68	−7.82%
Penn Virginia GP	PVG	8	$30.85	$37.60	21.88%
Anadarko Petroleum	APC	10	$51.54	$53.55	3.90%
Cohu	COHU	10	$21.89	$20.32	−7.17%
Pride International	PDE	10	$37.01	$36.39	−1.68%
Atwood Oceanics	ATW	10	$67.54	$80.57	19.29%
AVERAGE					**3.50%**
S&P 500 Index	$INX		1,503.35	1,525.75	1.49%

* Through September 21, 2007.

Yet that's why the market gods invented quantitative methods for us. You just need to shut your ears, close your eyes, and tap out the symbols on the keyboard while the ruckus rages around you. It's sort of like Odysseus passing the Sirens. Don't listen to all the calls for doom and gloom, just do your thing. Stand by your model, and your model will stand by you.

As you can see, StockScouter stuck with energy again in July, and added just a touch of technology. And once again, the diversity of the group was rather impressive: Cal Dive International (DVR), based in Houston, provides underwater construction services to shallow- and deep-water drillers in the Gulf of Mexico and the Middle East. Norsk Hydro (NHY), based in Norway, produces oil and natural gas in the North Sea, although its largest operations are in aluminum production in Europe, Canada, and Australia. Penn Virginia (PVG), based in Pennsylvania, is a master limited partnership focused on the management of coal properties and the gathering and processing of natural gas. Pride International (PDE), based in Houston, provides rigs and contract drilling services to oil and gas explorers on land in Latin America and in the sea off Africa, Europe, the southern United States, and the Middle East.

The electronics component for July didn't look very promising through September, but you never know. I'm constantly amazed at how StockScouter figures out strong prospects ahead of the crowd. United Micro (UMC) makes silicon wafers for use in logic, mixed-signal, and memory chips. United is one of the largest companies in the booming Taiwanese electronics industry. With customers like Texas Instruments (TXN) getting their groove back lately amid a rebound in wireless handset sales and an expansion under way in chips for solar energy and high-end computers, it could do great; you never know, so you never want to knock a stock off the list just because you have a bad feeling or don't like the chart.

August 2007 StockScouter Top 10

The StockScouter selections for August 2007 are shown in Table 5-9.

In August, as the credit crunch worsened, StockScouter continued to focus on mid-cap and large-cap energy and technology companies to the exclusion of all else. It's good to be single-minded sometimes. As you can see, Oceaneering (OII) (see Figure 5-8) and Core Laboratories (CLB) did an outstanding job for investors in the short period of time that this portfolio was in operation from August 1 through September 22, 2007.

What was going on there, really? Gasoline prices were near record highs, and unlike random consumers, who don't care about

Table 5-9 August 2007

StockScouter 10	Ticker	SS	Cost	Last	Chg*
ADC Telecom	ADCT	10	$19.07	$20.73	8.70%
Arris Group	ARRS	10	$15.00	$14.26	−4.93%
Apollo Group	APOL	10	$60.75	$58.72	−3.34%
Ceradyne	CRDN	10	$76.19	$74.58	−2.11%
Garmin Ltd.	GRMN	10	$79.90	$108.70	36.05%
Oceaneering Intl.	OII	10	$54.80	$73.85	34.76%
QUALCOMM	QCOM	10	$41.67	$40.83	−2.02%
Albemarle Corp.	ALB	10	$39.88	$42.67	7.00%
Core Laboratories	CLB	10	$102.67	$123.53	20.32%
Apple	AAPL	10	$143.85	$144.15	0.21%
AVERAGE					**9.46%**
S&P 500 Index	$INX		1,455.27	1,525.75	4.84%

* Through September 21, 2007.

Figure 5-8

the business of value creation, we had an opportunity to participate in a historic advance in the value of a commodity. There is, after all, really a shortage of refined oil products in the world marketplace today, and it was dawning on people that we were never, ever going back to the good old days of absolute abundance.

Higher prices at the pump were a matter of simple economics. U.S. refiners have the ability to churn out 17 million barrels of gasoline per day. Demand is around 22 million barrels per day. To make up the difference, we bring in gasoline from foreign refiners, which means that, at the margin, pump prices are set by import prices. Total U.S. demand for oil products was up 2.7 percent year to date, boosted in part by the surge of cold weather in February. But since we are far from the only country importing gasoline and other key refined products, we don't have a lot of say in what those prices are. Gasoline, like crude oil, is auctioned worldwide to the highest bidder, and with the dollar weak and overseas economic growth strong because of our fantastic appetite for iPods made in China and T-shirts made in Costa Rica, we have to pay up to keep our supply coming in. And that's all there is to it. With U.S. refinery capacity now at ridiculously low levels, in part because of lack of investment in new plants amid harsh environmental rules, any little change in the supply chain has an amazingly powerful effect.

If there's a blip in supply from Nigeria, where violence was raging in mid-2007, or there's a refinery accident that causes a kink in capacity, the amount of gasoline and diesel fuel available for American consumers shrinks dramatically. Price then becomes the great allocator of this scarce resource. At certain points in the summer of 2007, U.S. gasoline inventory hit record lows, with just 20 days' supply available.

If there's one thing you can pin on the oil companies, it's that during their long trek in the wilderness in the 1980s and 1990s, when prices fell dramatically, they failed to maintain their refineries adequately. This shortfall in investment led in part to the tragic 2005 explosion at the Texas City refinery of BP (BP), which killed 15 people, as well as a fire at the McKee refinery operated by leading refiner Valero Energy (VLO). Combine the poor maintenance with a stunning lack of qualified refinery engineers and some bad luck, and you had the 2007 mess, in which several of the nation's biggest refineries were running at half speed. As much as 500,000 barrels per day of gasoline capacity was unavailable.

The government, meanwhile, did not exactly cover itself with glory. For a variety of good reasons, for example, new federal rules have made a type of fuel used by farmers called ultralow-sulfur diesel difficult to transport nationwide in conventional pipelines.

So farmers have had to turn to more expensive grades of diesel that are refined and sold locally, while the cheaper diesel has been sent overseas, where transportation rules are less stringent. And what about ethanol, the supposed miracle fuel made from corn that President Bush has pushed as an alternative? It's kind of a bad joke. As a Deutsche Bank analyst pointed out at the time, ethanol is the energy equivalent of methadone—a palliative, not a cure. At present, ethanol requires huge tax subsidies to generate and transport, and the net savings in terms of foreign energy dependence are negligible, since corn, its feedstock, is farmed with oil-powered tractors and nourished with gas-based fertilizers and oil-based pesticides. Moreover, Deutsche Bank noted that ethanol is 30 percent less fuel-efficient than gasoline, which means that a car will travel only about two-thirds the distance on a gallon of ethanol as it does on a gallon of gasoline.

In a situation in which solutions are scant, it was easy for many people to just fall back on the easy ploy and accuse service-station operators of price gouging. But that really missed the point. Independent station owners are almost as much victims as consumers are, as they face escalating wholesale costs, rising credit card fees, and the enmity of their customers. Rather than complaining, consumers are better off figuring out how to make a buck off this turn of events, and StockScouter repeatedly pointed the way.

September 2007 StockScouter Top 10

The StockScouter selections for September 2007 are shown in Table 5-10.

Following a tumultuous August, with lots of strains all over the place, StockScouter threw all its cards in the air and picked a new

Table 5-10 September 2007

StockScouter 10	Ticker	SS	Cost	Last	Chg*
Textron	TXT	10	$56.79	$62.33	9.76%
Shenandoah Telecom	SHEN	10	$19.79	$22.40	13.19%
Navigators Group	NAVG	10	$53.29	$54.33	1.95%
Public Service Ent.	PEG	10	$85.87	$89.03	3.68%
Coca-Cola Femsa	KOF	10	$39.85	$39.31	−1.36%
United Fire & Casualty	UFCS	10	$38.47	$39.29	2.13%
Capital Trust	CT	10	$33.50	$36.63	9.34%
Lat Am Exp Bnk	BLX	10	$18.45	$18.42	−0.16%
Michael Baker Corp	BKR	10	$40.93	$51.45	25.70%
China Medical Technologies	CMED	10	$34.60	$39.55	14.31%
AVERAGE					**7.85%**
S&P 500 Index	$INX		1,473.99	1,525.75	3.51%

* Through September 21, 2007.

set of potential winners from a much wider range of sectors: capital goods, telecom, finance, utilities, energy, and health care. It was the most diverse portfolio of the year, and for at least the first month also the most consistent. Leading the charge was oil and gas platform construction services provider Michael Baker Corp. (BKR), but not too far behind were an ultrasound device maker based in Beijing called China Medical Technologies (CMED), a New York–based real estate investment trust called Capital Trust (CT), rural Virginia phone services provider Shenandoah Telecom (SHEN) and a heavy construction equipment maker called Textron (TEX). In this case, diversity worked fine, as the group was up 7.85 percent in its first three weeks, compared with +3.5 percent for the broad market.

The lesson is that the math behind StockScouter discovers opportunities so that you don't have to. Even active traders can buy and hold for six months while the power of math and compounding do their magic. Now let's look at one more model that has worked for the past dozen years in my research and practice.

Core Select—the Consistency Kings

Consistency is not an attribute normally associated with stocks, but there are a handful of companies that seem to get the job done year after year. Of the 5,500-plus stocks in the universe of stocks with market capitalizations over $100 million, only 15 recorded positive total returns (capital appreciation + dividends) in every one of the 10 years prior to 2007, and only 19 more were up in 9 of the past 10 years, with the single calendar-year loss being less than –9 percent.

Companies that have made a clean sweep of the past decade generally do their great work under the radar, although a few of them are well known. These stocks are not marketed heavily to investors largely because their business plans are so solid that they don't need to do secondary stock offerings or sell bonds to keep going. That makes them unattractive to brokerages, which need to generate fees by underwriting offerings. If a company doesn't need a brokerage's services, the brokerage usually won't initiate research—otherwise known as marketing—on it. It's a shady angle on the business, but it's the truth.

Despite their lack of fame, many of the stocks with unbeatable long-term records tend to have staying power. If they're up for 10 years straight, chances are they'll rise in the eleventh. My research shows that if you buy stocks of this type as a group and use a 20 percent stop in case the company finally stumbles, they have averaged an annual gain of 24 percent per year.

From a trading perspective, the best part about these "core" stocks is that once they get going again in your current year, they tend to have a strong, steady constituency for further buying. And furthermore, they tend to be the "go-to" stocks for institutional traders both during periods of extreme market stress and immediately after those stresses are relieved.

It's not easy to create the list of qualifying stocks, as you need a high-powered institutional database. I provide the list every year in my *Strategic Advantage* newsletter in the last week of the year. For traders, the best way to use this list is to simply establish positions on pullbacks and breakouts, focusing, as always, on the ones that begin the year in their usual strong uptrends or establish new uptrends after the start of the year. These companies are in a variety of businesses, ranging from international transportation services to Canadian banking and biotechnology. A few typical names are

WBK (Westpac Banking Corp.) NYSE   @ StockCharts.com
24-Sep-2007   **Op** 113.28 **Hi** 119.94 **Lo** 108.02 **Cl** 118.64 **Vol** 199.7K **Chg** +7.01 (+6.28%) ▲

The year-after-year strength of Westpac Banking over the past decade has made it a reliable play both on the Australian economy and on the concept of consistency itself.

Figure 5-9

Expeditors International of Washington (EXPD), Westpac Banking (WBK), Gilead Sciences (GILD), New Jersey Resources (NJR), Stryker (SYK), and Stericycle (SRCL). As you can see in the chart of Australian banking giant Westpac in Figure 5-9, these are stocks that can typically be counted on for daily and weekly trading in months where all else seems bleak. They are like trusted friends whom you can virtually always rely upon in bull markets, bear markets, flat markets, and flat-out crisis markets.

Now let's move on to my last set of ideas for active traders, which is lively groups of stocks that are taking advantage of deeply fundamental economic, social, cultural, or business change and working together like a pack of huskies pulling a sled through the Alaskan wilderness.

FRIDAY

N Power and Ecosystems

Friday afternoons are a time of rest and celebration in many businesses, but active traders should use the end of the last day of the week for concentrated reflection. With the week's trading activity, profits, successes, and discoveries fresh in your mind, go for a run or a swim after the closing bell and then come back to your desk to think about setting up a battle plan for the following week.

Two ideal subjects for Friday's contemplation are the lessons you have learned and the news you have observed in the past 5 days—and how they all fit together. A deliberate, contextual deep think on what's really new in the world will inform your daily trading not just for the next week, but for the next few months or more. It will help you zero in on the most powerful trends and sector moves in stocks and indexes, and reduce the level of random noise that tends to depress most daily traders' win ratios.

One of the most powerful and least understood forces at work in stocks is radical change in product cycles, business plans, management, and pricing. New management, new services, and new products—and, strictly from the market's point of view, new highs and new lows in price—are elements that catch investors' eyes and cause them, however subtly, to reassess the value of companies and industries. "N power," as I call it, is the secret motive force behind many great stock and sector moves, and learning to recognize key developments will help you immeasurably as a daily trader.

It's important to realize, after all, that change is threatening to an existing culture and point of view. Change is dangerous, it is unsettling, and it is uncomfortable, and it is for this reason that many market participants often simply ignore it. Yet once we recognize the strong effects of the new, and adjust for our rival investors' attempts to shove it into an ill-fitting conceptual box, then we can exploit it to our own benefit. I want you to train yourself to think hard about what is new in the marketplace, politics, economy, and culture, and determine if there are ways in which you can arbitrage the difference between what you see and what others are allowing to slip by. There is nothing more valuable for a trader than to develop an accurate "variant perception" about the world, as legendary hedge fund manager Michael Steinhardt puts it. The really big money is made when you have sensed a change before the rest of the herd has done so, taken a set of trading and long-term positions, and laid in wait for the rest of the world to move inexorably in your direction.

One of the real geniuses in helping investors comprehend and take advantage of this fundamentally human thinking process is Jim Williams of the Williams Inference Center in Massachusetts. He is a master at helping clients ranging from hedge fund traders to consumer brand managers develop an awareness of *anomalies* as a guide to early warnings of changes in social, political, and corporate trends and behavior. It's pretty tricky because there is a certain Zenlike quality to becoming aware of things around you that others consider just part of the environment. Jim has illuminated the process with a quote from a Robert Frost essay that states, "Poets stick to nothing deliberately, but let what will stick to them like burrs where they walk in the fields." Since we cannot literally walk through news broadcasts and publications, Williams helps us to see anomalies, or indicators of change, in what appear to be ordinary news stories.

Many of the examples in this chapter stem from ideas that I picked up while scanning the packs of news clips that Jim sends to clients every quarter, which are chock full of potential trend, mood, and culture change agents. Through a growing awareness of anomalies, he helped clients pick up on the amazing impact of digital cameras and camera phones several years before they were well understood as a trend that would wreck the business models of large companies like Eastman Kodak and create big new businesses for Sandisk, OmniVision, and Micron Technologies. He also helped clients understand the potential impact of ethanol as a fuel as far back as 2002, which led me to the U.S. corn and fertilizer industries at an early stage of their recent development. And his work also led to a very early understanding of the growing impact of China and India on U.S. business, as well as the fast-changing importance of natural gas, the tremendous growth of global ocean shipping, the huge impact that the rich have on the economy, and the reason that top consumer brands have been growing in value. Each of these insights came about as a result of the study of "what's new"—that seemingly harmless phrase that we so easily toss out.

The truly awesome thing about change is that it rarely happens in a vacuum. Not long after an important shift comes about, companies begin coalescing to serve it. There are large and small public companies associated with each of the changes, and they form little cooperative societies, if you will. Once you determine what is really new and surprising, in other words, you can next consider how these ideas, products, or services fit into a business "ecosystem." For more often than not, change occurs in waves within a sector or region or industrial niche, and materials producers, manufacturers, service entities, and consultants all individually conspire to benefit from it in their own way. Throwing yourself into these ecosystems as a trader puts the odds of success in your favor. You diminish the diversity of your portfolio but increase the likelihood of success.

As you'll see in a moment, a great example is the growth of interest in corn farming in 2006 and 2007 to meet the new demand for ethanol. A lot of fertilizer, seed, milling, and plant pollution control companies related to what I nicknamed the "corn industrial complex" sprang up to service the nascent ethanol industry, coalescing into an ecosystem of stocks whose success fed off one another. The range of companies involved makes this more than merely an agribusiness sector play. It is a wide-ranging opportunity involving suppliers, distributors, manufacturers, service providers, and banks. Likewise, the idea for a brand-new Boeing aircraft called the 787 Dreamliner kicked off the creation of a new ecosystem of titanium makers, forged metal parts makers, landing gear and cockpit makers, and the like. In this chapter, I want to help you identify these ecosystems as they develop and learn how to jump in and make money from them week after week in daily trading.

So now let's take a long look at several examples, and learn how they played out in the mid-2000s. Although all of these situations are historical, they should help you identify the new ecosystems that are forming in the world even as you read these words. They're out there, as long as you put yourself in a position to see and feel them. Once you do, create a holistic list of the stocks in the groups by using the screening software and methodologies described earlier, and trade them using charts with weekly bars to time yourself into high-return-potential trades using my recommended technical entry and exit methods.

Lighter Long-Range Commercial Jets

Sometimes it takes only a single product to launch a company to the next level. One insanely great idea, to paraphrase Steve Jobs, can spark customers' and investors' imaginations and ignite a multiyear rally in shares. For Apple, it was the iPod/iTunes combo. For Chipotle Mexican Grill, it was an all-natural burrito. For Crocs, it was those lightweight antifashion plastic shoes.

For Boeing, it was a product about 100,000 times larger: the 787 Dreamliner commercial jetliner. And yet there is also a jumbo-jet-sized difference between the first three ideas and Boeing's. Apple, Chipotle, and Crocs all reaped the benefit of their innovations *after* they had been released and enjoyed by the public. In contrast, Boeing shares rose 150 percent in four years even before it had built a single complete commercial 787 at the target weight for a customer, much less delivered one.

I know it sounds crazy, but what do you expect from Wall Street? Traders always count their chickens before they hatch. Indeed, only as the release date drew within a year did a burning question form in the minds of investors: Will the Dreamliner emerge from the most complex manufacturing assembly line in history without a hitch, or will Boeing be forced to delay at some point as a result of supply chain or engineering stumbles?

For a long time, plenty of big money was bet on both sides of this issue, but the preponderance voted in the affirmative with Boeing. Investors had essentially decided that Boeing was the greatest U.S. manufacturer of all time, considering that it had beaten back all domestic and foreign rivals to become the rarest of entities: a monopoly that had evaded the U.S. government's usual trust-busting impulse and pushed the envelope on both innovation and profitability. And what a result: between the time the Dreamliner was announced in April 2004 and the third quarter of 2007, Boeing shares rose four times more than the broad market, as shown in Figure 6-1.

Figure 6-1

The best industrial company ever? Why not? The Dreamliner was an unbelievably audacious gamble that planes could be built out of lightweight composite materials instead of heavy metal, that they could use two different manufacturers' engines interchangeably, that they could sport the largest windows ever inserted in planes, that they could be built in pieces at plants from Italy to Japan and then assembled in a single Washington State hangar, that they could fly more quietly and farther on less fuel than ever before—and that they could be churned out at the unprecedented rate of one every three days. The program blared out "new, new, new" everywhere you looked as you simply read daily headlines.

As Boeing sold the idea to customers from 2004 through 2007, the Dreamliner became the most successful new plane in aviation history, with $80 billion in orders on the books. At the very least, you've got to tip your hat to a sales staff that could vend a $175 million item to customers before they could touch or test it! The only four manufacturers that can compete with Boeing for the title of best U.S. industrial manufacturer ever are General Electric, United Technologies, 3M, and Intel, and yet none of them has so thoroughly dominated such a difficult global business by taking such big risks.

In the expectation that Boeing would leverage its epic success forward, the value that investors put on its shares ended up surprising a lot of people. Of course, Boeing had a lot more going for it than just the Dreamliner. Chief Executive Officer Jim McNerney pressured his managers to boost profit margins by reducing overhead costs. The long-term outlook for increased military aerospace spending was still strong, despite some real worries over cuts by the new Democratic leaders in Congress. Moreover, Boeing's shares were cheaper than they had been when they had approached previous earnings peaks in the past decade; they were selling at around 14 to 17 times estimated 2008 earnings despite annual earnings growth of 20 percent or more. (In the past, Boeing's earnings multiple had peaked in the low to mid-20s.)

The key thing for traders to comprehend at the time was that the aircraft replacement cycle was likely to last longer than equivalent cycles in the 1980s and 1990s because of the huge increase in the number of customers in emerging countries and aircraft leasing firms worldwide. By nosing around trade publications online, I learned that environmental and noise regulations at airports would force many airlines to ditch older planes in the next few years, before the end of their useful life. Because credit was more widely available at lower rates than in past cycles, airlines were also more capable of issuing debt to cover purchases. That was another anomaly.

And then there was that whole monopoly issue. In past cycles, Boeing had had to compete against the European joint venture that produces the Airbus. That outfit had fallen on hard times as a result of serious engineering and marketing slip-ups, allowing Boeing to move out to a big lead that its executives will be loath to relinquish. Strong competition was on the rise in Brazil and China, but only at the margins with lower-value aircraft as Boeing took advantage of its massive investment in research and development to keep its designs fresh, attractive, and efficient.

So, as you can see, Boeing's 787 represented a tectonic shift in the way commercial jets were designed, built, and sold, and it became clear very early that it would attract a profit ecosystem around it. For much like the transition from wood and fabric to aluminum in the 1920s, the adoption of composites as the aeronautical material of choice boosted the fortunes of not only Boeing and Airbus, but an entire constellation of related companies.

It became clear by 2005 that Boeing was at the center of an ecosystem that included separate companies creating state-of-the-art acoustics, new composite materials, lighting, broadband connectivity, wider seats, extra-large overhead bins, new large windows, and new cockpits. In addition, the composite fuselage material allows higher cabin pressure and higher humidity levels, which significantly improves passenger comfort — all guided by new electronic and air control equipment.

In its marketing material, the Dreamliner was sold as a plane that achieves its fuel efficiency and streamlined manufacturing costs through an unprecedented reliance on large quantities of titanium, aluminum, and carbon-fiber composites and a global supply chain held together by a new software system. Fear of the loss of a ready source of titanium was in large part behind the company's stunning pledge to spend $27 billion over the next three decades on engineering and raw materials in Russia, an economically and politically unstable country that happens to house most of the world's supply of the key metal. But there were at least three U.S. companies that supply titanium to Boeing as well, and they made terrific trades for more than four years as the ecosystem developed. Now let's bore a little deeper into the story to see the trades that were made available in the ecosystem.

Allegheny Technologies

A key insight for traders was the notion that titanium, an industrial metal that had had limited utility for years because of its high cost and limited applications, would undergo a profound shift in valuation once Boeing and Airbus designed it heavily into their next-generation airplanes. Composites have a number of benefits over traditional aluminum construction, including greater strength and lower weight, which translates into fuel and maintenance savings. And titanium is needed to bond composite components together, especially in high-stress load-bearing areas.

Because of its physical properties, titanium quickly became a popular resident of the periodic table. It's as strong as steel, but with only 45 percent of steel's weight. It is twice as strong as aluminum, but only 60 percent heavier. And it is compatible with high-tech carbon composites, whereas aluminum is corroded by composites. Titanium is also resistant to high temperatures and corrosion.

Surprisingly, titanium production is highly consolidated, with only five producers accounting for 83 percent of global production. Most titanium is actually consumed as titanium dioxide, a whitener used in unexciting applications like toothpaste and paint. Much of the remaining output is used to produce metal. This is the area of intense demand growth that is being driven by the aerospace sector. According to Deutsche Bank analysts, overall titanium demand will grow 47 percent between 2006 and 2010, to 107,000 metric tons, as increased global travel and rising jet fuel prices increase the popularity of new, more efficient airliners. (A metric ton is 1,000 kilograms, or 1.1 U.S. tons.)

As each new generation of commercial aircraft was engineered, the use of composites, and therefore titanium, increased. While there are only 20 metric tons of titanium in a Boeing 737, there are 120 in the new 787. The new Airbus A380 uses 80 metric tons, and the A350 XWB will use 100 tons.

By late 2005, it was evident from news reports that Airbus and Boeing were already running huge order backlogs: Deutsche Bank analysts put the number at 4,300 planes, which would require 150,000 metric tons of titanium to build over the new few years. For just the Boeing 737, the backlog had reached 1,442 planes by mid-2007, or five years of production. If you're in the market for a new Boeing 787 Dreamliner, the first available order slot is for a 2013 delivery. Do you see the anomalies piling up?

Most of the order demand was the result of the economic growth that was underway in Asia and the Middle East. American air carriers, which make up a little more than one-third of the global air fleet, had largely remained on the sidelines during this order cycle. But this was set to change. In early 2007, traders noted that Merrill Lynch analysts were looking for these carriers to put in big orders, replacing their twin-aisle aircraft first since they operate on key international routes and are really ancient. The analysts estimated that by 2013, over 60 percent of the U.S. twin-aisle fleet would be more than 20 years old.

The titanium producers were gearing up to meet the demand in a big way: one publication said that more than $2 billion would be spent on increasing industry capacity over the coming years. Of this, Allegheny was far and away the largest single contributor, investing over $500 million. In fact, Allegheny is set to become one of the top five titanium producers with its aggressive expansion plans.

Over the next four years, we saw repeated reports that led us to have more confidence concerning Allegheny's role in the ecosystem. For example, we learned in late 2006 that its production levels would increase tenfold over the next few years, to 17,800 annual metric tons. This would be accomplished by restarting an idled facility in Oregon and building a new facility in Utah. If demand dictated, another report said, capacity could be bumped up an additional 50 percent. At the time these projects were announced, everyone thought that Allegheny was nuts. But by mid-2007, its clairvoyance was deemed impressive. Much of this new capacity was already contracted to specific customers and won't enter the market. Allegheny signed a nine-year, $2.5 billion deal with Boeing, and that should keep the trade going for some time to come.

As you can see in Figure 6-2, there were at least four awesome opportunities to trade into the Allegheny Technologies story starting in 2004 as its role in the Boeing and Airbus construction cycle became clear: in the summer and fall of that year, in the spring of 2005, and again in the summer of 2006. Pullbacks to trendlines and breakouts to new highs were the triggers, just as they are in

Figure 6-2

most daily trading. A sale would only come on the violation of the weekly bars' uptrend.

Titanium Metals Corp.

More quickly now, let's take a look at the case of Titanium Metals (TIE), another top titanium maker. Once you heard that the Boeing planes would use gobs of titanium, you just needed to create a list of all the processors and forgers of the miracle metal and look for daily and weekly opportunities to ease into trades. Titanium Metals had just the name to help you make the connection. As with Allegheny, pullbacks and breakouts presented themselves repeatedly from 2004 through 2007 as the stock rode Boeing's coattails to a tenfold move higher and became a $5 billion company. The stock ultimately broke its uptrend in mid-2007. (See Figure 6-3.)

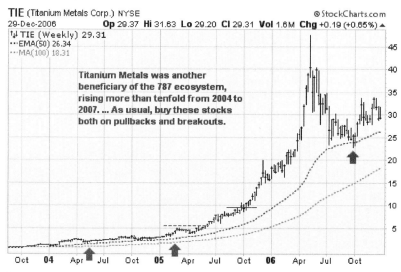

Figure 6-3

RTI International

RTI International (RTI) was a small-cap specialty metals provider when the Boeing and Airbus orders started coming in, and yet by mid-2005, it had begun trading like a momentum commodity stock. To meet demand from Airbus and Boeing commercial aircraft and the F-35 Joint Strike Fighter being built for the Pentagon, RTI announced in 2006 that it would spend nearly $100 million in capital improvements to its existing forging facilities and launch a $100 million expansion. (See Figure 6-4.)

Goodrich Corp.

Now I want you to look at a major aerospace parts maker, Goodrich Corp. (GR). The company engineers and manufactures dozens of airframe components, including wheels, brakes, landing gears, and steering systems. Its main focus is on thrust reversers, engine- and

Figure 6-4

pylon-installation systems, and nacelle components, which are covered housings independent of the fuselage.

You can see where I am going with this: the company ended up winning a large contract to supply all new Boeing 787s with nacelle components. In addition, Goodrich was awarded the engine nacelle and thrust reverser program for the Airbus A350 XWB, which, with aftermarket activity included, was worth a cool $10 billion over 20 years. With both the Boeing 787 and the A350 XWB, news reports suggested that Goodrich should have control of most of the nacelle and thrust reverser market for most of the world's leading long-range midsize aircraft.

That sounded new to me, and it was. Despite great growth in new aircraft sales, fleet growth has stayed low, which meant that new planes were replacing only a fraction of their mothballed planes. Quarterly reports showed that sales and earnings at Goodrich were growing at a 25 percent clip all of a sudden, almost entirely as a result of its role in the Boeing and Airbus ecosystem. By late 2007, it had ridden the aircraft production tailwind to an $8 billion market cap. (See Figure 6-5.)

Aircastle Ltd.

Next up is Aircastle, an aircraft lessor that provides passenger and cargo jets to passenger airliners and freight shippers around the world. By the third quarter of 2007, it was operating a fleet of 111 aircraft, a mix of various Boeing and Airbus models, which were leased to 48 customers in 27 countries. Collectively, the aircraft Aircastle manages are worth a total of $3.5 billion.

Aircastle spends a lot of time hunting for high-value aircraft to add to its air wing. Most of its purchases are 5- to 15-year-old

GR (Goodrich Corp.) NYSE · © StockCharts.com
14-Sep-2007 · **Op** 64.75 **Hi** 65.72 **Lo** 64.62 **Cl** 65.13 **Vol** 801.1K **Chg** -0.07 (-0.11%) ▾

ɪↀ GR (Daily) 65.13
···EMA(50) 61.81
—EMA(100) 59.44

Goodrich joined the ecosystem late. Daily
bars show a clear 50/100 MA crossover buy
signal in Oct. '06, then repeated new
opportunities on pullbacks and breakouts.
Shares rose 65% in 10 months.

Figure 6-5

U.S. jets that can be bought on the cheap, fixed up, and quickly
leased out. Think of it as searching for a Boeing 767 on a very
big clearance rack. Sure, it's not the latest model. And maybe
you had to look for it in somebody's aircraft storage facility out
in the Mojave Desert. But after replacing some upholstery, fix-
ing up the galley, and updating the avionics suite in the cockpit,
it can be a hot item.

This is especially true given the increasing demand for new
planes. As airlines returned to profitability worldwide, they told
reporters that they want to expand their operations with more frequent service and new routes. New aircraft orders perked up and
aircraft manufacturers' order books swelled, forcing many airlines
to turn to aircraft leasing as a stopgap alternative.

As you would expect, this has resulted in increased leasing rates;
they nearly doubled from 2003 to 2007. Aircastle managed to

bump up its average lease rate by 22 percent in 2007, and its fleet was fully contracted out with an average term of six years.

But the most important chapters of the Aircastle story are yet to be written, as production of the 787 Dreamliner won't really start ramping in a serious way until 2010, and that is when this lessor will really kick into gear. A majority of the new orders have been placed by airlines based in Asia and the Middle East, while American and European buyers have lagged behind. Through mid-2007, there were only 995 new planes for Western airlines on Boeing's order books, and most were replacement planes, not expansionary additions. By all measures, there simply will not be enough new jets to go around once the profitability cycle turns and U.S. carriers decide to buy en masse. And that is a real anomaly—more than worthy of putting Aircastle into our Boeing ecosystem.

Once you are aware of a story like that, the news pops out at you. Early in 2007, American Airlines announced that it wanted to push ahead its order for 47 Boeing 737s by four years, to a 2009–2012 delivery. American operates an older fleet of McDonnell Douglas MD-80s, which have higher fuel consumption than the new 737. Crude prices have begun moving higher, and the thought of being stuck with archaic, fuel-guzzling aircraft was scaring air carriers.

To prepare, Aircastle committed to acquire $1.3 billion in aircraft in 2007, and another $500 million in 2008—mostly from Boeing. Although management publicly expects $2.5 billion in total acquisitions over the next two years, if you add it all up, it looks as if something north of $3.3 billion is more likely. So you can see why you might have wished to trade Aircastle as part of this group, and there were many opportunities in 2007 after its initial public offering. This was primarily a dividend play, as the shares yielded

AYR (Aircastle Ltd.) NYSE   © StockCharts.com
14-Sep-2007   **Op** 33.74 **Hi** 34.00 **Lo** 33.33 **Cl** 33.45 **Vol** 358.5K **Chg** +0.16 (+0.48%)▲

Aircastle traded well after Aug. 07 IPO until a sell signal in Aug. '07. ... On recovery in Sept. '07, shares regained their uptrend: a new buy opportunity.

Figure 6-6

7.7 percent per year, but it offered plenty of chances to play it for capital appreciation too. (See Figure 6-6.)

Precision Castparts

Oregon-based Precision Castparts (PCP) emerged as a vital member of the 787 ecosystem very early in the process, as it had been a key Boeing supplier for many years. The company produces complex metal components, castings, forgings, and fasteners for aircraft as well as metal processing solutions. Its shares rose sixfold during the initial planning and preproduction stages of the Dreamliner, again before a single plane had ever been built and shipped to a customer. In the process, the company grew to be an $18 billion metal processing titan. As you can see in Figure 6-7, numerous pullbacks and breakouts arose in the weekly chart, all of which were appropriate for daily traders' interest.

PCP (Precision Castparts Corp.) NYSE   ® StockCharts.com
14-Sep-2007   **Op** 129.07 **Hi** 134.26 **Lo** 124.36 **Cl** 131.71 **Vol** 6.3M **Chg** +4.04 (+3.16%) ▲

Precision Castparts emerged as a key ecosystem member and traded beautifully for 4+ years with regular pullbacks and breakouts to permit new entries and adds.

Figure 6-7

BE Aerospace

Florida-based aircraft cabin interior manufacturer BE Aerospace sells both to airframe manufacturers like Boeing and directly to the airlines, which may wish to add their own superpremium or tourist-class seating arrangements to planes. It also makes a line of food preparation and storage equipment, lighting, and cabinetry products. It was well known that Boeing would choose BE for its interiors early in the process, and BE's shares rose sevenfold from 2004 through 2007. But as you can see in Figure 6-8, in 2006 and 2007 alone, BEAV shares nearly doubled as they rose in an ideal stair-step pattern for active daily traders.

I could go on and on with the Dreamliner ecosystem, but I think you get the idea. Once a big idea is firmly imprinted on the mind of the market, you can search for component makers, specialty

BEAV (BE Aerospace, Inc.) Nasdaq GS   © StockCharts.com
14-Sep-2007   **Op** 38.43 **Hi** 39.40 **Lo** 38.08 **Cl** 39.13 **Vol** 779.6K **Chg** +0.28 (+0.72%) ▲

BE Aerospace traded in an ideal
stairstep pattern in 2006 and 2007,
pulling back repeatedly to its 50- or
200-day MA for entries and adds.

Figure 6-8

finance companies, and the like to take advantage of that idea. This reduces the number of industries in which you need to become an expert and constantly provides you with stocks to play that are under accumulation by the largest institutions in the business. Now let's move on to a couple more ecosystems that emerged in the middle of the 2000s.

Corn Industrial Complex

After decades of decline and disrespect, corn suddenly became the hottest commodity in America in 2007. No longer just an ear to eat during the summer with salt and a square of butter, it was considered the answer to all the biggest problems of the day, from energy independence to global warming. Politicians praised it, Wall Street supported it, foreigners envied it, and farmers couldn't plant enough of it. America got yellow fever—an absolutely textbook anomaly—so you just knew that there had to be a way for cynical city folk to make a buck off it.

Check this out: as late as March 2007, the federal government reported that U.S. farmers intended to plant 90.5 million acres of corn that spring, which was the greatest amount of corn acreage since 95.5 million acres were planted in 1944. It was a 15 percent increase over the 2006 acreage of 78.3 million. Although every farm state indicated that it would grow more corn, the biggest boost was reported occur in the Southeast, where growers planned to switch from cotton. Elsewhere, farmers told reporters that they would switch tens of thousands of acres over from wheat and soybeans.

In plain English, that meant that there was a ton of corn on the way—and the boom has had a lot of unintended consequences that may not fit well with the primary agenda of those who believe in its role as a "green" alternative to imports of foreign oil and gas.

The driver for the corn frenzy was a huge boost in government support for the production of ethanol, a fuel that can take the place of gasoline in many cars. The Renewable Fuels Association pegged current annual U.S. ethanol production at 5.6 billion gallons, but it observes that an additional 6.4 billion gallons of capacity is either under construction or in development.

Now here is where the numbers get interesting. Bank of America analysts figured that ethanol production would jump to 10 billion gallons per year in 2010, or double the level of 2006. The analysts believe that this increase would require the production of an additional 2.25 billion bushels of corn per year, or about 21 percent of the entire 2006 harvest of 10.5 billion bushels. The production of corn outstripped the added demand in mid-2007. But Bank of America analysts said they figured that the supply-demand balance would shift over the next year, pushing corn prices up by $1.50 or more by 2008. That would put prices well above the record levels of $4 per bushel last seen in 1995.

The reason equity investors should have taken notice of news that normally only a commodity futures trader would care about was that every $1.50 increase in prices adds around $405,000 in annual income to a typical 2,000-acre farm. It would mean a real secular change to the farm belt, allowing farmers to buy more seeds, pesticides, and equipment—and lifting the value of everything from midwestern residential property to banks, retailers, and seeds.

In other words, it was easy to come to the conclusion that the new corn industrial complex would become a major nexus of investment and of success in the Midwest at a time when the manufacturing economy was disappearing. It was morning in Des Moines, investors.

If you doubted that such a big shift could really occur, all you needed to do was cast your mind ahead a year and consider the importance of Iowa to the presidential aspirations of a burgeoning field of both Democrats and Republicans. In an attempt to woo the farm families whose support at caucuses will make or break many campaigns, congressmen in the race were bending over backward to funnel federal grants and subsidies to the Corn Belt.

I hesitate to comment that they were all ears, because that's just a cheap joke, but what else can you say about someone like Sen. John McCain, an Arizona lawmaker who had long complained about corn and ethanol subsidies, suddenly trying to cozy up to the cobs? In November 2003, *Fortune* quoted McCain as saying, "Ethanol is a product that would not exist if Congress didn't create an artificial market for it. No one would be willing to buy it. . . . Ethanol does nothing to reduce fuel consumption, nothing to increase our energy independence, nothing to improve air quality."

But by the middle of 2006, his tone had changed, according to an Associated Press report. "I support ethanol, and I think it is a vital alternative energy source not only because of our dependency on foreign oil but its greenhouse gas reduction effects," he said in a speech in Iowa.

McCain's main beef, besides the subsidies, had been that ethanol produces less energy than the oil and gas used to generate it. And despite his flip-flop, he was largely correct. Not only does the corn refining process use a stunning amount of energy and produce a lot of toxic residue, but corn also happens to demand a lot more fertilizer and pesticides than wheat, cotton, and soybeans. It also has the effect of cutting way down on the amount of soybeans available for another key alternative energy source: biodiesel.

When capitalism combines with cronyism and do-goodism, there's no stopping the train, however. *Fortune* reported that more investment money poured into Iowa in 2006 than into New York, a state with six times the population, and that the unemployment rate there is essentially negligible, at less than 3.5 percent. Does that not scream investible anomaly?

The best way for equity investors to play the corn rush was clearly through companies that make fertilizer, seeds, and pesticides—the corn industrial ecosystem, as it were. Although most of these companies were already up a lot by the time this news hit in early 2007, many were still undervalued and had a long way to go. The market for fertilizer was pretty constrained, as farmers needed up to 20 percent more than usual to support the increase of 10 million acres of plantings, and environmental issues have cut the amount of phosphate and nitrogen produced. Corn uses nearly 50 percent more nitrogen per acre than cotton and 22 times more than the amount needed by soybeans. Corn already accounts for 40 percent of total U.S. fertilizer demand, so you had to figure that demand for all that stinky stuff was going to grow exponentially.

Now you can see how reading the news carefully leads to the discovery of anomalies, and then catapults you forward into determining the kinds of companies that can benefit. So now let's look at the companies that did grow exponentially in 2006 and 2007 as a result of the new Corn Age.

Monsanto Co.

Missouri-based Monsanto (MON) very quickly became recognized as the leading company of the corn boom. It was the Boeing of the Farm Belt, pumping out innovative brands through its Seeds and Genomics unit brands Dekalb and Asgrow. It also provided other seed companies with intellectual property, such as genetic material and lab-created traits for their own seed brands. Monsanto manufactured the leading herbicide, Roundup, and kept its growth path fertile by buying major companies to broaden its line, such as Delta & Pine Land Co. and Agroeste Sementes. By the middle of 2003, it was becoming clear that corn would ultimately become a very important fuel crop in the United States—not just a food. Monsanto scientists developed products that included a feature called "trait stacking," in which weed and pest control was bred into the seeds. The key product was YieldGard VT, which maximized yields and protection from insects. For farmers planting solely for ethanol, moreover, Monsanto developed Processor Preferred hybrids that helped maximize the amount of fuel contained in each stalk.

As you can see in Figure 6-9, which shows weekly bars, Monsanto shares doubled from 2003 to 2004, but it was just getting going. The further progress it made shows very clearly how vital it is for active traders not just to add on pullbacks when a major new product ecosystem is discovered, but also to add on major breakouts. Every time that Monsanto shares have moved sideways for a few months, they have ultimately intersected with their rising 50-week moving average and then been bought avidly by bulls. Through the middle of 2007, this pace was not abating, and considering that earnings have been strong, the pace could well continue through the rest of the decade.

Figure 6-9

Deere & Co.

You can't have an agricultural boom without tractors, and Deere & Co. (DE) is the leading U.S. brand. Drive anywhere in the midwestern part of the country, and you will see its familiar green and gold shield and hear its radio ads vowing that, "Nothing runs like a Deere." The company has four business segments in the ag space, selling mighty pieces of moving machinery like tillers, soil preparers, hay and forage equipment, and irrigation equipment. When you really drill into its Web site, you can see that Deere has been a fantastic innovator in every phase of the business, creating new "air seeders," "box drills," "drawn planters," and the like to help farmers maximize every inch of their acreage and every minute of their time.

The shares are up more than threefold since 2003, but the most exciting vertical push higher for Deere came once the full extent of the ethanol boom started to dawn on investors in late 2006. Following the soft spot for stocks in June and July 2006, Deere shares gained traction, if you will, and went on to double over the next 12 months. As you can see in Figure 6-10, the stock touched its 100-week moving average and then never looked back. Although it's a large-cap stock with 221 million shares outstanding, it traded just like a small-cap momentum stock, repeatedly bouncing off of its 13-week moving average on consolidations before breaking out again and moving higher. Once again, traders were buying both consolidations and breakouts to pyramid up this key player in the corn and ethanol ecosystem.

Syngenta AG

You had to recognize that the corn and ethanol boom had gone international when you observed the success of European seed and

DE (Deere & Co.) NYSE   @ StockCharts.com
14-Sep-2007   **Op** 136.74 **Hi** 140.52 **Lo** 134.30 **Cl** 137.93 **Vol** 11.7M **Chg** +2.07 (+1.52%) ▲

Deere shares tractored into their
100-week MA in Aug. '06, and then
took off, touching the 13-week MA on
each consolidation to permit traders
to add to positions on a 100% move.

Figure 6-10

pesticide manufacturers like big caps BASF (BF) and Syngenta AG
(SYT). The latter, based in Switzerland, was created in 2000 when
European pharmaceutical companies Novartis and AstraZeneca
merged their agricultural businesses to create a separate entity. The
new entity traded sideways for 2½ years until the corn boom started
to catch fire, and then its sales, earnings, and margins began to sky-
rocket. Syngenta became well known for its crop protection, seeds,
and basic plant science, but its specialty was herbicides, insecti-
cides, and fungicides focused on controlling weeds, pests, and dis-
ease. In mid-2004 it acquired a private Nebraska company called
Golden Harvest that owned 4 percent of the U.S. corn seed market and 3 percent of the U.S. soybean seed market. Combining that
with its acquisition of the Garst seeds unit of British agribusiness
giant Advanta, it became clear that Syngenta would zoom its market share up to 15 percent of corn seeds and 13 percent of soybean

seeds. That was good enough for investors, as they ramped Syngenta shares up fourfold over the next four years after the purchase was finalized.

As you can see in Figure 6-11, Syngenta shares let us know that they had entered high-momentum mode by trading up and consolidating repeatedly at their 13-week moving average. After longer consolidations, the shares came into their 50-week moving average, but the bulls never let them stay there for very long. The huge move in the mid-2000s is another great example of the value of finding stocks that are in the process of being re-rated higher as they benefit from participation in a successful fundamental ecosystem.

CECO Environmental

The corn and ethanol boom had a wide variety of tendrils in the economy. One of the more emblematic examples was CECO Envi-

Figure 6-11

ronmental (CECE), a century-old company focused on plant fil-
tration systems under the brand names Kirk & Blum, Busch International, and H.M. White. It turned out that all of the ethanol plants
being built across the Midwest needed heavy-duty filters to capture,
clean, and destroy airborne contaminants and prevent air pollution
damage to workers and industrial neighborhoods. As Figure 6-12
depicts, the stock took off in 2005 in tandem with the ethanol boom,
as well as on word of new business in China and Eastern Europe.
Revenue, cash flow, earnings, and margins all caught fire as the
company's backlog of business exploded to record levels.

This small-cap stock rose along its 13-week moving average during momentum swings higher, like many of the other corn-complex stocks we have looked at, and then never traded below its
60-week moving average during multimonth consolidations. Why
did I use the 60-week moving average here instead of the 50 or the

Figure 6-12

30? Every stock develops its own trading rhythm as it becomes beholden to a particular sponsor in the institutional investment community. If a standard moving average does not contain two of the recent lows, then lengthen the periods until you find the right level of support. Once an average has held a strong ecosystem-linked stock twice, it is likely to hold it again until the linkage is completely erased.

Terra Nitrogen

Iowa-based fertilizer producer Terra Nitrogen, which you may recall from Chapter 2, became one of the poster children for the corn-complex advance once it broke out of a two-year consolidation at $31 in late 2006. The stock was previously best known for its high dividend, which ranged from 7 percent to 12 percent as the stock price changed. Demand for Terra's nitrogen products rose dramatically because farmers knew that corn requires many times the amount of nitrogen fertilizer needed by the crops it replaced, such as cotton. In 2006 and 2007, quarterly earnings were up 200 percent over prior years, and on a fiscal year basis, earnings were up by more than 10,000 percent. Terra's ammonia and urea ammonia nitrate solutions were manufactured primarily at a plant in Oklahoma, and they sold primarily in the Corn Belt. Once traders glommed onto this idea, it ran like wildfire.

The key moment for the stock came in October 2006, when shares rose above their one-year consolidation zone at $30. After that, you just needed to hold on for the ride, as low-risk entry points were relatively few and far between. As you have seen with many of our ecosystem plays, consolidations were bought consistently at a particular support level characterized by an exponential moving average. The move in this case was so sharp that instead of buying on the 13- or 21-week moving average, buyers came in repeatedly on the 9-week line. Although the stock looked way overbought for months, successful traders realize that these group ecosystem momentum moves, if surprising enough to the majority of investors, can be as explosive as a match lit to a truck filled with ammonium fertilizer. Once this kind of advance has been established as the pattern, any one-week decline down and through that support level becomes both a sell signal and a sell short signal. In the case of Terra Nitrogen, a 300 percent up move was quickly followed by a 40 percent down move. That decline was contained at the most common support line of all, the 50-week or 200-day moving average, in mid-August. What happened next shocked a lot of people, but not us: the stock bounced back by 70 percent again in one month.

Now that is some serious corn pop.

TNH (Terra Nitrogen Co. L P) NYSE   ® StockCharts.com
14-Sep-2007   **Op** 113.95 **Hi** 117.68 **Lo** 104.05 **Cl** 113.59 **Vol** 1.9M **Chg** +3.17 (+2.87%) ▲
TNH (Weekly) 113.59
EMA(50) 71.62
EMA(150) 41.93
EMA(9) 102.32

Terra Nitrogen rose sixfold from Sept. '06 to July '07 as a key corn fertilizer play. The 9-week EMA gave traders entry points on consolidations, and ultimately a sell signal (down arrow). Next buy signal came on decline to 50-week EMA.

Figure 6-13

Potash Corp. of Saskatchewan

One of the most wildly successful corn-complex fertilizer providers also has the oddest name: Potash Corp. of Saskatchewan (POT). Its product is so humble, so simple, and so utterly ordinary that many traders may have legitimately looked at the chart in shock that it could be enjoying a move of such gigantic proportions. From 2003 through mid-2007, the shares were up more than 900 percent. And what was this amazing product—a music-playing sensation, an amazing semiconductor, software that cured the great ills of our time? Nope, just plain old potash—nitrogen and phosphate dug out of seven mines in Saskatchewan and New Brunswick in Canada. Potash is a key component of fertilizer and animal feed, and it made Potash Corp. the largest fertilizer company in the world, with a $28 billion market capitalization. Considering that its operations produce something like a fifth of all global potash capacity, it is essentially the Saudi Arabia of fertilizer.

From a trading perspective, once you recognized that Potash is El Primero when it comes to worldwide fertilizer supply, the decision to trade became pretty easy. As shown in Figure 6-14, shares jumped right away in 2003 along with the rising demand for agricultural products, came into their 100-week moving average for a nine-month rest from late 2005 through mid-2006, but then absolutely ramped in the fourth quarter of 2006 and went on to triple. In this case, the stock quickly established its 13- and 20-week moving averages as key support, providing numerous opportunities for anomaly-focused active traders to exploit interest in the corn industrial complex.

Well, I think you get the idea by now: corn. It's what's for dinner. And lunch. And breakfast—at least for traders wishing to feast

POT (Potash Corp. Saskatch, Inc.) NYSE @ StockCharts.com
14-Sep-2007 **Op** 88.00 **Hi** 90.69 **Lo** 85.66 **Cl** 89.01 **Vol** 9.1M **Chg** +1.59 (+1.82%) ▲

↑↓ POT (Weekly) 89.01
··· MA(100) 45.11
··· MA(20) 78.31

Potash Corp. of Saskatchewan was
another big-cap at the forefront of
the corn complex. Shares rose
ninefold over five years, offering
active traders entries on the 100-
and 20-week MAs.

Figure 6-14

on high-profit momentum moves with minimum risk. At least until ethanol is discredited as a fuel and Iowa diminishes as a key battleground for members of Congress and senators running for president.

Plastic Fantastic

The most famous career advice ever given to the baby-boom generation came in a single word in a 1967 movie: *plastics.* It was supposed to be funny, but it turned out to be prescient. Since the premiere of *The Graduate*, shares of plastics giant DuPont (DD) are up almost 2,400 percent, double the return of the broad market.

Forty years later, strangely enough, you could easily give the same advice, as the makers of everything from MP3 players and golf shirts to cars, corn, computers, and container ships are turning to plastics and advanced chemicals to cut weight, extend life, and improve durability. Another big blow for the primacy of polymers came in late 2006, when federal regulators approved the use of silicone in breast implants after a two-decade ban. It's good-bye wonders of nature, hello miracles of science. Synthetics or bust.

The beauty of plastic is more than skin deep, but it's so ubiquitous that we take it for granted. Consider that when you're marveling at the iPod, you're apt to praise its rich sound and sharp video. But really, how about that lovely case and vivid LCD screen? The device's smooth finish, light weight, bright color, and remarkable strength would not be possible without significant advances in the development of low-cost materials.

It's fashionable in some circles to complain about chemicals in food, water, and hair products, but just try to live without them. Engineers in labs have developed new pesticides and seeds that increase crop yields without poisoning the food chain, chewing gum that lasts longer and whitens teeth, soft polyester shirts that wick sweat away from skin at the gym, bombproof glass, and spongy but indestructible turf for kids' soccer games. The Stone Age was cool and everything for Neanderthals, but count me as happy to live in the Plastic Age.

Much of the time, the great work being done by chemical companies goes on unnoticed by investors unless a plant blows up and the toxic plume kills a thousand people. And yet that is the point: the new plastic era emerged without anyone ever writing a *Time* cover story. An entire ecosystem to build, feed, distribute, and use plastic emerged right under our noses. Fortunes were made, and destinies changed. It's more than merely the sort of sector move that I described in Chapter 2. Plastic, synthetics, and adhesives are everywhere and nowhere, and it's been incumbent upon traders to pay attention and play the group rather than look at each stock here and there at random.

To see how the market fails to recognize the importance of such hidden ecosystems, just take a look at the case of Celanese (CE), a Texas manufacturer of synthetic products that are the secret ingredients in many high-performance paints, electronics, detergents, lubricants, and even baked goods (see Figure 6-15). The company, which was founded in the 1920s, was taken private in 2003 by Blackstone Group, restructured, and then reoffered to the public early in 2006. By late 2006 it was well on the road to paying off its heavy debt, earning $500 million in 12 months on $6.5 billion in sales. Income was growing at a solid pace in the low double digits. Yet because of its checkered history, the stock traded at a forward-looking price-earnings multiple of around 7. That's the kind of valuation that the market typically gives a commodity chemical

Figure 6-15

maker, which is what Celanese was before being reshaped into a specialty polymers manufacturer.

The company suffered from the impression among many investors that it was overly exposed to the struggling automotive industry, but its largest customer in that industry was actually powerhouse Toyota, which had announced plans to ramp up U.S. production. Taking all this into consideration, I forecast that Celanese should have traded at a price-earnings multiple of more like 10 to 12 in a year as the market came around to my variant perception. If so, then applying this to a 2008 estimate of $3.19 took me to a forecast of $32 when the shares were $21. Instead, the shares actually leaped to $42, which was a double.

Ultrapar Participacoes SA

I could showcase a dozen more companies that surround, assist, and supply the plastic and synthetics business—all discovered via the Stock Screener tool at MSN Money described in Chapter 5— but instead I want to give you just one more. Ultrapar Participacoes, based in São Paulo, Brazil, is an example of how the ecosystem for a major economic development these days typically spreads out worldwide. One of the company's units is the largest producer of ethylene oxide and its derivatives in South America, which means that its products show up in paint, detergent, cosmetics, plastic packaging, textiles, and much more. The company also has a unit that transports, stores, and distributes chemicals and liquefied natural gas around South America. All told, it services something like 30,000 companies and 10 million households. When you are looking for trades in an industrial ecosystem, it really pays to look in regions of the world that are outperforming the United States—economically, anyway—as you can benefit from a double dose of positive vibes. In this case, picking up the stock upon its move over its critical 21-week exponential moving average, and on every dip back to that level, yielded a series of trades in 2006 and 2007 whose profit approached 100 percent. (See Figure 6-16.)

Pedal to the Metal

In the category of weirdest financial news stories of 2007, Philippine food conglomerate San Miguel announced in August that it planned to spin off its 117-year-old namesake brewery and use the proceeds to expand into mining. Chairman Eduardo Cojuangco said that the new underground venture, along with investments in infrastructure construction and real estate, would be the company's "new engines of growth."

Figure 6-16

Now think about that for a moment. If you can't make money selling ice-cold beer in a tropical steam bath like Manila, you probably aren't the shiniest 7-iron in the golf bag. So you almost certainly don't belong in the cutthroat world of metals and mining. Yet such was the fervor among executives of major industrial companies in the mid-2000s to grow faster, bigger, and stronger through investments in basic materials. It was almost as if ores the world over were casting a magnetic spell over boardrooms, luring otherwise intelligent managers to throw shareholder funds down holes in the ground and into blast furnaces that not too long ago were considered the last places any sane executive would wish to invest. Did companies go mad, or had the rules radically changed?

By the looks of the premiums that are being paid for rock and refining assets, it looks as if a whole new rule book has emerged, as governments in Asia, Eastern Europe, and South America threw off the chains of centralized economic control and allowed local entrepreneurs and mayors to industrialize and urbanize at breathtaking speed. Fueled by high middle-class savings rates, low interest rates, and new debt concoctions by financial engineers, unfettered businesspeople had the money to push their countries from the nineteenth century to the twenty-first century without a stop anywhere in the twentieth—building highways, factories, power plants, apartments, and shipyards everywhere in sight. In China alone, copper imports were up 52 percent in the first half of 2007. These were all vivid anomalies that active traders needed to latch onto with a vengeance.

In this period, large international metal miners and processors pulled out all the stops to lock up capacity anywhere they could find it—and paid record amounts to make deals. There was a sense that they hadn't a moment to lose in the race to hollow out and pave over the planet. But there was a cunning strategy here as well, as consolidation has created regional monopolies that can slash capacity to prevent profit-flattening price wars and rid the industry of cyclicality. Check out the mind-blowing size of a few deals of the era:

- British mining conglomerate Rio Tinto offered $38 billion in August 2007 for Canadian bauxite miner and aluminum smelter Alcan. Alcan traded exactly flat from 1997 through late 2005—a seemingly useless hunk of shiny junk—before shooting up 220 percent in the past 18 months.
- Brazilian steelmaker Gerdau Ameristeel offered $4.2 billion in July 2007 for Texas steel-mill operator Chaparral. Chaparral was up 800 percent from its initial public offering in mid-2005 to the date when Gerdau believed that it was a must-buy.
- Arizona mining conglomerate Freeport McMoRan Copper & Gold paid $25.9 billion in 2006 for copper miner Phelps Dodge, a company whose shares had languished for a decade before tripling from 2004 through late 2006.
- Swiss mining conglomerate Xstrata paid $22.5 billion for Canadian miner Falconbridge in 2006 after warding off several other buyers in a bidding war.
- Brazilian mining conglomerate Companhia Vale do Rio Doce bought Canadian nickel miner Inco for $17 billion in 2006 after another bidding war.
- Dutch steelmaker Mittal (MT) bought Luxembourg steel titan Arcelor in 2006 for $33.5 billion. It's now known as Arcelor Mittal.

The list goes on and on, but you get the idea. It's natural to conclude that every small and midsize metal miner and refiner in North America had become fair game for big global resource predators whose coffers are overflowing from the profits derived from skyrocketing commodity prices. As an independent active investor, you could almost say that because these companies were all in play, they were what golfers call *gimmes*, or tap-in putts—purchases that couldn't go wrong, given enough time.

There would be occasional corrections, but as long as you didn't hear reports that inventories of the commodities in question were rising materially, it was fair to guess that companies in the industry were solid bets. Copper prices were up 360 percent in the past four years, while aluminum doubled and nickel was up more than 1,100 percent. Hot-rolled steel prices firmed at $575 a ton in September 2007, up 225 percent from $175 a ton, the industry benchmark in 2001. The merry-go-round would end eventually, but while it lasted, it was a brilliant example of N power creating value.

So which were the right stocks to play? They were popping out right and left in the news to anyone paying attention, as it seemed that every major and minor miner, distributor, shipper, and equipment provider was mentioned as either an acquisition target or a buyer. Scans in the online Screener at MSN Money or in the Industry Analyzer at BigCharts.com for fast-growing companies in the metals complex provided a start for traders looking for plays, as did a review of charts in the Industry Analyzer tool at BigCharts.com or the Market Carpet of StockCharts.com.

For a more fundamental approach to understanding the entire ecosystem—and not just the sector—you needed to visit the Web sites of specialty trade magazines, which contained endless stories on the companies peripheral to the big dogs. In the second and third quarters of 2007, for instance, there were repeated stories in the papers about the notion that Pittsburgh aluminum giant Alcoa, trading at $40 at the time, would be bought in the next year or two. Australian mining and energy heavyweight BHP Billiton (Figure 6-17), which is five times Alcoa's size, was expected to be a buyer. But equally magnificent in their execution in the business were BHP's rival based in the United Kingdom, Rio Tinto (RTP), and its rival in Brazil, Compahia Vale do Rio Doce (RIO). From 2003 through September 2007, Billiton rose 500 percent, Rio Tinto rose 300 percent, and Vale do Rio Doce rose 1,110 percent to whopping market capitalizations in excess of $100 billion.

Likewise, at the same time there were repeated stories about the potential of Ohio steelmaker AKSteel as a target. But like most of the companies in this ecosystem, there was much more than just a

Figure 6-17

rising stock price at stake. There was also tremendous earnings growth. In the summer quarter of 2007, AKSteel reported that profits in the second quarter had tripled from a year earlier on higher prices and shipment volume. It was trading at a forward price-earnings multiple of 16 at a time when its earnings were growing at an annualized pace of better than 25 percent a year, which made it cheap despite a 530 percent advance in the previous three years. (See Figure 6-18.)

But it's really the industrial metals ecosystem that I want you to pay attention to, as that's what distinguishes this idea from an ordinary sector play. Included are copper miners such as Rio Tinto (RTP) and Southern Peru (PCU), transporters such as Excel Maritime (EXM), integrated steel giants such as Mittal Arcelor (MT), steel mill equipment providers like GrafTech Inc., and structural steel manufacturers like Chapparal (CHAP).

Figure 6-18

Southern Peru Copper

Southern Peru offers an ideal example of the value of broadening out beyond the most obvious ideas to find stocks that trade with a great institutional rhythm. Based in Arizona, the company operates four open-pit mines and three underground mines in Peru and Mexico. Though its name is not well known in the United States, it claims to have the world's largest reserves of copper. Its operations also include smelting and refining, as well as railroads and port storage facilities.

When copper prices were low, the stock stagnated. But when prices of the red metal began levitating amid ferocious demand from China to build out its urban plumbing and electrical systems, the stock began to charge higher. It broke out of a long consolidation late in 2005 and then hugged its 9-week exponential moving average en route to a 500 percent advance. Occasionally the 9-week support gave way, but the stock was then always supported at its 34-week moving average.

Let me repeat that as an active independent trader, you need to determine where institutional investors are coming into each individual stock. Don't get locked into a particular moving average. Be flexible and nimble. Regular purchases of Southern Peru on its rhythmical touches of the support levels shown in Figure 6-19 brought tremendous profits despite a long period of skepticism from most major brokerage analysts.

Arcelor Mittal

Arcelor Mittal became one of my favorite metal ecosystem plays in 2006 when it became clear that its growth path was wildly underappreciated by investors. Started by the Mittal family in

PCU (Southern Peru Copper Corp.) NYSE © StockCharts.com
14-Sep-2007 **Op** 105.00 **Hi** 110.64 **Lo** 102.06 **Cl** 110.17 **Vol** 7.9M **Chg** +5.52 (+5.27%) ▲
PCU (Weekly) 110.17
···EMA(9) 102.57
···EMA(34) 86.58

Southern Peru Copper soared fivefold
from 2005 to mid-2007, hugging its
9-week MA except for a few brief
excursions to its 34-week MA. The
9-week MA pattern was set by late 2005,
letting traders get the rhythm early.

Figure 6-19

India, the company became a global superstar by making shrewd purchases of rival steelmakers in countries around the world. Founder Lakshmi Mittal found ways to cuts costs and raise prices repeatedly, and he truly transformed the company by buying European goliath Arcelor in mid-2006 after a lengthy proxy and political battle.

The value of the combination of the two firms was again underappreciated, despite the fact that it controlled 10 percent of total world steel production, not to mention its own coal mines and transportation system, and therefore could finally start to squeeze the cyclicality of the industry's demand and price cycle. It mostly produces finished and semifinished carbon steel products like sheet steel, plate steel, bars, rods, and structural slabs. Fretting over the company reached its zenith in the summer of 2006, but you'll note in Figure 6-20 that the selling found sup-

MT (Arcelor Mittal) NYSE   @ StockCharts.com
14-Sep-2007   **Op** 63.61 **Hi** 68.63 **Lo** 62.06 **Cl** 68.25 **Vol** 9.7M **Chg** +4.27 (+6.67%) ▲
↑↓ MT (Weekly) 68.25
···EMA(13) 62.71
···EMA(100) 44.91

Arcelor Mittal doubled from 2005 to 2007, but traded somewhat erratically. Note that when a stock in a hot ecosystem starts hugging a short-term MA like the 13 (in late 2006) for several weeks, the new momentum persists for months.

Figure 6-20

port at the rising 100-week average, just as it had in late 2005. Not too long after that, the stock lifted a notch in momentum and began trading up along its 13-week moving average. That rhythm became clear by late 2006, allowing active traders to buy repeatedly in 2007 and ride the stock to gains of at least 100 percent. Short-term profits would have been taken on a decline down through the 13-week moving average in July 2007, but shares quickly regained their composure, leaving long-term positions intact.

I think you get probably get the picture now with the metals ecosystem. Once again, the telltale signs of an ecosystem move were the emergence of a wide range of stocks in the core and periphery of an industry in response to new fundamental demand and soaring earnings and margins.

Music to Our Ears

I have saved the best for the next to last. For the greatest recent example of the value the market puts on the creation of new products and the improvement of old ones comes from the folks at Apple Inc. (AAPL) in Cupertino, California. After years of doing business the wrong way—with executives merely making minor, incremental changes to an outdated lineup of products—Apple caught innovation fever in the early 2000s and created the iMac line of personal computers and the iPod line of personal music players. These first forays because runaway successes and were the harbingers of even greater things to come.

What really demands respect is the way the company grew beyond its roots as a niche maker of educational and graphic designer computer hardware and software to become the era's preeminent provider of consumer electronics. This shift amounted to a massively powerful anomaly. The change was formally recognized on January 9, 2007, when the company's name was changed from Apple Computer to just Apple, and, as you can see in Figure 6-21, that moment itself led to a tremendous 70 percent move higher in the shares.

This new product blitz was driven by the installation of a new management team (there's that word again). Steve Jobs reclaimed the reins of Apple in 1998 and saved it from certain oblivion. The "prodigal son" element of the tale adds a dramatic flair too, as Steve was banished from Apple in the 1980s and left to wander through the wilderness of Silicon Valley. To save Apple from the abyss, the turtle-necked messiah harnessed the element of change and brought the company's unique taste for attractive, user-focused design and usability to new segments of the marketplace.

AAPL (Apple, Inc.) Nasdaq GS   © StockCharts.com
14-Sep-2007   **Op** 136.99 **Hi** 139.40 **Lo** 133.75 **Cl** 138.81 **Vol** 169.3M **Chg** +7.04 (+5.34%) ▲
ᵗⱼ↓ AAPL (Weekly) 138.81
···EMA(100) 88.11
···EMA(34) 115.36

Apple shares repeatedly
consolidated and broke out from '03
to '07 as the company's power to
surprise with new products and
blowout earnings provided active
traders with numerous entry points.

Figure 6-21

What started with the iMac continued with the various iterations of the iPod, and the pedigree rolled on to make its mark with the iPhone and Apple TV. All of the devices evinced the company's rediscovered ability to merge robust and intuitive software with sexy, powerful, and thoughtfully designed hardware. It's like 1984 and the debut of the original Macintosh. No other company has been able to control a user's digital experience in such a holistic way, and no other company is so successfully expanding into new areas of the digital experience.

The real genius is that these new product lines eventually revived the fortunes of the company's original business: personal computers. I'm telling you all this as a reminder of what great marketing and salesmanship is all about. It's about finding ways to create a buzz of newness about old products: getting current customers to upgrade and getting new customers to buy for the first time.

Apple does this better than any other company right now, and it bears watching.

It's always interesting to see how well a company engages its customers. You love to see the ones that create a fantastic personal mystique and draw consumers into their mythology, news flow, and emotional web. Apple has managed to do this like no other firm on Earth in recent years, turning mundane product announcements into multimedia news events. Can you imagine that kind of news play for many other companies? I guarantee you that when Hewlett-Packard or Dell puts out a press release on its next round of new products, it does not get front-page treatment in the *Wall Street Journal*, as Apple does.

I have certainly seen Apple's magic engage my own kids. In 2006, when my 11-year-old daughter wanted an MP3 player, she had almost decided to go with the unit of an Apple rival because it had more capacity, features, battery life, and adaptability than the iPod. But then she tried to explain her choice to a friend on the phone, and she couldn't quite feel right. She couldn't explain it. It just felt impersonal, as if it was just an object. It had no marketing buzz. After the call, she turned to me and said, "Daddy, let's just get the iPod." It was then that I realized that Apple had created more than a product. It had created a language that helped kids and other consumers explain something about themselves.

In the past, much of Apple's performance was driven by the iPod/iTunes phenomenon. After all, half of its $19 billion in revenue in 2006 stemmed from digital music. Now that the company's products have become synonymous with digital music, and as the company becomes a force to be reckoned with in the consumer electronics space, it's easy to forget Apple's roots in computing. The

Mac lineup remains critical to the bottom line, as it carries higher prices and larger margins than the company's digital music players. The company's ability to sell computers truly determines its destiny.

Globally, Apple shipped out 1.76 million units of Macs of all sizes and shapes during the fiscal third quarter of 2007, for revenues of $2.53 billion. Sales of Macs were up 36 percent year over year, which was the best quarter ever for the unit. Macs were now selling at four times the growth rate of the PC market in the United States and at 2.5 times the growth rate in the rest of the world. Macs made up something like 9 percent of total PC sales in the United States and 3 percent worldwide in mid-2007—the highest levels ever. Not surprisingly, Apple's share of the computer market has increased. Bear Stearns analysts estimated in August 2007 that Apple's share increased 50 basis points over the prior year, to 2.57 percent. Although it may not seem like much, this is nearly a full percentage point improvement over where the company had been two years ago.

Normally, one might be tempted to write all this off as a bunch of holier-than-thou Mac users upgrading or expanding their arsenal of computers. However likely this may seem, according to Apple, over half of all Mac purchases were to people who are new to the platform. That's right, they were new converts to the realm previously reserved for unshaven graphic artists and schoolteachers. When you think about it, as more people get exposed—via the iPod—to the sexy designs, intuitive user interfaces, and robust software inherent in Apple's products, it's not surprising that curiosity about the Mac lineup would be piqued.

As Apple generates lust among current iPod and Mac owners and turns noncustomers into customers, it has found ways to create new subcategories of products and capture an ever-larger share of its customers' entertainment budget. Great examples of this include the video-enabled iPod and Apple TV, which has created a new industry in the micro-sales of individual television episodes and movies. Who would ever have thought that old episodes of *The A Team* were worth something? I must admit that the idea seemed completely ridiculous to me, but then, I am not the target audience. People who commute a lot on trains, planes, and buses are a terrific audience for these shows. To my teenage son, downloading an episode of some obscure cable TV show like *Psych* onto his iPod and watching it while traveling to a soccer or baseball tournament is totally normal.

This is the force that has made the iTunes service wildly successful. As of September 2007, there were over 110 million active iTunes users, many of whom had made significant investments in their digital media libraries. The service had already sold over 50 million television shows since 2005 and more than 1.3 million movies since late 2006.

Although a number of movie studios, including Paramount Pictures, Disney, and Miramax, are already offering their content, Apple was expected to add to the list over the coming years. Tough antipiracy controls and the large number of users makes iTunes an attractive venue for Hollywood to add incremental revenue; even more so now that Apple's portfolio of video-enabled devices continues to grow.

On the surface, the 2006–2007 period might have seemed like an odd time to be bullish on Apple prospects, with enthusiasm about its new devices at high boil. This was the time when you would normally expect a professional to have urged caution and recommend selling. Yet it cannot escape our notice that Apple's shares were simply not expensive for growth investors because of the company's extreme commitment to N power, and that there were several new catalysts on the horizon.

Throughout the mid-2000s period, in which its shares quadrupled, Apple's embrace of the new as a weapon against competitors like Nokia and Sony showed no signs of slowing or abating. And all the while, it chipped away at the market dominance of archrival Microsoft. Accompanied by a crack team of industrial designers and engineers, Steve Jobs has led one of the most successful flanking maneuvers in the history of industry, all focused on creating new objects for new customers.

Wall Street remained strangely skeptical about all this, which I found reminiscent of Dell back in the 1990s. Starting from a much lower base, Dell ultimately advanced 91,000 percent from January 1990 to December 1999, from a split-adjusted price of around 15 cents to around $52. Apple rose only 190 percent in the 1990s, and through the third quarter of 2007 it was still up only 395 percent in this decade. In both cases it was impossible to put your finger on one place on a chart and say, this is where the appreciation should stop. If you have a solid set of popular products, execute well on making them profitably, and are plugged into the spirit of your times, there are few limits on your success.

The Rich Get Richer, Thank Goodness

The superrich are different from you and me. It's not just that they have more money, it's that they spend more money. Much, much more. In fact, the superrich spend so much more of their mountains of money, according to a new line of thinking among academics, that they may provide a public service by smoothing out the little dents and valleys in the global economy. As scads of Russians, Chinese, Indians, and South Americans have joined the billionaires club as a result of the rise of emerging markets' industrial might, worldwide recessions have become much fewer in number and far slighter in severity than in past decades.

This makes sense, even if it doesn't make you feel better. For just when many average people in the United States or Europe are slowing down their consumption of goods and services because of the loss of a job or a pending home foreclosure, there are an increasing number of superrich worldwide to fill in the spending gap. It's sort of a perverse fulfillment of the trickle-down theory.

Rather than being resentful of the superrich, perhaps we should all be grateful to them. The next time you run into a superrich guy at your local Bentley dealer, give him a hug. The numbers are staggering and almost incomprehensible. According to research by Ajay Kapur, an analyst at Citigroup, the wealthiest 1 million people in the world account for as much spending as 60 million other households. The disparity between the bottom 99 percent and the top 1 percent has made any other class distinctions in the richest countries almost irrelevant. Welcome to the new world "plutonomy," where economic growth is powered by, and largely consumed by, the wealthy few. Now that is a real anomaly worthy of studying for the emergence of an investment ecosystem.

This was useful to know at a time of fears that a decline in U.S. home prices could sink the U.S. economy, as it takes only one new free-spending Mumbai or Moscow zillionaire to make up for tens of thousands of faltering Americans who are missing their mortgage payments. Fortunately, there are plenty more than that in Russia alone. The swift rise in the value of natural gas—sometimes called "blue gold"—as well as nickel, aluminum, and titanium has helped create at least two dozen Russian billionaires and thousands more multimillionaires who are spreading their wealth around.

The *Wall Street Journal* reported that the new "Blingsheviks" were buying castles in Germany, Warhol prints in New York, and polo ponies in Argentina. One in five homes in London's exclusive Mayfair district is now owned by a Russian, according to the *Journal*. A leader in this category is Roman Abramovich, the eleventh richest man in the world, who has three yachts that stretch 161 feet, 282 feet, and 377 feet, respectively, and who has commissioned a fourth that will eclipse the world's largest Arab-owned yacht at 525 feet plus. Sotheby's (BID) sold $3.65 billion worth of fine art at auction last year, 30 percent more than in 2005—and Russian art is a fast-growing category.

There are not a lot of Russian stocks to play in the U.S. markets to take advantage of the newfound Russian wealth, but one that traded well was major wireless services provider Vimpel Communications (VIP). As shown in Figure 6-22, shares of the company—which has emerged as a cellular service leader not just in Russia, but also in Ukraine, Tajikistan, Armenia, Kazakhstan, and Uzbekistan—took off in the fall of 2006. They emerged from a long consolidation to trade up along their 13-week moving average for a year, doubling in value.

China, meanwhile, is now home to 500,000 millionaires who are proud to show off their gold-plated toilets, Versace-designed bedrooms, and driveways loaded with BMWs, Escalades, and Ferraris. In India, where the economy is growing at 8 percent per year, *BusinessWeek* reports that 83,000 people were millionaires in 2007,

VIP (Vimpel Communications) NYSE   © StockCharts.com
14-Sep-2007   **Op** 24.94 **Hi** 27.71 **Lo** 24.55 **Cl** 26.98 **Vol** 16.4M **Chg** +2.29 (+9.28%) ▲

VIP (Weekly) 26.98
EMA(100) 15.16
EMA(13) 22.69

After a one-year consolidation, shares of
Russian cell service provider Vimpel Comm
broke out in mid-2006 and traded up along
their 13-week MA for a double. The sale on
a breakdown in June '07 was followed
quickly by a buy signal on a new high.

Figure 6-22

up 16 percent from two years before. To help them spend their fortunes, Louis Vuitton, Hugo Boss, Valentino, Gucci, and Fendi have opened stores in the major Indian cities.

In the United States, the share of total income going to the richest 1 percent of Americans rose to a record 17.4 percent in 2005. Meanwhile, the average worker's take-home pay, adjusted for inflation, has advanced just 0.3 percent since 2001, while the economy has swelled by 16 percent. If you exclude the value of primary residences, the United States has 2 million people with a net worth of over $1 million, according to Merrill Lynch; including primary residences, the number is around 8 million.

In addition to big yachts and big homes, the superrich are naturally into big jets, big vacations, big jewels, big art, and lots of fancy clothes. So when we look for the investment ecosystem, the plays range from jets to jewelry stores and auctioneers to any consumer items in

Russia. Three obvious plays have been jewelry retailer Tiffany (TIF), leather goods maker Coach (COH), and auctioneer Sotheby's—and all of them traded nicely to all-time highs in mid-2007.

A less well-exploited way to play the plutonomy is through the rapid advance of private jet aircraft. I mean, what's the point of being a billionaire unless you can zoom from your home in Monte Carlo to a meeting in Berlin without ever scuffing your Ferragamos in a public airport? In London alone, the number of private jet journeys has reached 300,000 a year and is growing by 10 percent annually, according to a published report. Some research online showed that the king of the skies in the 10-seat category is the Gulfstream 550, complete with sofa, two beds, and interior panels made from mahogany. No plastic allowed. That and numerous cousins are made by a division of General Dynamics (GD), which traded beautifully throughout much of this period, as shown in Figure 6-23.

Figure 6-23

A much riskier name in the business was Canada-based Bombardier (CA:BBD.A), which makes the Global Express jet, owned by director Steven Spielberg and steel magnate Lakshmi Mittal. The plane can fly between any two points in the world with only one stop, and zooms from New York to Tokyo without a break.

Keep up this kind of trading for a decade and you could buy your own Gulfstream or Global Express. Just remember who helped you, and stop by Seattle to say hi and have a latte sometime.

CONCLUSION

Now it is Saturday—a day of rest. And what a week it has been—exhausting, to be sure, but also lucrative and satisfying. We all know that the capital markets exist to provide companies with the funds they need if they are to expand, hire, produce, and grow. But traders learn that the markets are also the greatest money-making machine ever invented, so long as you learn how to work the levers.

Over the past six chapters, I have shown you numerous straightforward, systematic ways to make the machine work for you as an active trader every day of the week. None of these methods is extremely easy, but nor do any of them require an advanced degree. All you really need in order to succeed are curiosity, energy, a steadfast desire to win, the ability to repress your emotions while appreciating your instincts, and a stubborn streak that won't let you give up. Great traders are born, not made—just like great violinists and great athletes. But just about anyone can learn to be a pretty damned *good* trader—by which I mean a reliably successful trader—by passionately putting in the time to learn and practice.

The cool thing about the learning experience, I hope you'll agree by now, is that it can be incredibly interesting, and even fun. After you've spent your Monday afternoons studying relative strength in the market and discover that steel, copper, specialty chemicals, and fertilizer are all kicking butt in the broad market, you have truly learned something unique about world trade at that point in time. You are like the hawk that has sniffed the breeze, looked several miles down range, and become at one with his environment. The deep study of industry, politics, and culture for the purpose of making financial bets puts you directly in the flow of world events as few other jobs or hobbies will do.

Let's review the whole book briefly now, just to make sure that we're clear on the best plan of attack.

First of all, let me remind you that the *new* style of day trading amounts to active daily trading of equity markets for the purpose of finding successful multiday, multiweek, or multimonth holds. Active day traders are no longer afraid to keep positions overnight, or even over many nights, because they have confidence in their ability to find stocks and options that merit longer holds. Active day traders today recognize that more activity does not bring more success. Only more and better research, more and better conviction, and more and better self-knowledge bring more success. Day trading today means carving out of the day ample amounts of quiet time to discover variant perceptions about industries, companies, and markets that will lead us to take the right positions at the right time, just barely ahead of the crowd.

On Sundays, I recommend that you focus on timing. Look at the major U.S., European, and emerging-market indexes in daily, weekly, and monthly time frames and determine the major trends for each. Be clear, make decisions, write them down, and keep a record. Decide emphatically on Sundays whether you are going to trade primarily from the long side of the market or the short side, and promise to stick with those decisions no matter what new random special situation might arise during the rest of the week. Also make sure that you know whether market breadth and volume are working for bulls or bears. And keep track of the 20- and 40-week cycles: mark them down on a calendar, and prepare for them well ahead of their expected arrivals. Timing is a huge, huge part of this game, so make sure you are on top of it.

On Mondays, spend at least an hour going through the relative-strength charts, as described in Chapter 2. Make sure you totally understand which sectors, market-cap groups, style (growth vs. value), and regions are in favor in the daily, weekly, and monthly time frames. Promise yourself to fight only on the winning side. While it's sometimes tempting to try to be a contrarian and put yourself on the side of underdog groups that appear ready to turn the corner from weakness to strength, you must resist. The winning side is winning for a reason, and it will maintain its edge long enough for you to participate if you follow my instructions. It's so much harder to make money on groups that are fighting for their lives that it's really not worth your time and effort. Leave the peasants and losers to their misery, and throw in with the overlords.

On Tuesdays, spend at least an hour at Markethistory.com to understand which sectors, exchanges, commodities, and stocks are most likely to find success over the ensuing one or two months as a result of historical, intermarket, or price/volume tendencies. I cannot express to you enough how valuable this information is and how fortunate we are that it's available to noninstitutional traders for a reasonable fee. If there is one step you can take to make your success rate go way up, it is paying attention to well-entrenched relationships between the calendar, market events (such as earnings announcements and economic reports), and trading instruments. You ignore these relationships only at your peril. After you really get in tune with Markethistory on Tuesdays, you will never again be forced to suffer the market equivalent of swimming futilely against an incoming tide. These are facts, not opinions, and they will set you free to focus on reality and not wishful thinking.

On Wednesdays, spend at least an hour studying the charts, earnings reports, and stories of all the recent initial public offerings, spin-offs, postbankruptcy offerings, and reverse splits of the past 18 months. The market loves to trade things that are fresh and lively from both the long and the short side, so these equities are absolute gold mines for active players. Mark down your favorites in a trading journal each week, and track the progress of the ones that you did not trade as well as the ones that you did. Compare and contrast. Learn from both your successes and your failures. The market gives us ample opportunities to try again and again, and there's no reason you can't work diligently each week to make your victories more amazing and your misses less annoying.

On Thursdays, run the new StockScouter Top 10 lists at MSN Money as I describe in Chapter 5, or visit the monthly list that I provide in my weekly *Strategic Advantage* newsletter. These are stocks that have succeeded again and again for the past seven years as a result of their combination of fundamental, valuation, ownership, technical, and low-volatility factors. Even if you don't want to trade them as a "basket" as I describe, look at each name from long-term, medium-term, and short-term perspectives and determine which have the best opportunities to succeed over the next one week to six months, as I do for readers of my short-term-focused

Trader's Advantage newsletter. Don't be afraid to buy the strongest stocks at breakout highs even in flat to boring markets because they tend to be the ones that are in greatest demand for reasons that might not become clear for several more months.

And finally, on Fridays, take the time to think deeply about everything you have learned from the news, sector studies, IPO observations, StockScouter lists, and your own cultural observations. Determine which events add up to anomalies that might create persistent trading opportunities. Whether it's the potential for war, peace, genetic breakthroughs, a new type of media, religion, or a transformation in politics, really important change is happening all around us, and it takes only a few moments of quiet reflection every week to tease these new trends out of your mind. Write down your ideas in your trading journal, suggest some potential investment plays, and take action—and constantly review.

The most important element of active day trading, in the end, is to make systematic, fact-based decisions every day that are informed but not terrorized by your instincts or by random anecdotes. Willfully plan for success day by day, and you will be successful.

DOW JONES SECTOR AND INDUSTRY INDEXES

Symbol	Index
$DJUSAE	DJ US Aerospace & Defense Index
$DJUSAF	DJ US Delivery Services Index
$DJUSAG	DJ US Asset Managers Index
$DJUSAI	DJ US Electronic Equipment Index
$DJUSAL	DJ US Aluminum Index
$DJUSAM	DJ US Medical Equipment Index
$DJUSAP	DJ US Automobiles & Parts Index
$DJUSAR	DJ US Airlines Index
$DJUSAS	DJ US Aerospace Index
$DJUSAT	DJ US Auto Parts Index
$DJUSAU	DJ US Automobiles Index
$DJUSAV	DJ US Media Agencies Index
$DJUSBC	DJ US Broadcasting & Entertainment Index
$DJUSBD	DJ US Building Materials & Fixtures Index
$DJUSBE	DJ US Employment Agencies Index
$DJUSBK	DJ US Banks Index
$DJUSBM	DJ US Basic Materials Index
$DJUSBS	DJ US Basic Resources Index

Symbol	Index
$DJUSBT	DJ US Biotechnology Index
$DJUSBV	DJ US Beverages Index
$DJUSCA	DJ US Gambling Index
$DJUSCC	DJ US Commodity Chemicals Index
$DJUSCE	DJ US Consumer Electronics Index
$DJUSCF	DJ US Clothing & Accessories Index
$DJUSCG	DJ US Travel & Leisure Index
$DJUSCH	DJ US Chemicals Index
$DJUSCL	DJ US Coal Index
$DJUSCM	DJ US Personal Products Index
$DJUSCN	DJ US Construction & Materials Index
$DJUSCP	DJ US Containers & Packaging Index
$DJUSCR	DJ US Computer Hardware Index
$DJUSCS	DJ US Specialized Consumer Services Index
$DJUSCT	DJ US Telecommunications Equipment Index
$DJUSCX	DJ US Specialty Chemicals Index
$DJUSCY	DJ US Consumer Services Index
$DJUSDB	DJ US Brewers Index
$DJUSDN	DJ US Defense Index
$DJUSDR	DJ US Food & Drug Retailers Index
$DJUSDS	DJ US Industrial Suppliers Index
$DJUSDV	DJ US Computer Services Index
$DJUSEC	DJ US Electrical Components & Equipment Index
$DJUSEE	DJ US Electronic & Electrical Equipment Index
$DJUSEN	DJ US Oil & Gas Index
$DJUSEU	DJ US Electricity Index
$DJUSFA	DJ US Financial Administration Index
$DJUSFB	DJ US Food & Beverage Index
$DJUSFC	DJ US Fixed Line Telecommunications Index
$DJUSFD	DJ US Food Retailers & Wholesalers Index
$DJUSFE	DJ US Industrial Machinery Index

Symbol	Index
$DJUSFH	DJ US Furnishings Index
$DJUSFI	DJ US Financial Services Index
$DJUSFN	DJ US Financials Index
$DJUSFO	DJ US Food Producers Index
$DJUSFP	DJ US Food Products Index
$DJUSFR	DJ US Forestry & Paper Index
$DJUSFS	DJ US Forestry Index
$DJUSFT	DJ US Footwear Index
$DJUSFV	DJ US Financial Services Composite Index
$DJUSGF	DJ US General Financial Index
$DJUSGI	DJ US General Industrials Index
$DJUSGL	DJ US Large-Cap Growth Index
$DJUSGM	DJ US Mid-Cap Growth Index
$DJUSGR	DJ US Growth Index
$DJUSGS	DJ US Small-Cap Growth Index
$DJUSGT	DJ US General Retailers Index
$DJUSGU	DJ US Gas Distribution Index
$DJUSHB	DJ US Home Construction Index
$DJUSHC	DJ US Health Care Index
$DJUSHD	DJ US Durable Household Products Index
$DJUSHG	DJ US Household Goods Index
$DJUSHI	DJ US Home Improvement Retailers Index
$DJUSHN	DJ US Nondurable Household Products Index
$DJUSHP	DJ US Health Care Providers Index
$DJUSHR	DJ US Commercial Vehicles & Trucks Index
$DJUSHV	DJ US Heavy Construction Index
$DJUSIB	DJ US Insurance Brokers Index
$DJUSID	DJ US Diversified Industrials Index
$DJUSIF	DJ US Full Line Insurance Index
$DJUSIG	DJ US Industrial Goods & Services Index
$DJUSIL	DJ US Life Insurance Index

Symbol	Index
$DJUSIM	DJ US Industrial Metals Index
$DJUSIN	DJ US Industrials Index
$DJUSIP	DJ US Property & Casualty Insurance Index
$DJUSIQ	DJ US Industrial Engineering Index
$DJUSIR	DJ US Insurance Index
$DJUSIS	DJ US Support Services Index
$DJUSIT	DJ US Industrial Transportation Index
$DJUSIU	DJ US Reinsurance Index
$DJUSIV	DJ US Business Support Services Index
$DJUSIX	DJ US Nonlife Insurance Index
$DJUSL	DJ US Large-Cap Index
$DJUSLE	DJ US Leisure Goods Index
$DJUSLG	DJ US Hotels Index
$DJUSLT	DJ US Large-Cap TR Index
$DJUSLW	DJ US Low-Cap Index
$DJUSM	DJ US Mid-Cap Index
$DJUSMC	DJ US Health Care Equipment & Services Index
$DJUSMD	DJ US General Mining Index
$DJUSME	DJ US Media Index
$DJUSMF	DJ US Mortgage Finance Index
$DJUSMG	DJ US Mining Index
$DJUSMS	DJ US Medical Supplies Index
$DJUSMT	DJ US Marine Transportation Index
$DJUSMU	DJ US Multiutilities Index
$DJUSNC	DJ US Consumer Goods Index
$DJUSNF	DJ US Nonferrous Metals Index
$DJUSNG	DJ US Personal & Household Goods Index
$DJUSNS	DJ US Internet Index
$DJUSOE	DJ US Electronic Office Equipment Index
$DJUSOG	DJ US Oil & Gas Producers Index
$DJUSOI	DJ US Oil Equipment & Services Index

Symbol	Index
$DJUSOL	DJ US Integrated Oil & Gas Index
$DJUSOQ	DJ US Oil Equipment, Services & Distribution Index
$DJUSOS	DJ US Exploration & Production Index
$DJUSPB	DJ US Publishing Index
$DJUSPC	DJ US Waste & Disposal Services Index
$DJUSPG	DJ US Personal Goods Index
$DJUSPL	DJ US Pipelines Index
$DJUSPM	DJ US Gold Mining Index
$DJUSPN	DJ US Pharmaceuticals & Biotechnology Index
$DJUSPP	DJ US Paper Index
$DJUSPR	DJ US Pharmaceuticals Index
$DJUSPT	DJ US Platinum & Precious Metals Index
$DJUSRA	DJ US Apparel Retailers Index
$DJUSRB	DJ US Broadline Retailers Index
$DJUSRD	DJ US Drug Retailers Index
$DJUSRE	DJ US Real Estate Index
$DJUSRH	DJ US Real Estate Holding & Development Index
$DJUSRI	DJ US Real Estate Investment Trusts Index
$DJUSRP	DJ US Recreational Products Index
$DJUSRQ	DJ US Recreational Services Index
$DJUSRR	DJ US Railroad Index
$DJUSRS	DJ US Specialty Retailers Index
$DJUSRT	DJ US Retail Index
$DJUSRU	DJ US Restaurants & Bars Index
$DJUSS	DJ US Small-Cap Index
$DJUSSB	DJ US Investment Services Index
$DJUSSC	DJ US Semiconductors Index
$DJUSSD	DJ US Soft Drinks Index
$DJUSSF	DJ US Consumer Finance Index
$DJUSSP	DJ US Specialty Finance Index
$DJUSST	DJ US Steel Index

Symbol	Index
$DJUSSV	DJ US Software & Computer Services Index
$DJUSSW	DJ US Software Index
$DJUSTB	DJ US Tobacco Index
$DJUSTC	DJ US Technology Index
$DJUSTK	DJ US Trucking Index
$DJUSTL	DJ US Telecommunications Index
$DJUSTP	DJ US Top Cap Index
$DJUSTQ	DJ US Technology Hardware Index
$DJUSTR	DJ US Tires Index
$DJUSTS	DJ US Transportation Services Index
$DJUSTT	DJ US Travel & Tourism Index
$DJUSTY	DJ US Toys Index
$DJUSUO	DJ US Gas, Water & Multiutilities Index
$DJUSUT	DJ US Utilities Index
$DJUSVA	DJ US Value Index
$DJUSVL	DJ US Large-Cap Value Index
$DJUSVM	DJ US Mid-Cap Value Index
$DJUSVN	DJ US Distillers & Vintners Index
$DJUSVS	DJ US Small-Cap Value Index
$DJUSWC	DJ US Mobile Telecommunications Index
$DJUSWU	DJ US Water Index

ETFs

iShares

AGG	iShares Lehman Aggregate Bond
CFT	iShares Lehman Credit Bond
CIU	iShares Lehman Intermediate Credit Bond
CSJ	iShares Lehman 1-3 Year Credit Bond
DSI	iShares KLD 400 Social Index
DVY	iShares DJ Select Dividend Index
EEM	iShares MCSI Emerging Markets
EFA	EAFE Index iShares
EFV	iShares MSCI Value
EPP	iShares MSCI Pacific Ex-Japan Index
EWA	Australia iShares
EWC	Canada iShares
EWD	Sweden iShares
EWG	Germany iShares
EWH	HongKong iShares
EWI	Italy iShares
EWJ	Japan iShares
EWK	Belgium iShares
EWL	Switzerland iShares
EWM	Malaysia iShares

EWN	Netherlands iShares
EWO	Austria iShares
EWP	Spain iShares
EWQ	France iShares
EWS	Singapore iShares
EWT	Taiwan iShares
EWU	United Kingdom iShares
EWW	Mexico iShares
EWY	South Korea iShares
EWZ	Brazil iShares
EXI	iShares S&P Global Industrials Sector Index
EZA	South Africa iShares
EZU	EMU Index iShares
FIO	iShares FTSE NAREIT Industrial/Office
FTY	iShares FTSE NAREIT Real Estate 50
FXI	iShares FTSE/Xinhua China 25 Index
GBF	iShares Lehman Government/Credit Bond
GSG	Commodity iShares S&P/GSCI Index
GVI	iShares Lehman Intermediate Government/Credit Bond
HYG	iShares iBoxx $ High Yield Corporate Bond
IAI	iShares Dow Jones U.S. Broker-Dealers
IAK	iShares Dow Jones U.S. Insurance
IAT	iShares Dow Jones U.S. Regional Banks
IAU	iShares COMEX Gold Trust
IBB	Biotech iShares
ICF	Realty Major iShares
IDU	Utilities iShares
IDV	iShares Dow Jones EPAC Select Dividend
IEF	7–10 Year Treasury Bond
IEI	iShares Lehman 3–7 Year Treasury Bond
IEO	iShares Dow Jones U.S. Oil & Gas Exploration & Production
IEV	Europe 350 iShares
IEZ	iShares Dow Jones U.S. Oil Equipment & Services

IGE	Natural Resources iShares S&P/GSCI Index
IGM	Technology iShares S&P/GSTI Index
IGN	Network iShares S&P/GSTI Index
IGT.TO	iShares COMEX Gold Trust
IGV	Software iShares S&P/GSTI Index
IGW	Semiconductor iShares S&P/GSTI Index
IHE	iShares Dow Jones U.S. Pharmaceuticals
IHF	iShares Dow Jones U.S. Healthcare Providers
IHI	iShares Dow Jones U.S. Medical Devices
IJH	MidCap 400 iShares
IJJ	MidCap 400 Value iShares
IJK	MidCap 400 Growth iShares
IJR	SP SmCap 600 iShares
IJS	SmCap 600 Value iShares
IJT	SmCap 600 Growth iShares
ILF	Latin America 40 Index iShares
IOO	S&P Glbl 100 iShares
ISI	iShares S&P 1500 Index
ITA	iShares Dow Jones U.S. Aerospace & Defense
ITB	iShares Dow Jones U.S. Home Construction
ITF	TOPIX 150 Index iShares
IVE	S&P 500 Value iShares
IVV	S&P 500 iShares
IVW	S&P 500 Growth iShares
IWB	Russell 1000 iShares
IWC	iShares Russell Microcap Index
IWD	Russell 1000 Value iShares
IWF	Russell 1000 Growth iShares
IWM	Russell 2000 iShares
IWN	Russell 2000 Value iShares
IWO	Russell 2000 Growth iShares
IWP	Russell Mid-Cap Growth iShares
IWR	Russell Mid-Cap iShares

IWS	Russell Mid-Cap Value iShares
IWV	Russell 3000 iShares
IWW	Russell 3000 Value iShares
IWZ	Russell 3000 Growth iShares
IXC	iShares S&P Global Energy Sector Index
IXG	iShares S&P Global Financials Sector Index
IXJ	iShares S&P Global Healthcare Sector Index
IXN	iShares S&P Global Information Technology Sector
IXP	iShares S&P Global Telecommunications Sector Index
IYC	Consumer iShares
IYE	Energy iShares
IYF	Financial iShares
IYG	Financial Services iShares
IYH	Healthcare iShares
IYJ	Industrial iShares
IYM	Basic Matls iShares
IYR	Real Estate iShares
IYT	iShares DJ Transportation Average Index
IYW	Technology iShares (DJUS)
IYY	Total Market iShares
IYZ	Telecom iShares
JKD	iShares Morningstar Large Core Index
JKE	iShares Morningstar Large Growth Index
JKF	iShares Morningstar Large Value Index
JKG	iShares Morningstar Mid Core Index
JKH	iShares Morningstar Mid Growth Index
JKI	iShares Morningstar Mid Value Index
JKJ	iShares Morningstar Small Core Index
JKK	iShares Morningstar Small Growth Index
JKL	iShares Morningstar Small Value Index
JXI	iShares S&P Global Utilities Sector Index
KLD	iShares KLD Select Social Index
KXI	iShares S&P Global Consumer Staples Sector Index

LQD   iShares iBoxx $ Investment Grade Corporate Bond
MBB   iShares Lehman MBS Fixed-Rate Bond
MXI   iShares S&P Global Materials Sector Index
NY   iShares NYSE 100 Index
NYC   iShares NYSE Composite Index
OEF   S&P 100 Index—iShares
PFF   iShares S&P U.S. Preferred Stock Index
REZ   iShares FTSE NAREIT Residential
RTL   iShares FTSE NAREIT Retail
RXI   iShares S&P Global Consumer Discretionary Sector Index
SHV   iShares Lehman Short Treasury Bond
SHY   1–3 Year Treasury Bond (Leh) iShares
SLV   iShares Silver Trust
TIP   iShares Lehman TIPS Bond
TLH   iShares Lehman 10–20 Year Treasury Bond
TLT   20+ Year Treasury Bond iShares

ProShares ETFs

DDM   Ultra Dow 30 ProShares Fund
DIG   ProShares Ultra Oil And Gas
DOG   Short Dow 30 ProShares Fund
DUG   UltraShort Oil & Gas ProShares
DXD   ProShares Ultra Short Dow 30
MVV   Ultra MidCap 400 ProShares Fund
MYY   Short MidCap 400 ProShares Fund
MZZ   ProShares Ultra Short Mid Cap400
PSQ   Short QQQ ProShares Fund
QID   ProShares Ultra Short QQQ
QLD   Ultra QQQ ProShares Fund
REW   UltraShort Technology ProShares
ROM   ProShares Ultra Technology

RXD	UltraShort Health Care ProShares
RXL	ProShares Ultra Health Care
SCC	UltraShort Consumer Services ProShares
SDK	ProShares UltraShort Russell MidCap Growth
SDP	UltraShort Utilities ProShares
SDS	ProShares Ultra Short S&P 500
SFK	ProShares UltraShort Russell 1000 Growth
SH	Short S&P 500 ProShares Fund
SIJ	UltraShort Industrials ProShares
SJF	ProShares UltraShort Russell 1000 Value
SJH	ProShares UltraShort Russell 2000 Value
SJL	ProShares UltraShort Russell MidCap Value
SKF	UltraShort Financials ProShares
SKK	ProShares UltraShort Russell2000 Growth
SMN	UltraShort Basic Materials ProShares
SRS	Ultrashort RealEstate ProShares
SSO	Ultra S&P 500 ProShares Fund
SZK	UltraShort Consumer Goods ProShares
UCC	ProShares Ultra Consumer Services
UGE	ProShares Ultra Consumer Goods
UKF	ProShares Ultra Russell 1000 Growth
UKK	ProShares Ultra Russell 2000 Growth
UKW	ProShares Ultra Russell Midcap Growth
UPW	ProShares Ultra Utilities
URE	ProShares Ultra Real Estate
USD	ProShares Ultra Semiconductors
UVG	ProShares Ultra Russell 1000 Value
UVT	ProShares Ultra Russell2000 Value
UVU	ProShares Ultra Russell Midcap Value
UXI	ProShares Ultra Industrials
UYG	ProShares Ultra Financials
UYM	ProShares Ultra Basic Materials

Rydex Equal-Weight ETFs

RCD	Rydex S&P Equal Weight Consumer Discretionary
RFG	Rydex S&P Mid Cap 400 Pure Growth
RFV	Rydex S&P Mid Cap 400 Pure Value
RGI	Rydex S&P Equal Weight Industrials
RHS	Rydex S&P Equal Weight Consumer Staples
RPG	Rydex S&P 500 Pure Growth
RPV	Rydex S&P 500 Pure Value
RSP	Rydex S&P Equal Weight ETF
RTM	Rydex S&P Equal Weight Materials
RYE	Rydex S&P Equal Weight Energy
RYF	Rydex S&P Equal Weight Financials
RYH	Rydex S&P Equal Weight Health Care
RYT	Rydex S&P Equal Weight Technology
RYU	Rydex S&P Equal Weight Utilities
RZG	Rydex S&P Small Cap 600 Pure Growth
RZV	Rydex S&P Small Cap 600 Pure Value
XLG	Rydex Russell Top 50

Powershares ETFs

DBA	PowerShares DB Multi-Sector Commodity Trust Agriculture Fund
DBB	PowerShares DB Multi-Sector Commodity Trust Metals Fund
DBE	PowerShares DB Multi-Sector Commodity Trust Energy Fund
DBO	PowerShares DB Multi-Sector Commodity Trust Oil Fund
DBP	PowerShares DB Multi-Sector Commodity Trust Precious Metals Fund
DBS	PowerShares DB Multi-Sector Commodity Trust Silver Fund
DBV	PowerShares DB G10 Currency Harvest Fund
DGL	PowerShares DB Multi-Sector Commodity Trust Gold Fund
PAF	PowerShares FTSE RAFI Asia Pacific ex Japan Portfolio
PBD	PowerShares Global Clean Energy Portfolio

PBE	PowerShares Dynamic Biotech & Genome Portfolio
PBJ	PowerShares Dynamic Food & Beverage Portfolio
PBS	PowerShares Dynamic Media Portfolio
PBW	Powershares Wilderhill Clean Energy Portfolio
PDP	PowerShares DWA Techincal Leaders Portfolio
PEF	PowerShares FTSE RAFI Europe Portfolio
PEH	PowerShares Dynamic Europe Portfolio
PEJ	PowerShares Dynamic Leisure & Entertainment Portfolio
PEY	PowerShares High Yield Equity Dividend
PFA	PowerShares Dynamic Developed Intl Opportunities Portfolio
PFM	PowerShares Dividend Achievers Portfolio
PGF	PowerShares Financial Preferred Portfolio
PGJ	PowerShares Golden Dragon Halter USX China Portfolio
PGZ	Powershares Dynamic Aggressive Growth Portfolio
PHJ	PowerShares High Growth Rate Dividend Achievers Portfolio
PHO	PowerShares Water Resources Portfolio
PHW	Powershares Hardware & Consumer Electronics Portfolio
PIC	PowerShares Dynamic Insurance Portfolio
PID	PowerShares International Dividend Achievers Portfolio
PIO	PowerShares Global Water Portfolio
PIQ	PowerShares Dynamic Magni Quant Sector Portfolio
PIV	PowerShares ValueLine Timeliness Select Portfolio
PJB	PowerShares Dynamic Banking Sector Portfolio
PJF	PowerShares Dynamic Large Cap Portfolio
PJG	PowerShares Dynamic MidCap Portfolio
PJM	PowerShares Dynamic Small Cap Portfolio
PJO	PowerShares FTSE RAFI Japan Portfolio
PJP	PowerShares Dynamic Pharmaceuticals Portfolio
PKB	PowerShares Dynamic Building & Construction Portfolio
PKW	Powershares Buyback Achievers
PMR	PowerShares Dynamic Retail Portfolio
PPA	PowerShares Aerospace and Defense Portfolio
PRF	PowerShares FTSE RAFI U.S. 1000 Portfolio

PRFE	PowerShares FTSI RAFI Energy Sector Portfolio
PRFF	PowerShares FTSI RAFI Financials Sector Portfolio
PRFG	PowerShares FTSI RAFI Consumer Goods Sector Portfolio
PRFH	PowerShares FTSI RAFI Healthcare Sector Portfolio
PRFM	PowerShares FTSI RAFI Basic Materials Sector Portfolio
PRFN	PowerShares FTSI RAFI Industrials Sector Portfolio
PRFQ	PowerShares FTSI RAFI Telecommunications & Technology Sector Portfolio
PRFS	PowerShares FTSI RAFI Consumer Services Sector Portfolio
PRFU	PowerShares FTSI RAFI Utilities Sector Portfolio
PRFZ	PowerShares FTSI RAFI US 1500 Small-Mid Portfolio
PRN	PowerShares Dynamic Industrials Sector Portfolio
PSI	PowerShares Dynamic Semiconductors Portfolio
PSJ	PowerShares Dynamic Software Portfolio
PSP	PowerShares Listed Private Equity Portfolio
PTE	PowerShares Dynamic Telecom & Wireless Portfolio
PTF	PowerShares Dynamic Technology Sector Portfolio
PTJ	PowerShares Dynamic Healthcare Services Sector Portfolio
PUA	PowerShares Dynamic Asia Pacific Portfolio
PUI	PowerShares Dynamic Utilities Portfolio
PUW	PowerShares WilderHill Progressive Energy Index
PVM	Powershares Dynamic Deep Value Portfolio
PWB	Powershares Dynamic Large Cap
PWC	PowerShares Dynamic Market Portfolio
PWJ	Powershares Dynamic Mid Cap GR
PWO	PowerShares Dynamic OTC Portfolio
PWP	Powershares Dynamic Mid Cap VA
PWT	Powershares Dynamic Small Cap
PWV	Powershares Dynamic Large Cap
PWY	Powershares Dynamic Small Cap
PXE	Powershares Dynamic Energy Exploration & Production Portfolio
PXF	PowerShares FTSE RAFI Developed Markets ex-US Portfolio

PXJ   PowerShares Dynamic Oil & Gas Services Portfolio
PXN   PowerShares Lux Nanotech Portfolio
PXQ   PowerShares Dynamic Networking Portfolio
PYH   PowerShares Value Line Industry Rotation Portfolio
PZD   PowerShares Cleantech Portfolio
PZI   Powershares Zacks Microcap Index
QQQQ   PowerShares QQQ Trust
SSG   PowerShares UltraShort Semiconductors
UDN   PowerShares DB US Dollar Index Bearish Fund
UUP   PowerShares DB US Dollar Index Bullish Fund

Market Vectors

EVX   Market Vectors Environmental Services
GDX   Market Vectors Gold Miners
GEX   Market Vectors Global Alternative Energy Trust
MOO   Market Vectors Agribusiness
NLR   Market Vectors-Nuclear Energy
RSX   Market Vectors Russia Trust
SLX   Market Vectors Steel

INDEX